The New ER Files

THE NEW ER FILES

An Unauthorized Companion
By John Binns
& Mark Jones

CHAMELEON

First published in Great Britain in 1999 by
Chameleon Books
an imprint of André Deutsch Ltd
106 Great Russell Street
London
WC1B 3LJ
www.vci.co.uk

André Deutsch is a subsidiary of VCI plc

A catalogue record for this book is available from the British Library

Printed and bound by WBC, Bridgend
ISBN 0 233 99280 4
Inside pictures © Alpha and Corbis/Everett

FOREWORD

ER is one of the most successful television drama series of all time. Consistently at the top of the ratings charts in the United States and with an impressive number of Emmy nominations and awards, it has captured the imagination of millions of viewers around the world.

Why is it so popular? High standards of production certainly make ER one of the slickest shows on television, but what makes us come back week after week is a set of central characters who are complex, interesting and genuine. This is not a show about medical procedures or even, for the most part, the problems of patients: it is the story of the lives, both professional and personal, of the people who work in an Emergency Room.

This book is a guide for the ER viewer to the stories told so far about Doctors Greene, Ross, Carter and others, gathering together for the first time the events of four years of the show in the form of extracts from County General's confidential files. A series of dossiers on the hospital personnel, both major and minor, is followed by a complete guide to the events of every episode in series one to four. With the help of pointers showing the major players of each scene, the guide can be read either from start to finish, or with a focus on your favourite character or characters. It can easily be 'dipped into', flicked through, or searched for every mention of Greene, Ross, Carter, Lewis, Benton, Jeanie, Anna, Corday, Carol, or even Kerry Weaver!

From time to time we step 'out of character' to comment on ER as a television show, or to give pointers to particular episodes, and we have indicated this by using square brackets. As well as recommending what we think are some of the best episodes, we have added some information that definitely wouldnít be in the hospital files, including some of our favourite points of ER trivia! At the back, you'll find a table of episodes and a brief guide to the main actors, as well as a preview of the fifth series.

Some of you may be familiar with the previous version of this book which was released in November 1997 prior to the start of transmission of the fourth series in the UK. Rest assured, we have revised and updated every section, including the personnel files, to bring you up to date with the latest public and private affairs of all the characters. So now you can read about Anna Del Amico and Elizabeth Corday, and a host of less prominent characters such as Rocket Romano and Ellis West, as well as keeping up-to-date with the development of the more well established characters.

Finally, we would like to thank the following people, who have helped in various ways: John Ainsworth; David Bailey; Barbara, David and Helen Binns; Lisa Brattan; Jerry Cheung (without whom it really wouldnít have been possible); Jeremy Daw; Mike Evans; Sharon, Norman and Paul Jones; Victoria and Claudia Kielinger; Alex Leithes; Rebecca Levene; Lorraine Mann; Cassandra May; Lance Parkin; Natasha Prior; David Richardson; Gary Russell; Ethel Weston; Gareth Wigmore and Huw Wilkins. Special thanks to our editor at Andre Deutsch, Hannah MacDonald.

CONTENTS

PRIVATE & CONFIDENTIAL

MEMORANDUM

To: Mayor of Chicago

From: Henry Bradley –
County Health Services, ER Management

Following our meeting of 20th August 1998 herewith the requested personnel files and records. Since the merger with Southside Hospital in September 1996 and, more recently, the changing management of the ER following the illness and departure of Dr. David Morgenstern, we have been monitoring the productivity and effectiveness of Chicago County General's ER carefully.

As you will see from the files and records, the ER is a diverse department which makes tremendous demands on its staff. The doctors and nurses are a close team and, although occasionally unorthodox, they are extraordinarily dedicated. I do hope you will bear this in mind as your team compiles the Annual Health Service Review.

As you specifically requested detailed information on the core staff, I have taken the liberty of annotating the files with further information and comments on individuals. These notes may seem trivial but I think you'll find them fascinating! They should prove revealing on the dynamics of a high pressure hospital department.

I need hardly remind you that these files are extremely confidential and that great care must be taken they don't fall into the wrong hands . . .

Henry Bradley

SECTION ONE

Personnel Files
[The Main Characters]

Mark Greene . . . . *[Anthony Edwards]*

Douglas Ross . . . . *[George Clooney]*

Susan Lewis. . . . . *[Sherry Stringfield]*

John Carter . . . . *[Noah Wyle]*

Carol Hathaway. . . . . *[Julianna Margulies]*

Jeanie Boulet . . . . *[Gloria Reuben]*

Kerry Weaver . . . . *[Laura Innes]*

Anna Del Amico . . . . *[Maria Bello]*

Elizabeth Corday. . . . . *[Alex Kingston]*

Peter Benton . . . . *[Eriq la Salle]*

MARK GREENE, M.D.

AGE

34.

POSITION

Senior attending physician in ER. Formerly chief resident.

MEDICAL TRAINING AND CAREER TO DATE

Medical school: Four years. At some point concurrent with Dr Peter Benton.

Residency: Four years. Helicopter run regarded as highlight of residency. Fourth year served as chief resident in County General ER, responsible for running patient allocation board and staff morale. While chief resident was offered position at Dr Harris's private practice in Chicago and looked for positions in Milwaukee. Regarded as one of County's finest residents; recommended for attending by Dr David Morgenstern.

Note: Greene could have taken an almost $100,000 pay increase to join private practice but insisted he couldn't give up ER work .

Attending: Recommendation for attending approved by Dr William Swift (with reservations), 18th May 1995. First day as ER attending: 5th September 1995. Responsibilities: supervising residents, relations with other departments, presence at staff meetings, ER staff appointments and promotions. Joined by Dr Kerry Weaver as attending, July 1996. Greene has specific duties as patient ombudsman, runs mentoring programme, responsible for staff morale. Following Southside closure, Greene also responsible for chart review *[episode 3-3]*. Attending physician on the stroke team *[episode 3-20]*. Notoriously fails to call ER staff meetings.

Greene also seeking tenure position. Review Board holds reservations re Greene's inability to publish research, but takes note of recommendation of Dr Anspaugh. Reaction of prospective interns, January 1997, indicates suitable candidate *[episode 3-13]*.

3

Note: Anspaugh regards Greene as a better man-manager than Weaver but says he is less intelligent. Greene sarcastically dismisses pressures on him to produce articles: "Oh, yeah. Publish or perish."

Despite greater experience within the County ER, Greene was superseded by Dr Kerry Weaver as Acting Chief of ER following Dr Morgenstern's heart attack *[episode 4-1]*. Greene was pleased to allow Weaver to take precedence and welcomed the Synergix Physicians Group trial as a method of evading extra paperwork. Tenure position remains a possibility.

SIGNIFICANT CAREER EVENTS

1. Attempted suicide of Charge Nurse Hathaway, 17 March 1994 *[Pilot]*

Hathaway suicide attempt shocked ER staff. Important test for Greene as new chief resident: Morgenstern noted Greene sets the tone. Succeeded in steering ER 'unit' through tragedy. See Personnel file on Carol Hathaway.

2. Resident review: Dr Susan Lewis, January 1995 *[episodes 1-11 to 1-14]*

Treatment of Mr Vennerbeck extended conflict between Dr Lewis and Dr Kayson. Greene alerted Morgenstern to Lewis's lack of assertiveness, resulting in Morgenstern questioning her suitability for ER work. Results of Resident Review Board (and Lewis's subsequent treatment of Head of Cardiology - Kayson with tPA) allayed Greene's fears but uncomfortable working relationship with Lewis continued. Resolution following death of terminal cancer patient *[episode 1-14]*. See Personnel files on Dr Susan Lewis and Dr Jack Kayson.

Note: Conflict intensified by Greene's feelings for Lewis. Lewis angered along similar lines: "We're not married, we work together. Professional is personal."

3. Death of Jodi O'Brien, February 1995 *[episode 1-18, "Love's Labor Lost"]*

Case history (extracts)
Jodi O'Brien, 38th week pregnancy, suffering stomach pains

and need to urinate. Dr Greene misdiagnosed cystitis and incorrectly calculated weight of baby. Mrs O'Brien discharged with antibiotics but suffers seizure. Returned to ER; Greene recognized eclampsia. Ordered hyperventilation and foetal monitor. Baby's heart strong. Greene remained on duty despite end of shift. 9pm: indicated to Dr Coburn that eclampsia controlled. Delivery to begin in ER then O'Brien to be moved to OB. Labour began but concern for falling foetal heart-rate. 2.30am: OB ordered but no response (still no response by 4.13am). Forceps delivery aborted. C-section attempted but O'Brien suffered profuse internal bleeding from placental abruption. Baby saved but Jodi O'Brien died.

Concerns from members of ER staff indicated Greene suffered considerable guilt and loss of confidence. Refusal to treat pregnant patient. Full acknowledgement of misdiagnosis explained at subsequent O'Brien presentation *[episode 1-20]*. Considerable criticism from Dr Janet Coburn. Hospital served for malpractice: 18th May 1995. See Personnel file: Dr Janet Coburn and O'Brien case settlement (below).

Greene (at case presentation): "I've induced before, delivered babies before. I assumed that I could handle the situation. I was wrong."

4. Recommendation for attending position – concerns of Dr William Swift, February-March 1995 *[episodes 1-19 to 1-24]*
Greene not on duty: alleged to have 'flu'. Disagreement over diagnosis and treatment of patient with ultrasound. Dr Swift insisted that Greene give post-operative presentation on Jodi O'Brien. Dr Swift took responsibility for patient allocation board in light of Greene's inefficiency *[episode 1-22]*. Greene objected to being treated as med-student: Dr Swift regarded Greene as requiring an "attitude adjustment". Dr Lewis concurred *[episode 1-22]*. Following discovery of pulmonary embolism, against Swift's diagnosis of alcoholic cardiomyopathy, professional relationship improved. Morgenstern's recommendation for Greene as attending signed off by Dr Swift, dated 18th May 1995.

Ross to Greene: "If you lose [the post of attending] over this petty crap, buddy, you're a fool."

5. Patient: Loretta Sweet, September 1995 - July 1996 [episodes 2-1 to 2-22]

Loretta Sweet, prostitute, two children. Treated for contact dermatitis and pelvic inflammatory disorder, September 1995. Returned to ER shortly before job interview, November 1995. Cervical cancer discovered, end 1995. Caught early: five-year survival rate of over 90 per cent. Radiation therapy preceded radical hysterectomy: July 1996. Concern raised over lack of information given re side-effects. [episode 2-20]. Oncologist: Dr Lyle Howard.

Note: Greene looked after Loretta's children for one evening. Asked to be their guardian but Greene was unable to comply.

6. Supervision problems: Doctors Weaver and Lewis, from September 1995

Greene concerned for working relationship between Drs Weaver and Lewis on Weaver's arrival as Chief Resident County ER. Repeated disagreements in trauma invariably resulted in Greene backing Weaver [episode 2-3]. Greene gave Weaver full backing so long as no decision prevented any resident from doing their best [episode 2-4].

Subsequent problems with Dr Weaver regarding Greene's nomination of Susan Lewis for chief resident, February to June 1996 [episodes 2-13 to 2-22]. Significant reservations of Dr Weaver overturned when Greene dropped opposition to Weaver as new attending. Susan Lewis, however, rejected offer. Linda Martins appointed new chief resident [episode 2-22]. Further complications re innovations of Dr Anspaugh, supported by Dr Weaver [episode 3-3]. See relevant Personnel files.

Greene: "I'm philosophically opposed. That's my new motto - 'Change is not good'."

7. ER paediatric fellowship renewal: Dr Ross, November to December 1995 [episodes 2-5 to 2-8]

Dr Greene alerted Mei-Sun Loh to alternatives to traumatic treatment of her son prescribed by Dr Ross. However, alleged violation of teacher-student relationship by Ross not reported by Greene. Ross further defended by Greene against criticisms of Dr Bernstein [episode 2-6] and actions of Dr Benton in Bowman case *[episode 2-17].*

Note: Greene was concerned by Harper and Ross's one-night stand but brought no action. Ross reprimanded by Greene for falsifying charts: "If you're going to work for me, this cowboy crap has got to stop". Further concerns raised over alcohol and possible cocaine levels in Ross's bloodstream, though Ross tested negative for cocaine.

8. Malpractice case: O'Brien wrongful death suit. Settlement: December 1995-February 1996 *[episodes 2-10 to 2-13]*

> **Extracted from: Report of hospital attorney, Kathy Snyder, dated 1st February 1996, re Jodi O'Brien/Dr Mark Greene.**
> Hospital fears possible loss of $2million should suit go to court. Strong recommendation that Dr Greene agree to out-of-court settlement rejected. Dr Greene unwilling to see permanent record of his error on file. Dr Morgenstern concurs with hospital decision that Greene was at error in the O'Brien case. Postscript: Out-of-court settlement later accepted.

Greene's attitude altered by death of patient, 1st February 1996. Ross to Greene: "It's like there's you and the Pope - you guys are infallible. And, of course, there's the rest of us."

9. Night shift, March 1996 *[episode 2-18, "A Shift in the Night"]*

Other residents unavailable: Greene pulls fourth night shift in succession. Morgenstern refuses to close County to trauma. ER reaches maximum tolerance. Dr Greene treats patients in waiting room.

10. ER Dept decision re HIV-positive health-care workers, *[episodes 3-9 and 3-10]*

Greene illegally accessed Jeanie Boulet's personal file. Informed Dr Anspaugh of problem with HIV-positive worker in the ER. Policy decisions to be taken by each individual department. ER policy determined by attending physicians, Dr Greene and Dr Weaver.

Dr Anspaugh to Greene: "It's only suspicion - and, please, don't correct me if I'm wrong."

11. Meningitis case, January 1997 *[episode 3-11]*

Legal department criticized Greene for failing to co-sign cases. Further conflict as Greene disagreed with psych consult: performed lumbar puncture without consent. Tests concurred with diagnosis of meningitis resulting in mental disorder.

Note: Risked future prospects by bypassing opinion of psych consult. "I did my job and I can do my job somewhere, tenure or no tenure."

12. Accusations of racism, April 1997 *[episode 3-17]*

Dr Greene assumed black gun-shot wound victim (Kenny Law) would probably carry needles or weapons. Kenny innocent by-stander; white gun-shot wound was drugs dealer. Malik McGrath, Registered Nurse, objected to Greene requesting his presence when dealing with Law family.

Subsequent threatening of Dr Greene by Kenny Law dismissed. Investigation of attack on Greene *[episode 3-20]* revealed no connection to Chris Law case or any previous patients.

Chris Law: "Just another shot nigger's what you saw."

Note: Greene also unnecessarily curt with black woman – and was only prompted to regret it because he discovered she was wife of white patient.

Malpractice suit subsequently issued by Law family against hospital and civil suit against Greene. Former settled by out of court payment of $3 million. Latter dropped. Dr Greene close to dismissal over Kenny Law case.

Note: Greene hired Herb Speevak. The hospital is unaware of how Greene was able to pay Mr Speevak's expensive fees.

13. Assault on Dr Greene, summer 1997 *[episode 3-20 to 3-22]*

Dr Greene assaulted in men's bathroom, County ER. Discovered by Dr Ross. Treated for facial lacerations, broken hand and ribs. Extensive medical evaluations led by Ross and Weaver. Partial memory loss: no recollection of attacker. Hospital order installation of security cameras and bullet-proof glass in ER. One week after attack, Greene returned to work. Regarded attack as result of disgruntled patient: instigated measures to cut down waiting time. Police discovered no cause; Greene victim of random act. Concern of doctors Weaver and Pomerantz noted. Dr Ross feared imminent breakdown.

Greene to Weaver: "What I know is that everything I do, every day of my life, I do because I'm not the victim. I treat the victim, I cure the victim. I watch them roll the victim out like a piece of meat - but the truth is I'm the piece of meat."

14. Concerns over Dr Greene's competence, September to November 1997 *[episodes 4-1 to 4-7]*

Following assault, Dr Greene increasingly curt with staff and patients. Mood exacerbated by deteriorating relationship with ex-wife and daughter *[episode 4-4]* and pressures of Kenny Law malpractice and civil suits. Nurse Hathaway and Dr Doyle expressed concern that Greene may have inadequately treated bulimic girl *[episodes 4-2 and 4-3]*. PA Boulet objected to Dr Greene's refusal to finish physical examination of 65-year-old woman *[episode 4-5]*. Insensitive treatment of Mrs Scarlatti led to fear that Greene was suffering imminent nervous breakdown *[episode 4-6]*. However, brief vacation with Dr Ross (November 1997) led to change of mood noted by staff on his return.

Note: Greene admitted strains of assault in TV interview for PBS documentary on County ER. Feared losing control of what was outside the ER and within himself.

Greene: "The worst thing about it wasn't what it did to me. The worst thing was that some of the world's violence had leaked into our own ER. This is meant to be a safe place, for fixing people. Now it's vulnerable. And as an ER doctor, that's hard to accept."

Greene: "Trauma isn't something that happens to other people."

PROFESSIONAL ASSESSMENT

"The most impressive resident I've ever seen." (David Morgenstern to William Swift)

Strengths

Dr Greene is extremely well liked and easy to get along with, making him an excellent attending physician who pays close attention to the problems of individual residents and the morale of the unit as a whole. Furthermore, as an extremely strong man-manager and innovative emergency physician, he is ideally suited to a teaching position, should he desire it.

Weaknesses

Dr Morgenstern has noted specific problems relating to discipline, paperwork, and administration, and consequently suggested Dr Weaver to counteract these shortcomings. Greene has a particular hostility to calling staff meetings and occasionally makes scheduling errors. He also has a notable inability to manage his personal feelings and professional life, and has been attacked frequently by Dr Ross for his "sanctimonious" attitude to the private life of Ross and those of other members of staff. He is a little reactionary in terms of new initiatives, opposing several policies instigated in the ER by Dr Anspaugh and Dr Weaver. There have been accusations of unethical methods: Dr Greene lied to Dr Lewis about the origins of Dr Morgenstern's concerns over her assertiveness and he examined the personal medical file of Jeanie Boulet illegally. Furthermore he displays a degree of instinctive racism that is potentially worrying. Ultimately, Dr Greene's chief weaknesses stem from a belief in his own infallibility which allows any personal or professional problem to be magnified. His assault had far-reaching psychological consequences that adversely affected the efficiency and smooth running of the ER. However, Greene seems to have countered these problems in recent months and appears to have regained his confidence and authority within the ER.

Note: Greene is resentful that his personal pique may colour his professional decisions. Once described himself as a "sanctimonious, judgemental, self-righteous, sexually-frustrated little man", though Ross noted he is not little!

Prospects

Dr Greene should be encouraged to publish and to take a

permanent teaching position in the County General faculty. He may also wish to put his name forward for the post of ER Chief of Staff on the resignation of Dr Morgenstern.

PERSONAL INFORMATION

Family background

Father, David Greene, retired naval officer. Mark conceived after parents had dated only a couple of times; married soon afterwards. Mother, Ruth, admitted years later, relationship "had already started going wrong". Family had a number of homes while Greene was growing up, moving from Jacksonville to Norfolk, Corpus Christi then Washington DC. David Greene passed up promotion to admiral: returned home when wife wrote note re Mark's problems with bully at school. David Greene took desk job instead; "never once complained" about his decision.

Note: During David's first tour of Vietnam, Mark stared every night at model warplane hung up in his room. On his return, David pointed out that model was Phantom; he flew 86's: David bought Mark a replacement which Mark later tore down in anger.

Mother and father now live in San Diego, near naval base where David used to work. Mark visited infrequently until November 1997 when he and Doug Ross (in California for his own father's funeral) paid them a visit *[episode 4-7]*. Stay revived Greene's concerns re his parents' marriage and his father's health, both of which visibly deteriorating.

Note: Doug enamoured himself to Mrs Greene by praising her hummel figurines and super-sweet iced tea, after Mark had warned him about both!

Greene (and then girlfriend, Cynthia Hooper - see below) returned to San Diego in March 1998 *[episode 4-14]* when mother had series of small strokes after a fall: induced dementia. Greene also discovered mother had been seeing a psychiatrist, Dr Stanley Black, for a month. Mrs Greene's condition unlikely to improve; will continue to need wheelchair and constant care to protect her from risk of self-injury.

Note: Greene once told patient he was "the son of an agnostic Jew and a lapsed Catholic" [episode 2-10].

Ex-wife: Jennifer Greene

Daughter of a minister. Met when Greene was 16. Lived together only after marriage. Jenn went through night school for six years to finish college so Greene could continue med-school. Considerable strain on relationship after Greene became chief resident. Jenn returned to studying for her Bar exams: taken April 1994, passed the following month. Interviewed for jobs in Detroit and Milwaukee. Worked as clerk for federal judge. Angered by Greene's unilateral decision to accept post as attending physician in ER; consequently accepted renewed position for federal judge. Jenn left Mark, February 1995. December 1995: Greene discovered Jenn had fallen in love with Craig Simon and Greenes then divorced; Jenn given custody of daughter, Rachel. Custody battle settled amicably (see below). Craig and Jennifer married, September 1996.

Note: Greene once suggested that he and Jenn were married only to please their parents.

Note: Greene's mother always thought Jennifer had a sour streak about her; thinks Rachel may have picked it up too.

Note: Ross particularly disturbed by collapse of Greene's marriage. On hearing marriage is over: "Hey don't say that, you're my domestic role model!"

Daughter: Rachel Greene

Born: 16th February 1989 (during Greene's third year of med-school). First visited ER, October 1994. Both parents concerned for effect of separation on Rachel particularly after divorce papers issued, end 1995. Amicable settlement for Rachel agreed privately - neither Jenn nor Mark to leave the Chicago-Milwaukee area until Rachel has completed high school. Continuing emotional problems for Rachel: pretended to have leukaemia, April 1997.

Note: Dr Hemmings, a friend of Greene's from med-school now living in San Diego, considered him the most 'together' student in her class (she was the most driven): knew he wanted a family, and went for it. Greene told her despite the divorce, he had not given up on idea of having a family.

Personal relationships

Greene's interest in Susan Lewis noted, by Doug Ross, early in Greene's working relationship with her. Rumours about Greene and Lewis circulated February 1996. Confessed his love for her on her departure from Chicago at the end of 1996 but realized he was already too late. Relationship with Iris, an infomercial director *[episodes 2-17 to 2-19]*. Brief relationships with Chuni Marquez, Heather Morgan, and Polly Mackenzie (January 1997). Relationship with Dr Nina Pomerantz, County General psych consult, ended shortly after Dr Greene's assault.

Note: Following Susan's departure, Hathaway identified Greene as "Glasses, receding hairline, broken heart..."

Relationship with Cynthia Hooper started soon after his decision to hire her as ER desk clerk, despite disastrous interview. Over next few months she fell in love with him; suggested moving into his apartment when her lease expired. Greene generally happy with relationship (especially physical side), when Cynthia accompanied to San Diego after mother's fall, Greene forced to admit he was not in love with Cynthia. She left Chicago soon afterwards. (See also Personnel file of Cynthia Hooper.)

Greene to Cynthia (after she's told him he's a considerate lover!): "That's me, the caretaker. I'm like a magnet for needy people. They follow me wherever I go."

Health matters

Greene took up smoking after his assault; continued for several months despite several attempts to give up with help of nicotine patches, and a deal with Cynthia: for each cigarette smoked he would save $1 towards a Club Med holiday. After departure of Cynthia, Nurse Hathaway used more direct method: allocated Greene to patient with end stage lung cancer, prompting Greene to flush remaining cigarettes down toilet *[episode 4-16]*.

[*Trivia:* While at college he used to go to the Rathskeller every Friday night and drink huge pitchers of beer. He also tried to impress one girl by playing football but had to change his strategy when he regularly ended up at the bottom of the scrums. For Christmas in 1993, Mark bought Jenn a dust-buster. Greene was the star of the hospital teaching video 'How to Intubate...' When he started at the ER, he had blond hair. Jennifer was Mark's first sexual partner and he was never unfaithful to her. Mark invited everyone he ever met to their marriage; Jenn only got through it with drugs! He initially wanted to elope but "Jenn wanted Notre Dame". He once remarked "compromise is the soul of marriage" (just after Jenn had left him). Mark Greene is a terrible ice-skater. He has had dates with an aerobics instructor, a girl with a food-filled orthodontic brace, and narrowly averted a double-date with Ross, Holda, and the mysterious Inga. As a child, Greene's favourite toy was Mr Sunny Bear. He used to steal his mother's cigarettes, flush them down the toilet and then own up to her. Tommy Leadbetter used to beat him up every day during sixth form, and Mark became afraid to go to school until his father returned home to sort the situation out. He hated family summer holidays, especially the long drives to national parks and relatives, and idolised Kate Jackson. His father used to take him to the docks, where Mark was scared by kittyhawks. He was taught to slam dance by the younger sister of a friend he went to med-school with - he discovered she was brain-dead after a traffic accident. Mark once told Carter that sometimes he just wants to quit and do something else.

Anthony Edwards's Mark Greene remains the show's principal character, the single figure around whom much of the series revolves. Unlike any other character, Greene can be seen working with all members of staff, as befits his job description and character. His role as the ER's senior attending, and before that as chief resident, allows for the effective interplay of the personal and the professional. Mark's friendship with Doug Ross, and infatuation of a kind with Susan Lewis, make for excellent drama, as problems in the workplace extend to private confrontations. The underlying romance between Greene and Lewis was one of the series' finest and most frustrating storylines, culminating in Greene's desperately sad expression of his love for Susan, alas too late. His subsequent emotional problems, and those resulting from the brutal assault in 'Random Acts', make Greene one of the series' most interesting and human characters. It is as testament to this that Anthony Edwards is now paid a rumoured $400,000 per episode and has been signed by Warner Bros to appear in the program up to its seventh series.]

DOUGLAS ROSS, M.D.

AGE

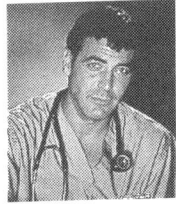

36.

POSITION

Holder of ER paediatric fellowship for over four years. Works full time in the ER. Funding supplied by paediatrics but underwritten by ER under arrangement settled between Doctors Morgenstern and Bernstein, summer 1997. Currently urging the creation of an ER paeds attending position, for which he would apply. Supervized by Dr Mark Greene.

Note: Greene and Ross close friends - can cause tension at times.

MEDICAL TRAINING AND CAREER TO DATE

Education prior to medical school notably successful, though uneven. Inclination to study often dependent on relationship with subject tutor; success through instinctive aptitude rather than hard work or memory.

Ross to Nurse Hathaway, re his pre-med physics exam: "They told us we could bring one sheet into the exam with all the formulas written on it. I brought in a really big sheet!"

Medical school: Four years. Years three and four: 'hands-on' training including paediatric and trauma rotations. Paediatric rotation at Southside Hospital under Dr Donald Anspaugh.

Residency: Four years. Included one year Mount Sinai Hospital concurrent with Kerry Weaver.

Note: possible professional conflict - Ross negative about Weaver's appointment as ER chief resident.

SIGNIFICANT CAREER EVENTS

1. Assault on patient's father, 16th February 1995 *[episode 1-16]*

Dr Ross examined baby girl ('fell' from building), found imprint of booted foot on child's back, concluded print was that of father. Failed to contact social services; assaulted father in waiting room. Restrained by his colleagues to prevent further assaults.

Disciplinary note

Report from Ms Diane Leeds, Risk Management Department. Resident Review Committee referred Ross to hospital psychiatrist, Dr Alan Murphy; arranged for compulsory consultation. Ross attended session with Dr Murphy 10th April 1995 *[episode 1-21]*; Dr Murphy reportedly satisfied Ross's "sloppy impulse control" not likely to be a major problem in future.

Note: Ms Leeds Ross's girlfriend at time.

2. Assault by patient's mother, 4th March 1995 *[episode 1-17]*

Risk management report by Ms Leeds: incident involving Dr Ross and Charge Nurse Carol Hathaway. Ross attended to young girl, Bonnie Howe, repeatedly abused by mother. Child and Family Services called to deal with child; police arrested mother. When dragged away from daughter, woman inflicted scratches to Ross's neck; treated in ER by Nurse Hathaway.

3. Treatment of Chia-Chia Loh, October/November 1995 *[episodes 2-3 to 2-5]*

Chia-Chia Loh, four-year-old boy with AIDS, brought in to ER early October 1995 *[episode 2-3]*: had become unconscious after medication overdose. Ross stabilized patient and found overdose due to fault in prescription given to boy's mother, Mei-Sun Loh, by Dr Neil Bernstein's clinic in County General. Ross instructed Mrs Loh to receive medication direct from him in ER in future; second visit mid-November 1995 *[episode 2-4]*. Dr Weaver reported visit not indicated on board in accordance with normal procedures.

Patient re-admitted nine days later *[episode 2-5]* with flu symptoms - tests revealed cryptococcal meningitis. Dr Ross persuaded Mrs Loh to consent to course of treatment. Dr Greene believed treatment inappropriate, given risk of side-effects and fact that Chia-Chia not expected to live for many more days. Given facts, Mrs Loh preferred to take Chia-Chia home. Greene reported that Dr Ross was unhappy with the outcome.

Ross to Greene: "If it was your kid, you would bet on a miracle."

4. Objections of Dr Neil Bernstein, autumn 1995 *[episodes 2-1 to 2-6]*

At staff meetings in 1995, Head of Paediatrics Dr Neil Bernstein expressed dissatisfaction with Dr Ross; particular reference to fact that fellowship paid for by paediatrics despite Ross being permanently in ER. Bernstein called Ross "arrogant", saying he persistently undermined Bernstein's authority (see Ross's call to Bernstein's clinic re prescription for Chia-Chia Loh). Meeting November 1995 *[episode 2-6]*: Dr Bernstein announced intention not to support renewal of Ross's fellowship on 31st December. Despite defence from Drs Greene and Morgenstern, Coburn agreed Ross "a loose cannon", becoming impossible to deal with. Ross therefore advised to find another post; December 1995, accepted position at private children's hospital.

5. Rescue of Ben Larkin/Channel Five news report, December 1995 *[episode 2-7]*

Taking time off from ER to attend job interview, Dr Ross alerted to plight of boy, Ben Larkin, trapped in storm drain during misadventure with brother, Joey. Drain was rapidly filling with water; Ben's leg caught in grille: risk of drowning and hypothermia. Ross instructed Joey to call for help. Showed commendable courage by single-handedly rescuing young Ben from the drain; built up rapport, prevented Ben losing hope while Ross removed grille. Sudden release of water engulfed Ben and Ross; Ben lost underwater for several seconds. Ross retrieved Ben; required emergency tracheotomy to re-start breathing. Ross performed tracheotomy using pen-knife.

Against advice of paramedics, allowed Channel Five News reporter to transport Ben and himself by helicopter to County General ER, where staff saved Ben's life. Dr Ross later presented with award for bravery; after discussion, decision taken to renew fellowship for another year.

Note: Ross turned down offer at private children's hospital - "Ninety grand a year and nobody dies," he told ER colleagues. Resented hypocrisy of board, especially Morgenstern and Bernstein; threw away award.

6. Failure to diagnose cancerous tumour, December 1995 (tumour finally discovered March 1996 *[episode 2-17])*

Dr Ross failed to see tumour developing in leg of Mr Bowman's grandson when first treated in December 1995. On advice from hospital attorney Kathy Snyder, Ross declined to inform Mr Bowman, who was told by Dr Benton instead. Unconfirmed reports say Dr Ross contributed significant amount to costs of boy's chemotherapy from his own funds.

7. Nadine Wilks, patient admitted 24th October 1996 *[episode 3-4]*

Miss Wilks brought in to ER by Dr Ross, with whom she had spent the night. Suffered seizure as result of cocaine overdose, complicated by epilepsy. Questions raised by Dr Weaver and Dr Greene re Dr Ross's ability to work later that day, though test for cocaine carried out on Ross came back negative.

8. Jad Houston, February 1997 *[episodes 3-14 and 3-16]*

Jad Houston, who had cystic fibrosis, brought to ER in February 1997 *[episode 3-14]* suffering from attack; treated by Dr Ross despite having signed DNR (do not resuscitate) order. Ross waited to check Mr Houston's age; 17, meaning that necessary consent for DNR order could only come from mother. Ross seemed to persuade Mrs Houston to agree to her son's wishes, but at last moment she demanded he be put back on respirator; Ross reluctantly did. On Mr Houston's 18th birthday *[episode 3-16]*, he requested Ross take him off respirator. Surprisingly Mr Houston able to breathe unaided and discharged himself.

9. Charlie, October 31st 1996 to summer 1997 *[episodes 3-5 to 3-22]*

Ross initially a reluctant participant in 'healthmobile' project pioneered by Dr Donald Anspaugh - though later organized immunization program as off-shoot. One patient Ross encountered in connection with scheme was Charlie. At time of immunization program, Charlie looking after housemate's baby son, Ahmed Lopez. Ross later operated on Ahmed to remove a tumour. Charlie often returned to ER and to Ross's home; once demanded money from Ross to pay off pimp. Arrived in ER January 1997 *[episode 3-11]*, battered and bruised, having been raped. Ross called social services - determined Charlie could not be returned to mother's home due to mother's history of violence. Charlie tried unsuccessfully to persuade Ross to adopt her. In summer 1997 *[episode 3-22]*, Charlie returned to ER: heroin overdose. Refused to see social worker; disappeared from hospital. Dr Ross and Dr Del Amico conducted unsuccessful search.

10. Review of funding and conflict with Dr Kerry Weaver, October 1997 onwards *[series 4]*.

Dr Weaver reviewed funding position as acting chief of ER during absence of Dr Morgenstern, as part of drive to cut budget deficit *[episode 4-3]*: instructed him to prepare a research project and/or secure independent funding, or lose fellowship. Ross prepared research project on PCA [patient controlled anaesthesia, a system of treatment which allows patients to control their own medication] and made presentation, but Weaver dissatisfied with research methods. Despite prompting, new research project or funding for Dr Ross still awaited as of summer 1998. Ross instead pushing for paediatric attending post.

11. Treatment of Sophie Marston during evacuation of ER, March 1998 *[episode 4-15]*.

Sophie Marston, aged eight, brought in to ER with acute renal failure - suspected E-coli - requiring dialysis. ER then evacuated due to benzine leak. Ross and Nurse Hathaway attempted to move Sophie to PICU using elevator, but power to elevator cut: Ross and Hathaway improvise treatment; oxygen supply close to exhaustion before rescue team arrived, but Sophie survived.

Note: Ross admitted to Sophie that he was "really scared" by the experience.

12. Eric and Adrian Reynolds, spring 1998 *[episode 4-16]*.

Adrian Reynolds, aged five, brought in with poisoning. Half-brother, Eric, had filled soda can with print developer and insecticide. Dr Ross found cigarette burns on Eric's arm; concluded he had been abused by step-father (Eric's father). Referred to social services, who then commit Eric to Edmonston for psychiatric assessment: no signs of remorse; cigarette burns may have been self-inflicted. Ross told he may be asked to testify against Eric.

Ross to Mary Jo Reynolds (Eric and Adrian's mother): "Don't worry, ma'am. We're going to take care of both of your kids."

Ross: "Sometimes working with kids is fine, but sometimes it really sucks."

13. Josh McNeil, June 1998 *[episodes 4-20 to 4-22]*.
Josh McNeil, crack baby, admitted by mother requiring methadone. Dr Ross suspected mother of using baby to obtain methadone for herself. Mother subsequently left baby in County ER. Foster mother, ex-nurse, found to take Josh and begin program of long-term withdrawal but when McNeil's mother moved in with aunt, baby to be returned to her by social services. Objections by County staff overruled. Dr Ross misled social worker that baby required additional tests and instead began unauthorized rapid detoxification under deep sedation, with aid of Nurse Hathaway. Complications led to discovery of baby in Dr Ross's care. Doctors Greene and Weaver voiced strong objections to Dr Ross's conduct but Doctors Anspaugh, Kayson and Rocher supported Ross. Case ongoing.

Ross (to Weaver): "I just want to make sure that this boy gets a decent shot at a normal life. I don't care about your rules or regulations."

PROFESSIONAL ASSESSMENT

Doug Ross to Jerry: "I'm a dedicated paediatric resident, struggling to fulfil the promise of a brilliant early career."

Strengths

Dr Ross is a highly skilled and hard-working paediatrician, who is invaluable to the ER, often putting in late and unsociable hours (though the reason for this has usually been a shortage of money). Of particular note is his excellent manner with children, from babies to teenagers, which puts the patients at their ease and helps them through the often traumatic process of treatment. Dr Ross accords children the same level of respect that the best doctors give to their adult patients, ensuring that they are never patronized or mistreated and that their needs are always catered for.

Weaknesses

On several occasions concern has been expressed about Dr Ross's attitude towards authority: Dr Bernstein is far from the only senior doctor he has clashed with. His attention to procedures and paperwork is also open to question. (His one day of deputizing for Greene as chief resident [episode 1-7] was not successful.) More importantly, he has a tendency to become emotionally involved in the plight of his patients, especially in cases of parental abuse or neglect, which can erupt into aggressive behaviour.

Note: Ross once told Greene that his problem was not the fact that Mark was his boss; it was the fact that anyone was his boss.

Prospects

The board is aware of Dr Ross's erratic employment record prior to joining County General, and considers that the ER is lucky to have kept hold of him for more than three years. However, the board is increasingly concerned by his persistent clashes with Dr Weaver, and his continuing failure to justify or fund the underwriting of his fellowship by the ER. While there may be some merit in the suggestion that the ER should have a permanent paediatrics attending physician, the Board is not impressed by Dr Ross's motive for making this proposal, or his methods of backing it up. There must come a point where the value of any physician, however gifted, is outweighed by the danger of having a member of the ER team who believes he is a law unto himself.

Note: Ross said that his "few years" in the ER was the longest commitment he had ever made, "to anything or anybody".

PERSONAL INFORMATION

Family background

Father: Ray Ross (deceased)

No contact for 22 years; Ray saw son on news in connection with rescue of Ben Larkin. Met socially a few times; Ray then disappeared abroad, with large amount of money stolen from girlfriend, Karen Hines.

November 1997, Ray Ross killed in automobile accident near Barstow. Ran a stop sign, 120 mph, hit pick-up truck. Driver of pick-up truck, Pedro Lopez, father of six, died at scene, as did Ross, Lopez and Ross's partner, Sheri Fox.

Note: Doug also has a son of his own, aged 12 [mentioned to a patient and overheard by Wendy], although he has never met him.

Note: Applied to join 'Big Brothers' agency in summer 1997, caring for disadvantaged children.

Personal relationships

Ross known to have had many, usually brief, relationships with women while working at County, some of them fellow employees. Two-year relationship with Charge Nurse Carol Hathaway ended, some time before March 1994, when he "replaced" her with someone else, action he now describes as "stupid, childish and immature". Other women dated by Ross: Linda Farrell, representative of Novell Pharmaceuticals *[episodes 1-5 to 2-7]*; Diane Leeds, risk management at County, mother of Jake *[episodes 1-13 to 1-23]*; Holda, Finnish flight attendant *[during series two]*; Karen Hines, father's girlfriend *[episodes 2-19 to 2-22]*; Heather, young doctor at County *[in third series]*. After death of Nadine Wilks, womanizing considerably toned down. Returned attention to Carol Hathaway.

Ross now appears seriously committed to relationship with Hathaway. Planned to marry her as a surprise, February 1998 *[episode 4-12]*, but she failed to turn up for their date; told him she had kissed paramedic Greg Powell. Later asked him for more time before setting marriage date; Ross, initially hurt and jealous, eventually calmed down and told her to "take all the time you need".

Carol, responding to Doug's charge that with the Greg Powell affair, she's embarassed him in front of his friends: ìWhat about the surgical tech in the on call room? Or the paeds nurse in the parking lot? Or the drug rep with the fake breasts and the big hair?"

Psychiatric report of Dr Alan Murphy (extracts)

Initial consultation after assault on patient's father, February 1995. Dr Ross's aggressive reaction towards people he sees as 'bad parents' could be traced back to perceived 'abandonment' of him and his mother by his father, when Dr Ross was a child. Ross clearly blames some of his personality traits on his father: like him, he claims, Ross never committed to anything in life. Job lets him "see people for a couple of minutes, fix them as best I can, and send them on their way. No fuss, no messy details". Possible connection with Dr Ross's general problems with authority figures?

[Trivia: In episode 2-14 Doug's birthday is in early February, which makes his starsign Aquarius. Discussing 'Winnie the Pooh' with Harper Tracy in series two, he revealed that his favourite character was always Eeyore (Harper's favourite was Tigger). Doug used to race TR7s to speeds of 120mph when he was young. Ross is affectionately known in the ER as 'Doctor Intercom', because of his reputation as the worst gossip in the hospital: he made sure that everyone knew about Susan's relationship with Div Cvetic, told everyone when it was Carol's birthday, and delighted in telling Mark and Susan about each other's blind dates. When Weaver told several people about the 'secret' meeting about hospital closures in episode 3-2, she told Greene: "I figured if you don't tell Doug Ross, you're okay!"

Doug Ross is rightly one of the most popular characters in ER, played by one of its best actors, George Clooney. The fact that George has stayed with the series so far despite a flourishing career in films like Batman and Robin *and* One Fine Day *shows his sincere commitment to the show, and it's a good thing: rarely has he had an opportunity in his films to play a character which has as much depth and ambiguity as Doug Ross. Although he is endearing in many ways, Doug is very much a flawed hero, often making disastrous mistakes in his personal and professional life. In the fourth series we saw him begin to succeed in his relationship with Carol, after spending most of the first three series telling her he loved her and wanted her back. Meanwhile, his professional situation seemed to become yet more precarious, with his maverick tendency causing more problems with Weaver and Greene. The fifth series, of course, is to be George Clooney's last, as his five-year contract comes to an end. It remains to be seen exactly how he will be written out, and it would be surprising if the possibility of occasional returns to the show was excluded, but one thing is for sure: once Clooney, and Ross, have left ER it won't be the same show again . .]*

SUSAN LEWIS, M.D.

Note: File closed, November 1997.

AGE

33.

POSITION

Medical resident, fifth year. Left County General autumn 1996 during her fourth year. Transferred to Phoenix General Hospital.

MEDICAL TRAINING AND CAREER TO DATE

Medical school: Four years. Years three and four 'hands-on' training including rotations at Mercy General and Lakeside Hospital, Chicago.

Residency: Three and a half years at County General.

SIGNIFICANT CAREER EVENTS

1. Clash with Dr Div Cvetic re patient with senile dementia, May 1994 *[episode 1-1]*
Dr Lewis treated patient for minor injuries; requested help from psychiatric dept as patient suffering from senile dementia. Dr Div Cvetic (Head of Psychiatrics) refused assistance; Dr Lewis herself then admitted patient to psychiatric service. Later clashed again with Dr Cvetic *[episode 1-7]* re drunk and disorderly patient committed by Dr Cvetic for forty-eight hours (after patient assaulted Dr Cvetic); Dr Lewis released patient as soon as sober.

Note: Lewis and Cvetic were then partners; Cvetic's unsympathetic actions probably relate to his own worsening mental state (see file on Dr Cvetic).

24

2. Full case review: Mr Vennerbeck, January 1995 *[episode 1-13]*

Dr Jack Kayson expressed concerns re Dr Lewis's competence on several cases. Lewis discharged Mr Vennerbeck after consultation with Kayson; Vennerbeck then re-admitted in cardiac arrest. Review found Dr Lewis should have appreciated risk of impending attack; however Kayson's consultation less than thorough.

Morgenstern to Lewis: "The specifics don't concern me nearly as much as your inability to assert yourself. You allowed Kayson to intimidate you...You must be an aggressive advocate for your patients."

Greene to Lewis: "When you go head to head with guys like Kayson and Benton, you tend to back down."

Note: Kayson himself later admitted with heart attack, and treated by Dr Lewis with tPA. Kayson told Lewis the experience had changed his life - even asked Lewis out to dinner! (She declined.)

3. Clashes with Dr Kerry Weaver

Turbulent relations with new chief resident Dr Weaver, especially during autumn 1995. Almost Weaver's first action in the ER was to call time of death on Lewis's patient against her wishes; Weaver disagreed with several subsequent decisions by Lewis; insisted Lewis check all procedures with her. Dr Greene forced to mediate.

Weaver to Lewis: "You have a tendency to become anger-locked and inflexible. If you feel yourself getting dug in, call me: I'm here to help."

Lewis to Greene, re Weaver: "She's irritating as hell! You'd think on her first day she would at least try to be nice."

4. Diagnosed case of lidocaine toxicity, December 1995 *[episode 2-9]*

Lewis identified rare instance of patient with toxic reaction to lidocaine. Weaver suggested presentation of case at conference; Lewis declined.

5. Concerns re personal and professional commitments

Dr Weaver expressed concern re Dr Lewis's ability to keep personal life separate from professional duty. Dr Morgenstern informed Dr Lewis that more commitment would be required to increase chances of promotion at County. Dr Lewis considered altering her residency to a part-time basis in order to adopt her niece (see Personal information), but child later returned to her mother.

Lewis to Weaver, after the latter assigned Lewis to routine cases because she noted she had "personal obligations": "I don't need any slack. If anything affects my ability to work, I'll let you know."

Lewis to Morgenstern: "I've taken on plenty of responsibility. So you'll have to forgive me if I don't stay after school these days to work for extra credit."

6. Candidacy for chief resident post

On suggestion of Dr Greene, Dr Lewis applied for post of chief resident from summer 1995. Dr Weaver at first resistant, but later supported Lewis's candidacy. Lewis was offered post, but she refused; Linda Martins appointed chief resident instead.

Note: Lewis told Greene that losing custody of baby Suzie had made her realize she needed to make more time for her personal life. Meanwhile Greene supported Weaver's candidacy for attending physician post on condition that she support Lewis as chief resident; told nurses "I think I just sold my soul to the Devil"!

PROFESSIONAL ASSESSMENT

Dr Lewis is a first-class medical resident, and her departure was a serious loss to County General and its ER. During her long-standing disputes with Drs Kayson and Weaver, concern was expressed about Dr Lewis's confidence in her own abilities, and her tendency to back down when confronted by a senior doctor. Since then she has become more forthright and sure of herself, culminating in her insistence, against the wishes of Dr Weaver, on an ultrasound for a pregnant patient on 2nd May 1996 *[episode 2-20]* which revealed that the woman had a tumour on her adrenal gland: something that would otherwise have been missed, with potentially fatal results.

Prospects

Dr Lewis is not expected to return to County and will probably stay in Phoenix for the time being, where she will no doubt go on to be an excellent attending physician. We wish her well.

PERSONAL INFORMATION

Family background

"We have ways of screwing people up in my family." (Susan Lewis)

Sister: Chloe Lewis

"She's thirty-four years old and she can't even part her hair." (Susan Lewis)

Has stayed with Susan for prolonged periods on at least two occasions, including several weeks leading up to and following the birth of her child, Suzie. Started course in computer skills at Midwest Business Academy, but dropped out; took up waitressing job for short period and left after argument with employer. Abandoned Suzie, leaving her with Susan, for five months from early October 1995 *[episode 2-3]* to early March 1996 *[episode 2-16]*. Criminal record includes arrests for drunk and disorderly behaviour (October 1994) and driving under the influence (April 1995). Returning to Suzie in March 1996 *[episode 2-16]*, explained she had been living in Phoenix and employed as a claims adjuster for four months; free of alcohol and drugs for five months. Became engaged to Joe, a police officer. Regained custody of baby Suzie, though Susan attempted to adopt her.

Chloe: "I want to be a mother to my child."
Susan: "Well that's too damn bad, because you abandoned your child. And that's the best thing that ever happened to her."

Niece: Suzie Lewis

Born May 12th 1995 - delivered by Dr Lewis herself in County ER. Dr Lewis looked after Suzie for five months after Chloe abandoned her; helped by their father, Henry, despite misgivings of mother, Cookie. Used day care facility at County. Began adoption proceedings; attempted to continue after Chloe's return, but advised she would lose custody; returned Suzie to Chloe in April 1996 *[episode 2-19]*.

Therapy notes (extracts)

Dr Lewis was deeply affected by her experience of looking after her niece for months and then having to give her up. She instinctively regards her sister as wayward and irresponsible, refusing to believe the possibility that she may have reformed. Over a period of months effectively standing in as Suzie's mother, Susan understandably 'fell in love' with the child and adjusted to the idea of parenting, so much so that she could contemplate changing her residency to a part-time basis and adopting Suzie. The main reason for her move to Phoenix was to be with Chloe, Joe and her niece.

Personal relationships

Only known romantic involvement: with Dr Div Cvetic, head of psychiatry, until his disappearance in November/December 1994 [between episodes 1-8 and 1-9] after a period of clinical depression. Relationship with Dr Mark Greene strongly rumoured at one time.

Note: Rumours of Greene and Lewis romance greatly exaggerated! Misunderstanding on part of John Carter, spread by Dr Ross. Lewis also involved with 'Paul' until March 1994 (overheard talking to him on phone).

[Trivia: Susan was a bridesmaid at Carol's wedding. Cookie Lewis apparently drank sangria and smoked four packets of 'Lucky Strikes' a day when bringing up Chloe and Susan. Lewis has, or had, a fear of flying: her planned holiday to Hawaii stopped short at Phoenix when she had to change planes (the attendants had to carry her off the plane); she overcame her fear to some extent when she flew in a helicopter for the first time to get to the site of a vehicle collision in episode 3-6. Susan also had a cat - which Greene looked after while she went on holiday - but we don't know whether or not she took it with her to Phoenix.

Lewis was one of the most likeable characters in the show, and is still sorely missed by many viewers. Her continuing struggle to gain confidence at work was an interesting, though understated, storyline, but she'll always be remembered for two things: first, the heart-rending story of her looking after and attempting to adopt baby Suzie; and second, our hopes for a romance with Greene, which were cruelly thwarted when she left for Phoenix. Strangely enough, Susan's stated intention to spend more time on her personal life, and not to be too wrapped up in work, mirrors Sherry Stringfield's reasons for leaving the show, which she said became something of a "treadmill" - especially considering all the fame that went with it.]

JOHN TRUMAN CARTER, M.D.

AGE

28

POSITION

One of County's 'home-grown' residents. Former third-year medical student and sub-intern under tutelage of Dr Peter Benton. Completed first year as surgical resident and member of Dr Benton's surgical blue team. Dr Anspaugh approved Carter's request to change specialty from surgery to emergency medicine. Repeated internship in County ER.

MEDICAL TRAINING AND CAREER TO DATE

Medical school, first and second years: Years one and two included psychiatry and dermatology rotations.

Note: Benton calls these "the well-dressed specialties".

Medical school, third and fourth years: Assigned to Dr Benton from 17th March 1994.

> **Medical school assessment (extracts)**
> During these two years, Dr Carter has excelled in many fields, showing exceptional ability in patient care, great competence in trauma situations in the ER and improved ability in general surgery, although Dr Benton has remarked on his inability to focus on occasion. His admission to the hospital's fourth year sub-internship program was complicated by his refusal of a place in the ER in favour of a surgical sub-internship which only became available at the last moment *[episodes 1-22 to 1-24]*. Attached to Dr Vucelich's 'clamp and run' research, through Dr Benton.

29

Though scheduled to finish his sub-internship with a plastics rotation, administration discovered that Dr Carter was deficient in certain areas of medicine and instead required that he complete a four week paediatrics rotation with Dr Ross in the ER *[episodes 2-20 to 2-22]*.

Internship [First Year Residency]: Member of Dr Benton's 'blue' team: general surgery, ER, proctology. Joined Dr Hicks's team, January 1997 *[episode 3-13]*. Involved in paediatric surgery, through Benton's association with Dr Abby Keaton. Transferred in summer 1997 to emergency medicine under supervision of Dr Mark Greene. All procedures run past Dr Maggie Doyle.

SIGNIFICANT CAREER EVENTS

1. Incorrect identification of GSW victim, May 1994 *[episode 1-3]*

Failed to identify anonymous gun-shot wound victim correctly from year book photographs; contacted wrong parents. Carter apparently distracted by nature of the injuries and prospect of notifying relatives of deceased patient for first time. Corrected mistake and informed second set of parents. On same day, Dr Carter successfully delivered a baby for first time.

2. Suicide of 'Miss Carlton', 17th November 1994 *[episode 1-8]*

Male transvestite, Carlton, admitted to the ER having sustained injuries in car accident. Dr Carter's uncomfortable personal feelings surrounding patient's sexuality interfered with ability to listen to Carlton's problems. Carlton later jumped from hospital roof, despite attempt by Carter to prevent it.

3. Complaint to Mark Greene, chief resident, 1st January 1995 *[episode 1-11]*

Dr Carter complained re basic nature of 'scut work' given by Benton. Dr Mark Greene encouraged Benton to allow Carter to intubate and later attend his first gall bladder surgery. Unfortunately, Dr Carter contaminated himself and was unable to assist.

4. Treatment of Caleb, 18th May 1995 *[episode 1-24]*

Carter's compassionate treatment of young boy with leukaemia mirrored events in own childhood [see Personal information].

5. First patient: Ed Menke, October 1995 *[episode 2-3]*

Carter performed lumbar puncture on Mr Ed Menke; accidentally pierced patient's liver, requiring immediate surgery. Attempts to reinvigorate Menke's collapsed liver successful, but there were further medical complications which could only be discovered during exploratory surgery: Doctors Hicks and Benton unable to save patient. Mr Menke's liver given to Dr Carter to be sent to County laboratory for cirosis studies.

6. Treatment of Mrs Rubadoux, December 1995 to February 1996 *[episodes 2-10 to 2-12 and 2-14]*

Shortly before Christmas 1995, Mrs Rubadoux brought to County suffering from dissecting aneurism. Dr Carter explained to husband choice of surgical methods available; recommended Dr Vucelich's pioneering 'clamp and run' procedure, but gave warning ofpossible heart attack and paralysis. Dr Benton completed surgery in record time but Mrs Rubadoux suffered post-operative symptoms of partial paraplegia, congestive heart failure, renal insufficiency - therefore required full time care. Dr Carter put in charge of continued care but it became clear that Mrs Rubadoux was dying. Ordered to make Mrs Rubadoux comfortable, Carter gave patient dibutamine and sent her to permanent care facility. Mrs Rubadoux suffered stroke at nursing home and was returned to County, in Dr Carter's care, on insistence of Mr Rubadoux. Benton ordered that Mrs Rubadoux be admitted for final days: Carter arranged for her to be taken by Neurology for nerve stimulation study but failed to inform Mr Rubadoux of seriousness of his wife's condition. Mr Rubadoux angrily confronted Dr Carter re lack of candidness on 25th January; Mrs Rubadoux died 1st February 1996.

Note: Carter attempted to clear his conscience by attending Mrs Rubadoux's memorial service.

7. Accepted as resident, 20th March 1996 *[episodes 2-15 to 2-17]*

Offered post of first year resident at County General following impressive interview on 15th February 1996 and glowing recommendations of Dr Carl Vucelich and Dr Peter Benton. Carter celebrated with alcohol while on duty, against hospital policy. Dr

Hicks considered this grounds for expulsion, but disciplinary review committee not organized; indiscretion allowed to pass.

8. Death of Dr Gant *[episode 3-11]*

Sought counselling after suicide of colleague, also intern supervised by Benton. Dr Carter expressed feelings of guilt that he had not been more of a friend to Dr Gant, failing to act on realization that he was working himself too hard. Also see personnel file on Dr Dennis Gant.

9. Conflict with Dr Anspaugh: treatment of Mr Bartok, 17 April 1997 *[episode 3-18]*

Disagreement with Dr Anspaugh over need for preventative surgery for Mr Bartok, high-risk candidate. Carter lied to Dr Hicks to have man taken to surgery. During surgery, Dr Carter encouraged Hicks to continue operating despite septic stomach, and after Dr Anspaugh discovered Bartok admitted against Anspaugh's wishes. After operation, Carter put on probation but not removed from surgical program, despite Hicks's desire to see him expelled.

Dr Anspaugh came into conflict with Dr Carter on two further cases. Case of Mr Lensky *[episode 3-21]*: Dr Carter disagreed with Dr Anspaugh's intention to operate on perforated ulcer in favour of non-operative treatment in accordance with patient's wishes. Secondly, arranging nursing home for Mr and Mrs Kromkey *[episode 3-22]*, Dr Carter refused to attend Dr Anspaugh's surgical rounds.

Carter to Anspaugh, re Mr Lensky: "I don't believe I should cut someone open just because I can."

In light of these events, and his increasing concern for personal requirements of patients, Dr Carter requested to be transferred from the surgical program and to join ER medical program for second year of residency. Transferred to emergency medicine but downgraded to intern status.

10. Professional conflicts with Dr Peter Benton, autumn 1997 *[episodes 4-1 to 4-4]*.

Dr Carter complained of Benton's abrupt manner with him following his transfer from the surgical program to residency in emergency medicine. Confusion partly arising from Dr Carter's superior skills contrasted with his position as an intern for second year and his knowledge and experience of surgical procedures contrasted with the requirements of an ER intern. Conflict settled privately.

Note: Carter confronted Benton re deteriorating relations. Benton objected to Carter's decision to approach Anspaugh rather than talk to him about changing his specialty. Benton would have appreciated opportunity to talk Carter out of it.

Benton: "You don't want to be treated like my student, stop seeking my approval."

11. First student, George Henry, autumn 1997 *[episodes 4-2 to 4-10]*.

Assigned first student, George Henry, studying for medical PhD in brain research on compulsory ER rotation. Due to inadequate formal training prior to rotation and inattentiveness, Dr Carter unable to evaluate Henry on a number of procedures. Henry forced to repeat rotation following Carter's report. Passed on 24th December 1997.

Note: Henry was resuscitated by Doctors Carter and Del Amico after suffering arrest following exposure to latex triggered by allergy. Henry now brings non-latex gloves to work.

Carter: "Do me a favour, Henry. Stick to brain research."

12. Alleged withholding of treatment from Jack Dar, February 1998 *[episode 4-13]*.

Dar was a serial rapist whose victims had been treated at County ER for several weeks, including by Carter. Security guard who stopped last rape shot by Dar, admitted to ER and died of wounds. Victim, woman of 72, admitted to ER, hips dislocated. Dar apprehended by police and admitted to ER: multiple gun-shot wounds. Serious blood shortage; Carter decided to use Dar's own blood for transfusion rather than use low supply. Dar survived, but Dr Del Amico questioned decision.

Carter: "It was my decision, and I made it. If he'd died, I don't know how I'd feel. But I can't say that I'm sorry."

13. Dealing with benzine emergency and ER evacuation, March 1998 *[episode 4-15]*.

Fire and explosion in chemical warehouse: victims admitted to ER; chemical spill discovered: benzine leak (highly toxic). Disaster manual missing. Dr Weaver collapsed. Carter organized evacuation: closed ER to all new admits; contaminated patients and staff to ambulance bay; non urgent cases turned away; patients requiring X-rays and stitches to lobby; critical patients to cafeteria. Called for portable monitors, oxygen cylinders. Liaised with Captain Daniker of fire service. Daniker praised Carter's role in difficult circumstances.

PROFESSIONAL ASSESSMENT

"An exceptional student, well-trained, superior diagnostic skills, fast learner, dedicated, selfless, excellent bed-side manner with patients, far more successful at dealing with the patient's emotional needs than this instructor, highly intelligent... One of the finest students I've ever had the opportunity to work with. Recommend high honours." (Dr Peter Benton)

Strengths

Compassionate patient care, illustrated in the cases of Joseph Klein *[episode 1-17]*, Mary Kavanagh *[episodes 1-2 and 1-10]*, and T C Lucas *[episodes 2-21 and 2-22]* for whom Dr Carter missed his graduation and graduation party. Inspired diagnostic skills, including correcting the diagnosis of the hospital chief of staff, Dr Donald Anspaugh *[episode 3-16]*, and correctly deducing the surgical risk involved in one further borderline patient *[Mr Bartok, episode 3-18]*. A keen interest in the emotional well-being of the patient, and post-operative care, made Dr Carter an unusually sensitive member of the surgical staff. Dr Carter's skills appear to be better suited to emergency medicine although his experience of surgical procedures, while on one level an advantage, have led to confusion and to error *[episode 4-1]*.

Weaknesses

His candidness is sometimes questionable (see case of Mrs Rubadoux) and he has once taken credit for another student's work *[episode 2-13]*. Dr Hicks has raised two disciplinary points against Dr Carter: for drinking while on duty, and for admitting a high-risk candidate for surgery although the patient had already been rejected (see above). Occasional lapses in punctuality have not gone unpunished – Carter was, at one point, made to hold a man's arm upright for the duration of surgery *[episode 2-2]*. Dr Carter has reprimanded himself for his use of patients as guinea pigs and his extreme competitiveness. In extreme cases, may let emotional reaction get in the way of dispassionate clinical assessment *[episode 4-13]*.

Prospects

In Dr Carter's first year at County, Dr Benton expressed the feeling that Carter was "wasting his time" as a surgical intern candidate. Similar observations had been made by medical student Debra Chen and hospital Chief of Staff, Dr Donald Anspaugh. Late in his first year at County, Dr Carter stated that, although he was uncertain whether or not he was capable of being a surgeon, he intended to find out. Although there was no reason to doubt Dr Carter's capacity to become a competent surgeon, his desire to be involved to the fullest extent in a patient's emotional and medical treatment suggested a promising career in emergency medicine. It is for this reason that his transfer was approved although Dr Carter was consequently required to repeat his internship in the ER. As a second year resident he would seem to be an ideal candidate to teach new medical students.

Note: Benton told Carter that he did not think like a surgeon. Carter replied: "Why, because I don't think like you?"

PERSONAL INFORMATION

Family background

The Carters are one of Chicago's richest families: Roland Carter, John's father, has net worth of $178 million. Family home surrounded by a large private estate. Close friends of family include Mayor of Chicago and Greg Davies, a multi-millionaire and one of County General's principal benefactors.

Older brother, Bobby, suffered from leukaemia when John at school. Despite treatment, Bobby died. Carter's observation of doctors at work convinced him to enter medical profession.

Note: Abby Keaton suggested that this experience explained in part John's natural affinity for treating children.

Grandmother (Millicent Carter) and grandfather, trustees of Carter Foundation: beneficiaries of trust include County General clinic. Grandfather, director of major corporation. Cousin, Chase Carter, talented photographer but became addicted to heroin. Carter tried unsuccessfully (with help of Dr Del Amico) to end addiction, but Chase unwilling to attend detoxification centre or inform grandparents of addiction. Overdosed; treated at County General ER. Respiratory centre depressed and went into cardiac arrest, leading to unquantifiable brain damage. Currently unable to dress or eat independently.

Dr Carter's financial situation changed significantly in recent months. Presently out of favour with grandparents over Chase Carter issue: trust fund withdrawn by Millicent Carter, after Carter accused her of withdrawing clinic funding due to personal differences between them. Unpaid by ER for repeat internship. Refused bank loan.

Millicent Carter: "All your lives you've been indulged and considered it oppression."

Psychological evaluation (extracts)

Carter's motivation and the pressures on him seem to stem greatly from his family background. Carter has always entertained an interest in the more rarefied specialties: psychiatry, dermatology and plastic surgery. His family were set on cardiology *[episode 1-14]* and at the end of his second year at County his favoured specialties included cardio-vascular surgery and plastics. However, a year later, Carter's sights were set firmly on the ER, with his request to leave the surgical service in pursuit of a career in emergency medicine. As of summer 1997 *[episode 3-22]*, Carter worked in the ER for no wages. It is ironic, considering Carter's affluent background and the family pressures placed on him to move into the more well-paid specialties, that he seems ideally suited for a position in paediatrics, notoriously the worst paid specialty. Perhaps his proven skills and boosted confidence under Dr Keaton will eventually lead him towards paediatric surgery.

Personal relationships

Has always had amicable relationships with fellow med-students and interns, although often fierce competitiveness can endanger these friendships. Debra Chen came from similar prominent and affluent background, seemed ideal competition (see Personnel file on Debra Chen). Romance with Harper Tracy did not reduce his need to compete with her. Though clearly concerned by lapse in attention to patient care and overt competitiveness after Rubadoux case *[episode 2-17]*, arrival of Harvard med-student Dale Edson *[episode 2-19]* merely encouraged revival of this instinct: Harper then ended relationship. Rivalry with Maggie Doyle dominated intern year: seems set to continue, perhaps grow, especially if Carter leaves surgical service and joins her in ER. Most tragically, shortcomings in friendship with Dennis Gant may have contributed to Gant's suicide.

Romantic interest in Susan Lewis. Though intentions ultimately unrequited *[episodes 1-6 to 1-10]*, Carter always appeared to take Susan's words to heart, notably after she alerted him to his change of character after death of Mrs Rubadoux. During sub-internship, involved with fellow med-student Harper Tracy but relationship ended when she became frustrated with Carter's competitiveness and constant 'sucking up' to members of surgical staff. Brief relationship with Dr Abby Keaton, Southside's foremost paediatric surgeon who joined County after staff merger in October 1996. Attempt to date fellow intern Dr Maggie Doyle clearly doomed to failure...

Note: Carter had brief but passionate romance with the flirtatious Liz - ended with results of STD tests being pinned to ER noticeboard and Liz making move on Dr Kayson!

Flirtation with Anna Del Amico. Apparently lied to her, or at least failed to disclose the nature of his background and financial standing. Del Amico briefly upset at Carter's insensitivity. Carter revealed his feelings at ER banquet *[episode 4-18]*, but Del Amico unwilling to enter relationship - still had feelings for ex-boyfriend, Dr Max Rocher. Advances halted by arrival of Rocher in ER, summer 1998. (See also Personnel file of Anna Del Amico.)

*[**Trivia:** According to Benton's mother, Carter's family may have once been slave-owners in Tennessee and owned Benton's ancestors [episode 1-6]. Carter used to wrestle at junior varsity and was an accomplished dressage competitor. He won several rossettes on his horse, Marigold, at Temple Farms in 1985. He is a Gemini, and perhaps a little superstitious. Carter was at school with the son of Greg Davies, one of the hospital's wealthy benefactors. On his arrival in the ER, Mark Greene noted that Carter's was the first tailored white coat he had ever seen. In attempting to escape from a round of carol singing, Carter claimed to suffer from "chronic tone deafness and acute stage fright". After performing an appendectomy on his teacher, Carter now has Benton's appendix in a jar on his mantlepiece; he also has a number of photographs taken during the operation!*

When a child, Carter used to pretend that Faberge eggs were his Weeble family's household pets. Carter has no idea how a tumble dryer works. In 1990 he was a crewmember in the Whitbread yacht race - his team's yacht capsized between Sydney and Auckland. He was jokingly referred to as 'John Carter the Third' by Anna on account of his riches.

From the start of the first series, John Carter has been the audience's eyes and ears. Not only is he the character with whom we begin and end each season, but also it's through Carter that we are introduced to the mainstays of the series' action in the trauma room, such as intubation, IV's, and resuscitation. Noah Wyle's superb performance neatly encompasses the gradual changes in the character of John Carter - from the uncomfortable third year med-student, unable to put on surgical gloves, to the compassionate, competent surgical resident who gleefully performs Benton's appendectomy. Ironically, in the fourth series, Carter's competence as a surgeon led him to be over-confident and to ignore procedure in the ER, ultimately leading to at least one death [episode 4-1]. *Carter is still a wonderfully fallible character, pummelled by expectations from colleagues and family alike. As a second year resident in the fifth series he will be as senior as Benton was in the first, and it will be interesting to see how he copes with med-students coming his way.]*

CAROL HATHAWAY, R.N.

AGE

31.

POSITION

Charge Nurse County General ER for over four years. Member of hospital-wide re-engineering committee. Responsible for ER nursing schedule, budget, and supplies. Currently organizes free health-care clinic using ER treatment rooms two to three times per week, funded by Carter Family Foundation.

MEDICAL TRAINING AND CAREER TO DATE

Extremely capable student at St Monica's with promising future (studied history with Maggie Doyle's older sister). Fully qualified registered nurse. Interested in possible career as doctor. Started prestigious pre-med night school course, Malcolm X Community College, 31st October 1996. Took medical school entrance examinations, February 1997. Results in top 15 per cent but, as of April 1997, Dr Weaver reports Hathaway has decided not to pursue med-school ambitions further.

Note: Carol clearly influenced by Maggie Doyle, in both positive and negative way. Grew up in same area and took same pre-med course; irritated by Doyle's youth and authority over her in the ER. Carol once noted nurses teach interns how to earn four times as much as they do. Dr Ross was supportive of Carol's endeavours: "If I can make it anyone can."

Note: Confrontation with Weaver over care for Andrea Thompson confirmed Hathaway's skills as nurse above desire to become doctor.

SIGNIFICANT CAREER EVENTS

1. Attempted suicide, 17 March 1994 *[Pilot episode]*
Following overdose of barbiturates, Nurse Hathaway admitted as patient by new flatmate, 17th March 1994. No suicide note left. Ross devastated. Hathaway narrowly survived. Returned to work, 12 May 1994. Began therapy which lasted over nine months.

Emotionally reassured and inspired by attitudes/outlook of leukaemia patient, Mrs Packer *[episode 1-2]* and Mr Gasner *[episode 1-4]*.

Note: Reason for attempted suicide unclear. There have been suggestions that she became over-reliant on certain pharmaceutical drugs. Carol to Doug: "There are more depressing events in my life than you... Lots of things built up." Didn't leave suicide note because "didn't know what to say."

Hathaway to Greg Powell: "I thought about everybody but me when I tried to kill myself. I just got wrapped up in everyone else's expectations of me . . . I forgot who I was."

2. Rape patient *[episode 1-7]*
Hathaway convinced rape patient named Jamie to give evidence against two of her boyfriend's friends who raped her.

Carol to Jamie: "You've got to take care of things. If you don't, they come back. They always do."

3. Attempted adoption of Tatiana, *[episodes 1-15 to 1-17]*
Tatiana adopted by Mrs Hall in St Petersburg, 4th February 1995; girl admitted to County ER suffering from coughing and fever, 14th February 1995. Diagnosed with AIDS. Tatiana abandoned by Mrs Hall: Hathaway waits for social services to collect Tatiana. Decides to adopt: passes first stage of adoption procedure but rejected on grounds of attempted suicide less than one year ago.

Note: Following rejection of adoption, Carol visited Ross, not Taglieri, her fiancé. Ross drove her home.

4. Rehabilitation of alcoholic father, Mr Krosset, 5th September 1995 *[episode 2-1]*
Mr Krosset admitted with alcohol poisoning: son, Noah, called 911 - not first time. Father stabilized but suffered breathlessness when tried to leave. Hathaway encouraged rehabilitation. Advice apparently unheeded until Kenny Krosset, other son, admitted for minor injuries 25th January 1996 *[episode 2-12]*. Mr Krosset reformed character.

Note: Ross did not believe Krosset had changed; Carol insisted if Ross wants to beat up on a father, he should call his own. See personnel file on Dr Douglas Ross.

5. Attempted suicide of Julia Kasler, December 1995 *[episode 2-8]*

Teenage girl brought in having taken drugs overdose. Hathaway and Williams performed stomach pump; Hathaway discovered Julia Kasler pregnant by brother Kyle; accidentally informed Mr Kasler; Hathaway reprimanded by Greene for breach of patient confidentiality.

Note: Shep, Carol's then boyfriend, noted people who overdose on pills don't seriously mean to commit suicide, but taken aback when Carol said that she had meant it.

6. Death of Raul Melendez, March 1996 *[episode 2-16]*

Shepherd and Melendez rescued from burning building; admitted to County General. Shepherd stabilized; Melendez 90 per cent third degree burns, diagnosed as fatal. Shepherd exhibited increasingly violent behaviour, resulting in near fatal assaults on homeless 'Button Man', and a drunk. Also came close to attacking Hathaway *[episode 2-19]*. Subsequent attack on Arn Nuan by Shepherd became subject of incident report logged by Fireman Reilly *[episode 2-20]*. Investigation conducted by David Haskall dismissed concerns of paramedic Reilly and vindicated actions of Shepherd.

Note: Hathaway's personal relationship with Shepherd resulted in her lying to defend him. Reilly pointed out she was doing Shepherd no favours. They broke up after Shepherd failed to accept the need for psychiatric help.

7. Resignation, 3rd July 1996 *[episode 2-22]*

Hathaway enraged by decision to send baby home before serious heart problem diagnosed. Dr Weaver and Dr Lewis defended hospital policy in general terms. Subsequent frustration over failure to care for 46-year-old cancer patient without medical insurance, and desire of insurance company to move patient with painful leg fracture to another hospital for treatment, resulted in resignation.

Note: Greene told Carol she'd feel foolish about this and regret it in the morning. As predicted, she returned to work the next day!

8. Opposition to nurse 'floating' scheme *[episodes 3-6 to 3-9]*

Hathaway logged complaint re Rhonda Sterling, registered nurse, 'floated' from med-surgery to cover Nurse Haleh Adams' vacation. Sterling incorrectly administered potassium - almost stopped patient's heart. Later responsible for loss of man's foot. Management scheme to 'float' nurses indicated attempts to dismiss most experienced nursing staff before full pension maturity. Meeting with Mary Cain, nurse administrator *[episode 3-8]*, led to flotation of nurses only to departments with comparable duties. Hathaway requested as member of hospital-wide re-engineering committee: later arranges for ER exemption from nurse 'flotation' scheme *[episode 3-9]*.

9. Illicit ER nursing strike/Death of homeless patient, January 1997 *[episodes 3-12 to 3-16]*

Hathaway's afternoon shift reported 'sick'. Management organized temporary nurses; alerted other members of staff. Drs Greene and Weaver insisted County be closed to trauma. Homeless man admitted. Hathaway administered wrong blood resulting in death of patient. Following possible use of incident for leverage in nursing contracts review, Hathaway reported full story to newspaper, resulting in immediate suspension.

Disciplinary note

Dr Greene and Dr Weaver duly reported incident on Nurse Hathaway's request. Hathaway suspended during course of investigation: Haleh Adams, RN, appointed temporary Charge Nurse (see personnel file). Management and Safety Committee review concurred with initial assessment of accidental death. Nurse Hathaway reinstated February 1997.

Note: During suspension, Hathaway hostage in bungled store hold-up. Police report indicated Hathaway provided invaluable assistance and saved the life of one man.

10. Formation and management of free health-care clinic, October 1998 *[from episode 4-3]*.

Nurse Hathaway increasingly conscious of failure of ER to treat some patients. Experiences with bulimic girl *[episodes 4-2 and 4-3]* and drug addict *[episodes 4-1 and 4-4]* prompted Hathaway to form

CAROL HATHAWAY, R.N.

clinic. Dr Weaver supportive but unwilling to provide resources other than examination room two to three times per week. Approached Carter Family Foundation. Application successful: $75,000 initial grant. Given further $150,000 on 24th December 1997 following inspection of clinic by Millicent Carter. Clinic currently staffed by members of ER staff outside normal hours (acceptable so long as no interference in nursing schedule).

Hathaway (responding to Greene's comment that the ER can't help those who can't help themselves): "No, Mark, they're precisely the people we should be helping."

Note: Clinic funding temporarily cut off, summer 1998 [episode 4-18], but rapidly reinstated. Cause remains unknown but perhaps relates to deteriorating relations between Carter family and Hathaway's colleague, Dr John Carter.

11. Confidentiality issues re underage intercourse, Natalie Vaughan, April 1998 *[episode 4-17].*
Hathaway gave birth control advice and contraceptives to Natalie Vaughan, a minor, as part of clinic duties. Natalie's mother later arrived in ER demanding to know why; Hathaway cited nurse-patient confidentiality. Natalie then told Hathaway she was having sex with her teacher, aged forty. Hathaway reported this to police.

Hathaway: "She thought her secret was safe." Ross: "Birth control is one thing. This is sexual abuse."

12. Josh McNeil incident, June 1998 [episodes 4-20 to 4-22].
June 1997 assisted Dr Ross in illegal rapid detoxification of methadone baby Josh McNeil. Greene encouraged Hathaway to report that she acted as a nurse assisting a doctor. Hathaway insisted that her actions were based on knowledge of consequences and approval of Dr Ross's actions. Pending formal enquiry.

Note: Support of Dr Ross founded on their personal relationship.

PROFESSIONAL ASSESSMENT

Strengths

Nurse Hathaway is one of the finest, most dedicated members of staff at County. Highly intelligent and capable (see also medical school admissions examination results), her compassionate treatment of every patient has pushed her away from a promising career as a doctor. She is also well liked and her attempted suicide shocked and traumatized the ER staff. Her ability to stay calm in stressful or emotional situations saved the lives of several in a shop hold-up *[episode 3-15]*. In this dangerous siege situation and, whilst off duty, she displayed re-markable courage and clear thinking. The emergency medicine she administered was improvised and risky but none the less inspired. For Hathaway, nursing is a natural instinct. Hathaway is also noted for her absolute honesty, condemning Dr Ross for lying rather than telling the difficult truth *[episode 1-3]* and insisting upon an incident report in the case of accidental death, despite the vindication of her actions by colleagues and management at the time. Most importantly, Nurse Hathaway has consistently assisted and defended her nursing staff in the best tradition of a Charge Nurse.

Carol to Benton, following Benton's condemnation of Haleh Adams: "Step off that pedestal you put yourself on and you'll see the nurses make this place work, not you."

Weaknesses

Nurse Hathaway can frequently seem hemmed in by the limitations of her job, resenting the inability to provide more substantial care for some (most notably Tatiana, a Russian girl she wanted to adopt) or even basic care in the case of those without medical insurance. In such situations, she can be confrontational and has on one occasion resigned over these issues.

PERSONAL INFORMATION

Family background
Hathaway family originally from Ukraine. Father deceased; relationship with her mother is occasionally strained. Helen Hathaway is keen that her daughter keeps links with the family's roots and tried to teach young Carol how to speak Russian. Carol has an Uncle Michel, who gave Carol away at her wedding, in place of father. Carol grew up with her two sisters on the west side of Chicago.

Note: Uncle Michel made money in real estate - unmarried with no children. Helen Hathaway suggested Carol become replacement daughter for Michel to escape her financial troubles!

Carol to Ross, when wedding reception takes place without the wedding: "You know my family - what's a little humiliation when there's free food and drink?"

Personal relationships

Carol Hathaway dated Doug Ross for two years before her suicide attempt. Separated when Ross "replaced her". Hathaway dated and became engaged to Dr John Taglieri, County General orthopod. Moved in with him: marriage scheduled for June 1994. Slept with Ross while dating Taglieri, winter 1993/4. After Hathaway's attempted suicide, Ross attempted to get Carol back, 25 August 1994, but Hathaway would not risk the same rejection. Tag asked Carol to move back in with him, but had second thoughts (October 1994): Hathaway insisted second thoughts had nothing to do with her feelings for Ross but kissed him two weeks later when she was about to move in with Tag. Ross gate-crashed engagement party; assaulted by Taglieri. Carol again had second thoughts about marriage, January 1995. Further complications over Hathaway's desire to adopt Tatiana, during which Carol wanted to return to Ross, February 1995. Wedding failed to take place: Carol agreed with Tag that she doesn't love him as much as he loves her (18th May 1995). Expressed concern that she couldn't fall in love with "a nice guy": wanted to be happy, but afraid she never would be. Continued to resist attempts by Doug Ross to rekindle relationship.

Note: Carol dismissed Doug as "a little kid - he always wants what he can't have."

Introduced to Shepherd, 5th September 1995. Joined him for paramedic run. Began dating, October 1995. Moved out of her mother's house (mother later moved to suburbs) and bought her own place *[episode 2-5]*. Shep asked Carol to have his babies *[episode 2-10]*. Death of Melendez *[episode 2-16]*. Broke up with Shep after his refusal to get psychiatric help.

Reunited with Doug Ross for approx one year, following Doug's change in outlook after death of Nadine Wilks. Hathaway unwilling to commit to wedding date, despite Doug's eagerness to do so. Brief flirtation with paramedic Greg Powell *[episode 4-12]* led to confrontation with Doug, February 1998 *[episode 4-13]*. Relationship currently appears stable, helped by good working relationship.

Carol to Doug: "This is about me needing some time, and you being really pissed off that things aren't working out exactly as you planned. I've spent years - years of my life changing to fit your needs, working around your schedules, your insecurities, your inability to commit. Well you know what Doug, it's not all about you. I know that may come as a shock. But a relationship is give and take, two people as equals, and right now I need something. So you can grow up and accept it, or you can go on being the same selfish, self-centred bastard you've always been and refuse to give me the one thing, one thing I've ever asked you for." *Doug to Carol:* "Take all the time you need."

*[**Trivia:** Carol used to climb television poles to heights of 200 - 300 feet. Linda Farrell estimated that Carol's engagement ring cost Taglieri about $12,000. Carol has been stuck with a dirty syringe five times. Carol's PAI ('provocation to assault interval') is 21 seconds, putting her in the top percentage. Carol is allergic to a certain flavour of edible massage oil and comes out in a rash. Carol slept with Ross on their first date: "He rang the door bell - next thing I knew we were on the kitchen floor!" Carol Hathaway speaks limited Russian and is a genius at simple mathematics. Carol's brief attempt at worm cultivation ended when they all 'croaked'. At Christmas 1996, eight drunken members of Carol's Ukranian family re-enacted the Purges in her front room. Carol was Doug Ross's character referee for his 'Big Brothers' application.*

When one views the series as a whole, it's easy to see why Carol Hathaway didn't die in the pilot episode - despite being clinically dead! Julianna Margulies's portrayal of Carol Hathaway is one of the strongest regular performances of the show. Most of Carol's storylines follow her personal relationships, from Tag and Shep to what appears to be her destiny with Doug Ross, giving her, and the series as a whole, greater emotional depth. Her bumpy relationship with Tag (and Ross) led to one of the finest and most emotional episodes of the show, 'Everything Old Is New Again', where her aborted marriage, and Shep's mental breakdown, created some of the unhappiest scenes. The third series explored her motivations and talents more fully, principally her role as nurse manager

and her desire to prove herself as a match for any doctor, while cautiously pursuing her renewed relationship with Doug Ross. Series four saw her take control of her life still further, even managing to keep control of her renewed relationship with Doug. But will the happy ccouple ever tie the knot?

JEANIE BOULET, P.A.

AGE

32.

POSITION

Physician's assistant in County General ER.

MEDICAL TRAINING AND CAREER TO DATE

Physical trainer, worked part time County General physical therapy. Prior experience: rehabilitation and private nursing care. Trained as physician's assistant. First day as PA in ER: 30th November 1995. Dismissed by Dr Weaver as part of ER cutbacks, November 1997. Reinstated by Dr Anspaugh following claims of wrongful dismissal, December 1998 (see Significant Career Events).

Important medical note
Tested positive for HIV, 3rd July 1996. Failed to give details at County General HIV-AIDS outpatient services, 4th July 1996. Falsely notified Dr Kerry Weaver of negative test result on same day (may have indicated truth to Dr Benton). From October attended up-state clinic at Highland Park. Initial lab results indicated positive assessment; new drug cocktail prescribed. Side-effects, especially nausea, experienced after three weeks. Informed Dr Weaver of positive test, 21st October 1996.

December 1996: Al Boulet treated by Dr Greene, senior attending, ER. Greene accessed Jeanie Boulet medical file (breach of confidentiality; see below). Legal department recommended departmental policy decisions re HIV-positive health-care workers (see Significant career events). Positive test result made public, 24th December 1996. Subsequent lab results indicated no viral nodes, suggesting drug cocktail successful. Dr Greg Fischer, County infectious diseases department, as private HIV-treatment supervisor (from start 1997). Viral nodes dropped, February 1997, but rose again, 17th April 1997. As of summer 1998, drug cocktail working satisfactorily although personal problems and use of other medication led to temporary forgetfulness which briefly endangered regularity of treatment timetable.

Note: No initial insurance claim against cocktail, despite estimated $16,000 annual cost: indicated unwillingness to inform hospital authorities.

Note: Conflicting reactions from ER colleagues. Benton refused Boulet access to his patients or traumas. Weaver supportive - "It'd be a real loss to the patients if you quit".

Boulet to Greene, regarding Greene's improper access of her file: "It's better this way. You know about me, and I know a hell of a lot more about you."

SIGNIFICANT CAREER EVENTS

1. First day as Physician's Assistant, ER, 30th November 1995 *[episode 2-6]*
Applications made to most hospitals in Chicago for ER rotation. Dr Weaver noted difficulties in professional relationship with Dr Peter Benton; further difficulties reported December 1995.

2. Concerns raised by Nurse Hathaway and Dr Benton, December 1995 *[episode 2-11]*
First student analysis, provided by Nurse Hathaway, indicated possible unsuitability for trauma work. Supervisor reassured by Boulet. Subsequent actions indicate improved assertiveness and initiative *[episode 2-14]*. Made 'Employee of the Month', March 1996 *[episode 2-17]*. Continued problems regarding Benton. Personal relationship complications noted by nurses.

Boulet to Benton: "If this is about you and me, get over it. If it's about

something else, get over that too... I'm sick of it. That boy in there needs
compassion - if you can't find that in yourself then get out of medicine."

3. Treatment of Mrs Mendoza, April 1996 *[episode 2-19]*
Initial diagnosis of probable appendectomy dismissed by Dr Benton.
Subsequent emergency appendectomy performed. Claims of
inadequate initial observations made by Boulet dismissed by Hicks;
Dr Benton reprimanded.

Note: Personal problems interfering in work.
Jeanie to Benton: "I'm sorry that I hurt you, but I thought by now you'd
be past it."
Benton: "I am past it - way past it."

4. Death of Mrs Jennings, 31 October 1996 *[episode 3-5]*
Mrs Jennings, elderly patient, assisted in suicide attempt by
husband. Treated by Boulet but not resuscitated (DNR order) -
activities questioned by Dr Margaret Doyle.

Jeanie to Al: "We didn't have that kind of marriage, did we Al? We didn't
love, we didn't cherish, we didn't respect. And now you've killed me."

5. Medical condition revealed, November/December 1996
[episode 3-9]
Dr Greene treated Al Boulet for AIDS-related illness. Subsequently
accessed Jeanie Boulet's medical records without consent. Boulet's
condition brought to attention of Dr Donald Anspaugh: Drs Weaver
and Greene to decide ER's departmental policy on HIV-positive
health-care workers. Result: continued use of universal precautions;
no work to be undertaken on deep penetrating, poorly visualized
cavities; Dr Weaver assigned as physician's monitor. (See also
Personnel file on Dr Mark Greene).

6. Treatment of Suzanne Alner, 17th April 1997 *[episode 3-18]*
Patient overdosed on AIDS drugs. Attempts to make Alner
comfortable in final moments hampered by lack of actions by Dr
Greg Fisher. Mr Roger Alner expressed satisfaction at wife's death.

Note: Instrumental in re-establishing relationship with Al Boulet.
Jeanie to Al: "I don't hate you. I don't want to be angry anymore, I don't
want to be that kind of person."

7. Breach of restrictions on HIV-infected personnel, October 1997 *[episode 4-4]*.

Elderly male admitted by son. Fell from roof. Boulet administered aid but man became unresponsive and required chest tube. As inserting tube in darkened cavity by hand would break regulations governing care given by HIV-infected hospital workers, Boulet called for assistance. Lack of prompt assistance, however, led Boulet to insert tube herself. Dr Weaver took over care of patient; reprimanded Boulet.

Note: On examination, Boulet found that her gloves had not split and that her hands did not have any cuts, making cross-infection impossible.

8. Aborted wrongful dismissal case, November-December 1997 *[episodes 4-6 to 4-9]*.

PA Boulet sacked by Dr Kerry Weaver in consequence of ER overspending. Most recently hired Physicians Assistant. Following hiring of new RN in ER and increase in Dr Weaver's salary (covering extra duties in consequence of Dr Morgenstern's illness), Boulet felt that her dismissal was a consequence of her HIV status and her recent breach of rules (see above). Wrongful dismissal case begun against hospital but Boulet reinstated by Anspaugh. Case dropped.

Weaver: "You and I know this had nothing to do with your HIV status."
Boulet: "Do we?"

9. Private duty care giver to Scott Anspaugh, January to May 1998 *[episodes 4-11 to 4-18]*.

Scott Anspaugh, son of Dr Donald Anspaugh, admitted to ER January 1998 with abdominal pains - diagnosed as resurgence of cancer treated early 1997. Boulet's rapport with Scott led Dr Anspaugh to appoint her as private duty care giver during chemotherapy. Remained friends after course of treatment finished, but Scott re-admitted soon afterwards with low blood cell count *[episode 4-17]*; bone marrow biopsy revealed cancer was back. Attempts to find donor for bone marrow transfusion unsuccessful. Scott at first said willing to undergo experimental chemotherapy, but Dr Ross indicated to Boulet he thought Scott was doing it for her. Died May 1998, aged 12.

Note: Jeanie didn't tell Scott about her HIV status, but Dr Anspaugh thought he sensed it somehow; respected her as a kindred spirit.

Note: Jeanie sang Green Day's 'Time of Your Life', one of Scott's favourite songs, at his funeral.

PROFESSIONAL ASSESSMENT

"Lacks assertiveness, and needs to take control if she is to be more useful... Good skills, but may not be suited to work in the ER." (Carol Hathaway)

Strengths

Jeanie Boulet is an extremely capable physician's assistant, whose extensive training in rehabilitation has resulted in an excellent bedside manner. Her personal battle against the HIV virus and her decision to continue to work display courage and professionalism, as does her questioning of colleagues' attitudes, not least those of Dr Peter Benton. Dr Kerry Weaver has noted that had Jeanie decided to stop working in the ER, it would have been a considerable loss to her patients. She was rewarded for her efforts in the ER by being named 'Employee of the Month' for March 1996. Though Jeanie's compassion can often lead her to dangerous situations (her recent breach of hospital regulations re HIV status workers was a consequence of this), it is this deep intuitive capacity for care and generous spirit which makes her an excellent physician's assistant. Employee of the month, October 1997. Highly recommended by Dr Donald Anspaugh.

Weaknesses

Her prior training in rehabilitation, and desire to work for the complete physical and mental recovery of the patient, is often at odds with the 'treat 'em and street 'em' attitude necessary in any ER. It may also be because of Jeanie's prior training that Charge Nurse Carol Hathaway initially regarded Jeanie as lacking the proactive attitude necessary for trauma work.

Prospects

Jeanie Boulet has shown a considered, cautious and level-headed attitude to living with HIV-infection and, two years on from having tested HIV positive, she has clearly made a decision not to let the virus run her life. The board is convinced that, with Dr Weaver's continued supervision, Jeanie can remain an integral part of County's emergency services but fears that the conditions and stipulations placed on her represent an oppressive burden. Perhaps Boulet should be encouraged to take more cases such as that of Scott Anspaugh in which she showed the utmost skill and compassion. And hopes that the conditions and stipulations placed on her will not restrict or hamper the good work she is already doing.

PERSONAL INFORMATION

Family background

Immediate family: Possibly unhappy upbringing. Implied dislike of her mother; younger sister given preferential treatment.

Husband: Al Boulet. Married 17th April 1988. Significant marital problems: Jeanie's unrequited desire for children; Al's extensive adultery. Difficulties accelerated by Jeanie's relationship with Peter Benton. By December 1995, Jeanie and Al separated. May/June 1995 Al Boulet tested HIV positive; may have been positive for ten years. Jeanie tested positive early July 1996. By December 1996, Jeanie and Al divorced. Treatment of Suzanne Alner forced Jeanie to reconsider attitude towards Al *[episode 3-18]*. Jeanie and Al lived together once more until revelation of Al's HIV status at work resulted in dismissal from his job. Currently separated once again. Al now in Atlanta with his sister *[episode 3-22]*.

Al on his many sexual partners, asked to produce a list after HIV result: "It's not much to be proud of now."
Jeanie: "It wasn't much to be proud of then."

Personal relationships

Affair with Peter Benton during final months of marriage to Al. Benton asked Jeanie to tell Al but she was unwilling and they separated (early October 1995). Cause of increased tension in ER: other ER rotations and rescheduling attempted but failed. Benton still emotionally involved by December 1995 but Jeanie did not inform of separation from Al. Indications of continued tension, April 1996 *[episode 2-19]*. Increased conflict from July 1996 over Jeanie continuing work without notification of hospital authorities. Following examination of suspected ebola case, relationship with Dr Greg Fischer, County General infectious diseases department *[episode 3-12]*. Recommended as personal doctor for HIV treatment. Conflict over Patterson and Alner cases *[episodes 3-13 and 3-18]*. Al Boulet put on HIV treatment trial in infectious diseases, alerting Fischer to Jeanie's continued relationship with Al.

Note: Jeanie indicated Peter not the cause of her problems with Al. Breakdown of marriage in part blamed on failure to communicate.

*[**Trivia:** Jeanie's mother's preference for her younger sister used to annoy her. Al thought Jeanie was the over-achiever. When Jeanie graduated from college her father was so delighted he danced on a table. She worked for a vet during high school, and can perform 'mouth-to-mouse' resuscitation. Interests shared with Scott Anspaugh include John Woo movies, hockey (specifically Blackhog Islanders), and the soap opera 'Days of Our Lives'.*

At first used to chip away Benton's veneer, Jeanie Boulet has grown to become one of the series most endearing yet tragic characters. Her battle with her doomed marriage in the second series, and with HIV in the third, has tended to shift Jeanie away from the central action of the series - but given us some wonderful moments of high drama as well. Gloria Reuben balances the tragedy of Jeanie's condition with her fiery and defiant spirit. Her developing relationship with Scott Anspaugh was the finest storyline of the fourth series and by far the most harrowing. With strong emotional stories of high quality regularly given to her, Jeanie remains one of the most powerful and watchable figures in the series.]

KERRY WEAVER, M.D.

AGE

35.

POSITION

ER attending physician and acting ER chief.

Responsibilities

Include scheduling, daily summaries and managing budget. Responsible for chart review until transferred to Dr Greene upon arrival of Dr Anspaugh.

Note: Anspaugh formed impression that Weaver was doing all the work!

MEDICAL TRAINING AND CAREER TO DATE

Medical school: Four years. Two years' 'hands-on' training included rotations at Mercy and Lakeside Hospitals. Worked with Doug Ross.

Residency: Three years at Mount Sinai General Hospital; one year as ER chief resident at County General.

SIGNIFICANT CAREER EVENTS

1. Appointment as ER chief resident - began work September 1995 *[episode 2-1]*

Note: News of her appointment greeted with dread from most staff, except Benton who called it "definitely a step in the right direction".

Appointed to compensate for weaknesses of Dr Greene, ER attending physician and former chief resident, particularly in relation to: discipline, paperwork and administration. Early suggestions: doctors to write down orders when they give them, not wait until three hours later and blame nurses if they are not done; residents to clean up after procedures; residents to be prevented

54

sifting through charts looking for the best cases. Suggestions approved by Nurse Carol Hathaway. Also banned personal use of fax machine; decided residents should take at least four patients at any time.

Weaver to Lewis: "The nurses here are downright great...They deserve that from the rest of us."

2. Conflict with Dr Susan Lewis

Problematic working relationship began as soon as Weaver arrived; almost first action was to call time of death on one of Lewis's patients. Demanded Lewis keep her charts up-to-date; ordered her to run all procedures past her. Greene asked to mediate; informed Weaver her authoritativeness could be a problem. Lewis later criticized Weaver for assigning her to routine cases due to personal obligations. Weaver at first resisted Lewis's candidacy for chief resident.

Lewis to Weaver: "If being chief resident means having you breathe down my back, to hell with it. Stay out of my way."
Weaver: "That's the first time I've seen you act like a chief resident. Maybe Morgenstern was right."

3. Conflict with Dr Doug Ross *[episode 2-2, 3-4]*

September 1995 *[episode 2-2]:* Ross treated Byron Fields, young boy with burnt hand, after he set fire to motel room. Ross called Jack Chandler, child psychiatrist and personal friend of Ross, for kerbside consult. Weaver cancelled, and called general psychiatrist, Dr Myers, instead. Child left alone, sets fire to examination room. Ross and Weaver blamed each other.

24th October 1996 *[episode 3-4]:* Weaver disagreed with Ross continuing shift after bringing in Nadine Wilks, a patient known to Ross, who died from cocaine overdose complicated by epilepsy. Ordered Ross tested for cocaine and alcohol.

4. Appointment as attending physician - July 1996 *[episode 2-22]*

Note: Greene supported Weaver's candidacy as attending in return for Weaver's support of Lewis for chief resident (although she turned the post down). Nurses were heard to comment that it was going to be "a long year".

Early (aborted) suggestions: new format for admissions board, using two-letter acronyms instead of patient complaints and social security numbers instead of names; formalizing chart review for "quality assurance, monitoring and feedback"; dividing duties of attendings between surgical and medical cases. Also suggested Tuesday and Thursday lunchtime meetings for attendings to improve communication.

Greene to Weaver in response to suggestion re formalizing chart review: "Our residents' diagnostic skills are pretty terrific the way they are. They don't need more supervision, they need more vacation."

5. Treatment of Al Boulet and support of Jeanie Boulet re HIV status *[episode 3-3, 3-9]*
Dr Weaver treated Al Boulet, husband of Jeanie Boulet, Physician's Assistant in ER, for flu symptoms; diagnosed AIDS. Ms Boulet then tested positive for HIV but did not inform Dr Weaver until reluctance to take part in a dangerous surgical situation alerted Weaver to Ms Boulet's condition. Did not inform Dr Greene; heavily criticized him for illicitly inspecting Ms Boulet's medical file. Supported Ms Boulet during review of policy towards HIV-positive staff members; took responsibility for monitoring her for signs of dementia.

Weaver to Jeanie Boulet (supposedly talking about Al): "Must be tough to be sick all alone . . . It's got to be hard to carry that around all day." Jeanie: "It is."
Weaver: "I'm glad you decided to keep working. It'd be a real loss to the patients if you quit."

6. Application for academic tenure *[episode 3-11]*
Conducted much research, including study of effect of exercise on circadian rhythms of night shift workers (with help from Nurse Wendy Goldman and physician assistant, Jeanie Boulet); wrote several articles including 'The Woman Who Ate the ER' about patient, Iva Blender, who swallowed surgical instruments because she wanted to undergo surgery. Tour for prospective interns less

promising: no students signed up for County after 'progress of a urine sample' lecture.

7. Period deputizing as ER chief for Dr David Morgenstern, October 1997 to April 1998 *[episodes 4-2 to 4-17]*.

Dr Weaver eagerly seized opportunity to act as ER chief. Attempts to balance budget technically perfect but politically flawed, giving rise to conflict with Dr Ross and claims of wrongful dismissal by PA Jeanie Boulet (see respective Personnel files).

Note: Weaver also raised her own salary by $25,000!

8. Support for Synergix Physicians Group management consultancy, November 1997 to February 1998 *[episodes 4-6 to 4-13]*.

Dr Weaver's attitude to Synergix initially sceptical: had already made good progress on balancing ER budget as acting ER chief (see above). Attended presentation by Dr Ellis West; later supported Synergix application to manage ER, but withdrew support after discovered evidence of dubious cost control techniques by Synergix at other hospitals: had closed down 60% of their trauma centres in Mid West. Weaver accused Synergix of putting profits before patient care. Rallied support of ER attendings against Synergix after County board voted to begin negotiations; Synergix withdrew contract. Situation complicated by romantic relationship with Dr West.

Weaver: "I'm willing to make hard choices, Ellis. I'm not willing to endanger patients."

PROFESSIONAL ASSESSMENT

Strengths

Dr Weaver is disciplined and well organized, adopting a diligent attitude towards her work, both medical/surgical and managerial. Has an excellent manner with even the most difficult patients, offering calm reassurance and information where required. Takes an interest in the less popular, routine issues of the hospital. Particularly strong interest in balancing ER budget without jeopardising patient care, with remarkable success despite some problems (see below).

Note: Method of dealing with irritable Ethel Garvey involved answering all questions in full detail, with aid of diagrams and a flip-chart!

Note: In her first week as attending physician, attended a lecture (by Donald Anspaugh) on 'Modern architecture for emergency medicine management'.

Note: Weaver offered to lend Greene her copy of Managing Through Example: Twelve Steps to a More Efficient Workplace. "A number of passages are highlighted; I hope you don't find that too distracting."

Weaknesses

"If you're considering violence, count me in! There is no politically correct way to describe that woman" (Doug Ross).

Note: On her day off, the remaining staff held a party to celebrate a 'Happy No-Weaver Day'.

Dr Weaver is unfortunately not popular among other staff members, and has been described as patronizing and irritating. So far, however, there has been no appreciable effect on the department's efficiency. Needs to take a more pragmatic approach to issues that are politically sensitive, such as dismissal of PA Jeanie Boulet *[episodes 4-6 to 4-9]*. Dr Anspaugh cited "Ellis West-Synergix fiasco" as concern counting against her bid to become ER chief *[episode 4-22]*.

Prospects

Dr Weaver will be retained as ER attending physician for as long as she is willing to stay. Also clear contender for the now vacant post of ER chief, although recent problems have exposed potential weaknesses in Dr Weaver's approach, and County may prefer to keep its options open.

Personal information

Only known romantic partner while working at ER: Dr Ellis West of Synergix Physicians Group (see above). Relationship ended acrimoniously when Weaver withdrew support for Synergix.

West: "Synergix provides the most care for the most people, and if that means giving them an Oldsmobile instead of a Rolls, then so be it."

West: "I only wanted the contract if it meant working closely with you, Kerry . . . You are a smart, beautiful, sexy woman, and I don't want you believing that I used you, because I didn't. And I never underestimated you; never once. You underestimate yourself."

Note: Visited by Mlungusi Christmas 1995; gave him affectionate welcome; immediately cancelled work over Christmas period. Asked how she knew Mlungusi Weaver merely replied: "I had a farm in Africa..."

*[**Trivia:** Weaver walks with a crutch, and to date no reason has been given. She is suspected to have written a lurid romantic novel based on the ER, which includes a Weaver-like character: "Witchcraft attracted her as a child when Zulu tribesmen on her father's game preserve tried sorcery to heal her shrivelled leg." According to Maggie Doyle, the novel had to be written by "an incurable romantic who is very warped." Weaver loaded an audio program onto the ER computer, using her own voice - irritating Lewis and others. Her locker is next to Carter's.*

Weaver has received some long overdue attention in the fourth series. Since her arrival she had been little more than an object of hatred and ridicule for the other staff, but the Ellis West storyline gave the excellent Laura Innes a chance to show Weaver's human side. West may not have been particularly likeable, but it's nevertheless a shame that they had to break up: their last scene together suggests a side of Kerry that never expected to have a successful relationship, and it would be nice to see her proved wrong. She'll always remain a spiky and difficult character, but her support of Jeanie in the third series, and her attitude to Synergix in the fourth, show that she has a strong sense of morality and compassion underneath that harsh exterior. Hopefully in the fifth series we may get to see more of her hidden depths. The possibility that she could have written the romantic novel found lying around in the ER is intriguing, as is the fact that in it the Weaver character has the hots for a Dr Martin Bean...]

ANNA DEL AMICO, M.D.

Note: File closed, Summer 1998. Has since returned to Philadelphia to work in a paediatric ER.

AGE

29.

POSITION

Paediatrics resident (beginning second year residency). Has recently completed internship in ER. Paediatrics supervisor: Dr Ross; Emergency medicine supervisor: Dr Greene.

MEDICAL TRAINING AND CAREER TO DATE

Completed four years undergraduate study and four years at medical school. Three-four years in paediatrics. Left Philadelphia (where her attending was Dr Max Rocher) to join County as paediatrician double boarding in emergency medicine. Pursued emergency paediatrics elective in County ER before starting residency in July 1997.

SIGNIFICANT CAREER EVENTS

1. Delivery of Benton baby, summer 1997 *[episode 3-21]*.
Carla Rees admitted in early stages of labour; two months premature. Dr Coburn assisted in delivery room by Dr Del Amico. Vacuum extraction ordered. Baby boy delivered unable to breathe. Emergency resuscitation by Dr Del Amico successful; baby intubated. Transferred to NICU under care of Dr Tabash.

Note: Dr Del Amico working under significant pressure of Dr Benton's presence. Rees Benton later taken off life support and released, autumn 1997.

2. Professional conflict with Dr Ross, summer-autumn 1997 *[episodes 3-21 to 4-5.]*
Dr Ross objected to number of tests ordered by Dr Del Amico leading to tension over treatment of other patients *[episode 3-22]*. Dr

Ross also objected to lack of adult patients treated by Dr Del Amico *[episode 4-2]*. Further clashes over nature of treatment ordered and failure to communicate diagnosis to Dr Ross. Problems over preferences of patients: grandmother preferred familiar face of Dr Ross to Dr Del Amico, causing added tension *[episode 4-4]*. However, Del Amico's persistence with patients has led to bond of trust with them, see Brett, 20-year-old athlete, diagnosed with testicular cancer *[episode 4-5]*.

Ross to Weaver (having shown Del Amico the ER): "Kerry, will you take Dr Del Amico back. I'm intimidated enough already" [episode 3-20].

3. Treatment of Tom Dibble, transfer from Bellerman Memorial Hospital, March 1998 *[episode 4-16]*.

Unidentified drunken male with head injuries after motor vehicle accident, transferred by Dr Zachariah from Bellerman Memorial Hospital to County General ER. Unconscious; suffered subarachnoid haemmhorage leading to swelling of frontal lobes of brain. Dr Del Amico expressed anger at transfer - not trauma case. Son arrived, identified patient as Tom Dibble. Dr Del Amico told son that partial frontal labectomy may save his life, but Dr Mack, head of neurosurgery, advised no chance of success. Dr Zachariah then agreed to operation, possibly due to Dibble's excellent medical insurance status.

Del Amico: "I knew it was a dump, but this is gross negligence."

4. Refusal to perform abortion, May 1998 *[episode 4-19]*.

Patients admitted with various injuries following explosion at abortion clinic. Dr Weaver and Dr Del Amico treated woman in second trimester. On discovery that woman was in middle of abortion, Dr Weaver opted to conclude procedure. Dr Del Amico refused.

Note: Later confronted by Weaver about incident. Del Amico insists has "no moral objection to abortion." Weaver: "Well something happened in there."

PROFESSIONAL ASSESSMENT

Strengths

An excellent paediatrician whose enthusiasm and compassion for the care of children rivals that of Dr Ross. Anna has demonstrated consummate abilities under Dr Ross's tutelage. She may, however, require further experience with adult patients.

Weaknesses

Dr Del Amico has shown a marked tendency to pursue her own treatment of patients and tends to resent the involvement of others. In some cases, her failure to bring her findings to the attention of other members of staff, and her moral outlook, have undermined standards of patient care. Anna has often given too high a priority to proving herself. Dr Ross's supervision of Anna has shown an awareness of these problems and made efforts to correct them.

Prospects

Dr Del Amico should be encouraged to stay within the County ER. Perhaps a place could be found for her in the proposed paediatrics emergency department, should it be formed?

Note (summer 1998, on closure of file): Dr Del Amico's abrupt departure partly due to lack of paediatrics emergency department at County General.

PERSONAL INFORMATION

Family background

Dr Del Amico is Italian, comes from South Philadelphia; family still lives there. Has seven brothers (including Hank) and seven sisters-in-law. Has a stepmother and an Aunt Tessa.

Anna: "I'm the family freak. Aunt Tessa bursts into tears every time she sees me."

Anna: "I wrap a mean diaper."
Personal relationships

Relationship while at previous hospital with Dr Max Rocher, the paediatrics attending there. Rocher was a percodan addict; Anna helped him beat it. Dr Max Rocher now consultant to hospital emergency facilities; grades suitability of ERs for specialist paediatrics units. Arrived in County ER, spring 1998. Assessed County as suitable venue for specialist unit.

Possible relationship with Dr John Carter. Del Amico particular concerned for Dr Carter's well being following his arrest for obstruction of justice. Anna bailed him out *[episode 4-9]*. However, Del Amico was apparently unaware of Carter's family background and inheritance and was annoyed that Carter misled her. Carter however apologised. Likely romance apparently cut short by arrival of Dr Max Rocher in County ER.

*[**Trivia:** On arrival in Chicago, Anna lived in a motel but came into work to avoid the noise of her amorous neighbours who were "working on some kind of record." She stopped counting the number of babies she has delivered when it topped 200. Anna was pushed out of her window by her brothers when a child. She became infatuated with a tamagotchi she found in the ER. It died and emergency CPR (banging it on the reception desk) failed to bring it back to life! Her idea of a good breakfast is scrambled eggs, weak toast, blueberry pancakes and orange juice.*

Seeming at first like a hasty addition to the cast to help make up for the departure of Lewis in series three, Anna became more likable and interesting as series four developed, and a particularly good foil for Carter: her reaction to his decision not to use the scant blood supplies for rapist Jack Dar was particularly effective, especially given the obvious chemistry between them and Carter's growing infatuation with her. Ironically though, as Maria Bello unexpectedly departed the show between the fourth and fifth series, it seems Anna has left us just as we were beginning to get to know her . . .]

ELIZABETH CORDAY, F.R.C.S.

AGE

34.

POSITION

Surgical lecturer in orthopedics and trauma (Great Britain). Visiting US on BTA scheme: fellowship sponsored by Dr Robert Romano. Roughly equivalent position to senior surgical resident. Has also signed on for nights and weekends in trauma.

MEDICAL TRAINING AND CAREER TO DATE

Trained in UK: degree in medicine (equivalent to US medical school). Fellow of Royal College of Surgeons. Not qualified to resident status in US. Studies undertaken at County General include ER haemo-A study (see below) and femur transplant research.

SIGNIFICANT CAREER EVENTS

1. Professional conflict with Dr Peter Benton, autumn 1997 *[episodes 4-2 to 4-8].*
Dr Hicks asked Dr Benton to be guide to Dr Corday. Benton initially underestimated Corday's attention in trauma. Later suspected Corday of using Benton's need to be with son as means of securing best surgery for herself. Apparently retaliated by encouraging Dr Corday to perform appendectomy without surgical attending present *[episode 4-6].* Benton's actions based on misinterpretation of Corday's intention and pressure of competition.

Benton: "So I guess you were paying attention earlier?"
Corday: "Always."

Note: Doctors Benton and Corday currently an item!

2. Treatment of Allison Beaumont, December 1997 to May 1998 *[episodes 4-9 to 4-19].*
Allison Beaumont and mother admitted December 1997. Mother

seriously injured; died in ER. Allison stabilized but major injuries to leg. Dr Benton recommended amputation; Dr Corday and Dr Romano advocated fibula transplant. Surgery undertaken but length of time taken on transplant resulted in need for emergency measures. Dr Corday told to step out and let Dr Benton take over. Allison stabilized but in coma. 24th December 1997, second stage of tib-fib transplant undertaken by Doctors Corday and Romano; Dr Corday's misgivings noted. Following surgery, Allison woke from coma but with vocal chord injuries. Dr Romano recommended collagen injection; Dr Corday opted for surgery. Specialist Dr Kotlowitz given special dispensation to perform surgery in County. Operation successful.

Note: Corday uncertain whether she chose to perform transplant rather than amputate out of best care for patient or lust for challenging surgery.

Allison Beaumont now training to be paramedic, readmitted, May 1998, with rib fractures and internal bleeding resulting from attempts to assist patients at scene of accident. Dr Corday performed successful emergency surgery.

Corday: "You can put them back together, but you can't keep them that way."

3. Rescue of Leo Leipziger, March 1998 *[episode 4-15]*.
Corday on paramedic ridealong, attended collapsed building. Leipziger trapped under rubble; Corday and paramedic Dewey attempted rescue against advice. Leipziger's arm pinned under debris. Corday administered morphine IV; succeeded in freeing Lepziger without amputating arm, but amputation necessary in later surgery. Chicago Sun Times ran report praising Corday's 'heroic' rescue.

4. ER Haemo-A study, April 1998 *[episode 4-17]*.
Corday carried out study of artificial blood in ER with Dr Mark Greene as faculty advisor, despite status of Dr Robert Romano as Corday's supervisor. Successfully used haemo-A on patient, Mr Jang (store owner with gun-shot wounds), and responded to objections of patient's son.

PROFESSIONAL ASSESSMENT

Strengths

Dr Corday has been highly praised by several senior staff at County, including Doctors Greene and Anspaugh, who said Corday had "raised the bar" of surgical standards at County since her arrival. A combination of personal ambition, a desire to innovate and a genuine care for patients have made her an extremely valuable member of the team during her stay here.

Weaknesses

Romano: "She always has something to prove, often at the expense of the case at hand. She's not detail-orientated."

Dr Romano's six-month evaluation was less positive, criticizing her lack of focus and particularly citing her over-involvement in the case of Allison Beaumont *[episode 4-16]*. Romano's opinion is uncorroborated but nevertheless important, as his sponsorship will determine whether Dr Corday is able to stay at County.

Prospects

Corday was offered two good positions in spring 1998: Chicago area coordinator of Dr Romano's haemo-A OR study, and senior lecturer at Gloucestershire Royal Hospital in the UK. She declined both, electing to stay at County General for as long as possible *[episodes 4-17 and 4-18]*. At time of writing, Dr Romano has indicated he is not willing to renew her fellowship, and the deadline for obtaining fellowship from other sources has passed. Corday is therefore attempting to obtain sponsorship from another surgeon in order to stay at County.

Corday, refusing Romano's offer of a position on his Haemo-A OR study: "I'm staying put. It may not be the smartest political move, but it feels like the right thing to do."

PERSONAL INFORMATION

Family background

Corday says got into medicine to please her father and rattle her mother. Father a surgeon, as was grandfather. Was given to nurse after she was born and mother went away to South Spain for three weeks; then cared for by nannies, and sent to boarding school when aged five.

Personal relationships

Split up with Jeremy, a "self-possessed dermatologist". Dr Benton reluctant to respond to Corday's advances at first, but relationship begun after night out at British-themed bar, February 1998 [episode 4-12], and has strengthened since despite Dr Benton's apparent problems accepting a white girlfriend (see Personnel file of Dr Benton).

Note: Also approached by Dr Romano, but brushed off: Romano assumed Corday had a policy against dating colleagues, and later found out she was dating Benton. May have something to do with non-renewal of fellowship...

*[**Trivia:** Corday is a darts expert, able to score a 25 while throwing backwards with her eyes closed! She is a big fan of practical jokes, and makes regular purchases from a joke shop down the street from her apartment. She also told Benton she enjoyed the smell of talcum powder on a man . . .*

When Corday first appeared it looked as if her only role would be to draw attention to the differences in terminology and practice between Britain and the United States, but thankfully she turned out to be much more. Her rocky relationship with Romano has been a joy to behold, but the writers' real stroke of genius was to pair her off with Benton, showing a new side to to him while also endearing her to us as perhaps the only person who can bring him out of his shell. Without giving too much away for those who haven't seen the relevant episodes yet, Dr Corday will be with us for series five, and hopefully beyond despite the lack of a fellowship.]

PETER BENJAMIN BENTON, M.D.

AGE

32.

POSITION

Sixth-year surgical resident.

Responsibilities

Though assigned to surgical service, covering the ER represents large proportion of duties. Has also been responsible for teaching medical students and interns. Joined Dr Hicks's 'red' surgical team, spring 1997. Joined Dr Robert Romano's surgical team, December 1997.

MEDICAL TRAINING AND CAREER TO DATE

Medical school: Five years, included two years 'hands-on' training. Last two years included obstetrics rotation at Lakeside; period working alongside Dr Mark Greene, currently attending physician in ER.

Note: Greene told Carter that he was at med-school with Benton; Benton "got sick all the time" during procedures.

Residency: Five years to date. ER rotation in first year at Mount Sinai hospital concurrent with Dr Kerry Weaver. Years two to five at County General.

SIGNIFICANT CAREER EVENTS

1. Ivan Gregor, May to October 1994 *[episodes 1-1 to 1-5]*
Liquor store owner Ivan Gregor came to ER several times May to October 1994 - injuries sustained in armed hold-ups of his store. Eventually decided to purchase a firearm; accidentally injured himself and re-admitted to ER. Mr Gregor came to know Benton by name; specifically requested his presence several times. October 1994, Mr Gregor shot 14-year-old boy who had menaced him.

Reported to police by Dr Benton.

2. Application for Starzl fellowship, August to November 1994 [episodes 1-3 to 1-7]
August 1994: Benton applied for Starzl fellowship, despite being only second-year resident. Developed strongly competitive attitude towards rival, Dr Sarah Langworthy, with whom he worked in the ER. Both noted to be over-zealous on occasion: made strenuous efforts to revive one patient who was dead on arrival [episode 1-3]. Dr Benton strong candidate but lost out to Dr Langworthy who had more experience of procedures.

Note: Benton clearly upset when didn't get fellowship. Intervened in one of Dr Ross's cases, boy with epiglottitis, cutting airway before strictly necessary. When confronted Benton admitted he was wrong and apologized (somewhat unusual!).

3. Teddy Powell, 24th December 1994 [episode 1-10]
Dr Benton narrowly avoided being unable to harvest from organ donor, Teddy Powell, after already informing other hospitals organs were available. Drs Hicks and Greene noted foolishness of assumption: Powell himself indicated consent on driver's licence, but estranged wife yet to be contacted; upon arrival refused to allow harvest. Benton persuaded Mrs Powell to consent with help from Dr Greene.

4. Concerns of Dr Hicks over swapping shifts with other doctors, February/March 1995 [episodes 1-16 to 1-17]
Dr Hicks noted Benton had arranged informal shift swaps with other doctors over several weeks. Benton explained he needed to take time to care for his ailing mother. Dr Hicks pointed out practice of swapping shifts frowned upon; told Benton if he needed to spend more time with his mother, should take one year's break from residency. Dr Benton claimed not necessary, but later found to have undertaken a 48-hour shift. Hicks believed long shift without adequate rest presented danger to Dr Benton and patients. Benton agreed to take two hours' sleep - after which performance in surgery remarkable.

Note: Benton only took a few minutes' sleep - just avoided Hicks for two hours. Shift took its toll on Benton later: failed to wake in time to give his mother medication; mother fell and broke hip.

5. The Vucelich study, late November 1995 to early March *[episodes 2-6 to 2-16]*

November 1995, Dr Benton applied for position on research study of 'clamp and run' procedure led by Dr Carl Vucelich. Benton stayed with study for ten weeks; according to Dr Vucelich performed with excellence. Benton left study suddenly in early February, stating he and Dr Vucelich "experiencing some differences in style". However Dr Vucelich's nomination instrumental in board's decision to award Dr Benton title of 'Resident of the Year', May 1996.

Note: Real reason why Benton left 'clamp and run' study not officially recognized, to protect him from damage to career. Benton suspected some patients on whom procedure was unsuccessful, including Mrs Rubadoux (see file on Dr John Carter), were being omitted. Checked and found at least three had been incorrectly excluded - possibly resulting in too favourable conclusion to study when published. Benton took concerns to Vucelich; was then effectively pushed off study. Consulted Hicks and Greene who advised extreme caution. Benton told brother-in-law, Walt, he backed out of a meeting with Dean at last moment: "I'm stupid enough to ruin my career, but I don't even have the courage to do it the right way." Later wrote letter to ethics committee outlining concerns. Luckily, matter settled privately: Vucelich published addendum to article detailing excluded cases. Benton's letter returned to him.

6. Elective in paediatric surgery under Dr Abby Keaton, October 1996 to January 1997 *[episodes 3-3 to 3-11]*

Dr Benton applied for a fellowship in paediatric surgery; one rotation under Dr Abby Keaton, recently transferred from Southside General Hospital following its closure.

Note: Carter said applying for paediatric surgery rotation "typical" of Benton: notoriously difficult specialty and impossible to get into!

Dr Keaton's assessment of Benton's work overwhelmingly positive in terms of surgical skills, but raised serious concerns about ability to deal with children and parents on an emotional level. Also doubted whether Benton had sufficient enthusiasm for paediatrics for its own sake rather than as an intellectual challenge. Keaton noted over-confidence and lack of humility in Benton's approach; particular reference to treatment of ten-day-old patient Megan Herlihy, November 1996 *[episode 3-6]*. Asked to close on abdominal surgery which Drs Benton and Keaton performed together; Dr Benton unwittingly damaged child's liver and caused severe bleeding; sent into shock, respiratory failure. Child survived, but Dr Keaton heavily criticized Benton's actions, particularly delay in calling her after realizing that he had reached limits of his experience. Keaton therefore did not recommend second paediatric rotation for Dr Benton.

8. Death of Dr Dennis Gant, intern assigned to Dr Benton, January 1997 *[episode 3-11]*

Questions raised by members of ER staff after suspected suicide of Dr Gant, intern working under supervision of Dr Benton. Benton's written assessment of Gant positive, but often heard to be extremely critical. Gant known to be working strenuously hard in last few weeks to avoid further criticism.

Note: Without confirmed cause of death or further evidence from other students, no conclusions can fairly be drawn from this tragic event.

Note: Benton's failure to be recommended by Keaton, near-fatal mistake with baby Megan and Gant's apparent suicide appeared to take toll on Benton's confidence. Spent several weeks doing very little surgery. Student Dr John Carter requested to transfer from 'blue' surgical team (Benton) to 'red' team (Hicks). Benton later accepted Hicks's offer to join red team also and abandoned ambitions in paediatric surgery.

9. Rodney Price, November 1997 *[episode 4-8]*.

Rodney Price, aged twelve, admitted following hit and run accident. Damage to internal organs; x-ray revealed rare genetic condition that reversed abdominal organs. Doctors Romano and Corday assisted Dr Benton in surgery. Rodney stabilized. Dr Benton known to father, Isaac Price (former classmates). Mr Price agreed that tests be conducted. Apparently told blood samples to be taken to aid Rodney's recovery but actually to assist genetic research as planned. Complications in PICU; Rodney died despite extreme efforts of Dr Benton.

Note: Dr Romano asked for autopsy to aid research but Dr Benton refused to ask Mr Price. Felt he had abused his position of trust with father enough.

10. Laporoscopy on Dr L. Swanson, May 1998 *[episode 4-17]*.

Assisted Dr Morgenstern in surgery; pushed him aside and took over when Morgenstern allegedly cut gastric artery. Benton unable to stop bleeding; Dr Swanson died. Residents review committee suspended Dr Benton from surgical rotation pending results of an enquiry, but Dr Morgenstern recommended reinstatement prior to resignation, effectively admitting fault for Swanson's death. (See also Personnel file of Dr Morgenstern.)

Benton: "I lost my mentor today, and the hospital – they lost a great surgeon."

PROFESSIONAL ASSESSMENT

"A man of many talents, all unproven." (Dr Steven Flint)

"That's what I like about you, Peter. Naked ambition tempered by arrogance." (Dr David Morgenstern.)

"Arrogant as hell." (Dr Carl Vucelich.)

Strengths

Dr Benton's dedication to his work is beyond question, as evidenced by the long shifts he has often worked and the clear diligence he shows in his attitude towards studying and practice. The result is a remarkable level of surgical skill, and a breadth of knowledge which sets a high standard for his students.

Note: Has been heard muttering medical jargon in his sleep; listens to surgical education tapes in spare time. Usually reluctant to take time off. Even resents having to sleep for more than few hours: "Anything more than three hours, and I'm sluggish all day."

Note: Has spent noticeably less time on work since birth of Rees; concerns expressed by Dr Anspaugh, but County recognizes importance of family commitments. Dr Benton generally strikes fair balance between the two.

Teaching

"Dr Benton is an intern's worst nightmare. He's smarter than you, he never eats, he never sleeps, and he reads every medical journal no matter how obscure. He is the Antichrist, Beelzebub, Lucifer...You will go to sleep at night wishing plague and pestilence on his unborn children, and you will wake up every morning praying for his approval. You won't get it." (Dr Melvoyne)

"The man is a sadist." (Dr Dennis Gant)

Despite concerns about his occasional harshness, students' assessments of Dr Benton have been overwhelmingly positive. Although his insistence on high standards and his reluctance to give any kind of approval can be demoralizing at first, they produce an impressive result. Dr Morgenstern has stated that Dr Benton's students come out of his rotations stronger than any others he has seen *[episode 1-6]*.

Weaknesses

"You're a gifted surgeon; it's outside the operating room where you need work. That mother needed something from you today and you acted as if your job was over as soon as you took the surgical gloves off. You've got great hands. Now you've got to show some heart." (Dr Abby Keaton)

"You have the arrogance of a great surgeon, the ego, and someday one hopes the talent, but what you don't have is the ability to get along, to be one of the team." (Dr Angela Hicks)

Dr Benton himself concedes that he is not adept at dealing with the emotional needs of patients. It has also been noted that he is less than popular among his colleagues, and on several occasions has clashed with Drs Greene, Ross and Lewis. As described above, Dr Keaton has also noted his occasional lack of patience and humility, as well as a marked inability to get on with children *[episode 3-5]*.

Benton's third-year assessment of Carter: "Far more successful at dealing with the emotional needs of patients than this instructor."

Note: Benton may not consider emotional needs important. Told Debra Chen not to let her course, 'Dealing with Patients as People' , interfere with work!

Prospects

Dr Benton has repeatedly stated his ambition to become chief surgical resident at County General, a post for which he is intellectually suited but which would probably require better social skills than Dr Benton has so far presented. The board's current intention is to retain Dr Benton at County General for as long as is possible, by means of either a fellowship or a post as an attending physician.

PERSONAL INFORMATION

Family background

Dr Benton's mother treated at County General in March 1995 for fractured hip, then moved to Melville nursing home. Died May 1995.

Elder sister Jackie married to Walt, with two children. Walt and Jackie own car repair business inherited from Dr Benton's father. Were responsible for the care of Mrs Benton for several years before she moved to the Melville home.

Son born at County, summer 1997 *[episode 3-21]*, named Rees Benton. Son's mother: Carla Rees. (See Personal relationships.)

Note: Dr Benton's father died when Benton was a child. Jackie shocked when Dr Benton admitted he missed him shortly after birth of Benton's son.

Personal relationships

Became close to Jeanie Boulet (now physician's assistant in ER) while she was working as physical therapist for Mrs Benton. However, Ms Boulet married to Mr Al Boulet.

Note: Benton and Jeanie continued affair for several months; Benton

demanded Jeanie choose between him and Al; she told him she would not
leave her husband (though they did separate shortly afterwards).

Note: Benton tested for HIV when told Al Boulet had AIDS. Tested
negative. Reluctant to allow Jeanie to participate in surgery when heard
her test was positive.

Relationship with Carla Rees. Owner of Caribbean restaurant. Gave
birth to son, summer 1997 *[episode 3-21]*. Many complications
including gestational diabetes, premature delivery (by two months);
birth with use of vacuum extraction. Immediate resuscitation
required; possible blood infection; lungs weak; possible impairment
of sight. Oxygen starvation during experimental treatment to relieve
lung problems may have resulted in mental retardation.

Note: Carla brought in to ER after involved in rear-end shunt from truck.
Treated by Jeanie Boulet and Dr Coburn: stitches needed to arm. Test
needed to rule out compatibility problems with baby. Jeanie needed to
know blood type; Carla told her father was Benton.

Note: Benton's interference in birth of child similar to interference in
treatment of his mother. Reluctant to trust other doctors with
treatment of loved ones.

Note: At first Carla told Benton she didn't expect even financial help
from him for their child; but child's poor health may mean she needs
much more support than she ever expected.

Current relationship with Dr Elizabeth Corday. Benton admits to
problems with dating a white woman; also said to be non-commital
re relationship, asking Corday to consider work in other hospitals
and other regions of US. But colleagues note combined effect of
fatherhood and Corday relationship has made Benton happier and
more relaxed.

Psychological evaluation (extracts)
Has occasionally expressed deep resentment of system of training
and evaluating doctors. Blames own tendency to overwork on need
to log all procedures.

Hicks and Benton's exchange during Benton's 48-hour shift (Hicks criticizes Benton for over-zealously assigning procedures to himself):
Hicks: "It's not a competition."
Benton: "So why are we required to keep logs of every procedure that we do?"
Hicks: "As a record, not a score card!"
Benton: "Yeah, right. You're keeping score, and you know it."

Anger at perceived racism in system; strong opponent of positive discrimination.

Note: Arguing re respective responsibilities of (black) parents and state, paramedic Shepherd said 'the system' worked well for Benton as a doctor. Benton responded angrily that it did not.

Note: Benton told Gant that black students, interns (and residents?) had to work "twice as hard, stay twice a late, to be twice as good" to prove they had not been hired "to fill a quota". Benton himself did not tick the 'African-American' box on his application. Gant: "Maybe you should just tell people. So you don't have to go around keep proving it all the time."

Concern expressed about Dr Benton's lack of 'support systems'. He has few friends, if any: tends to refuse offers of friendship (eg Carter). Shaky relationship with Walt and Jackie.

Note: At desperate times, turns to religion - see faltering recital of Lord's Prayer during treatment of Megan Herlihy; visits chapel during early problems with son.

*[**Trivia:** Benton's mother raised him and his sister at home. When Benton was ten years old, staying at a boys' club camp, he reported another boy who had stolen money from the equipment fund after he had shown him the money. The other boys broke his nose and didn't talk to him for the rest of the summer. Benton tells Jeanie that his mother stood up and applauded at his med-school graduation, although he told Carter that he missed his graduation because he was in surgery. Until his first date with Dr Corday, Benton hadn't drunk alchohol for years: he told her it was because he didn't like the taste, to which she replied, "So, it's not a control thing then?" She proceeded to get him very drunk, albeit on just two glasses of Pimm's. He also doesn't smoke, and hasn't eaten meat*

for six years. In 1994 he told Carol his salary was $23,739 before taxes; in 1998 he told Corday his take-home pay was $675 a week.

Prior to the fourth series, Benton shared with Weaver the position of regular character least likely to win a popularity contest. He treated Carter with contempt from the beginning, although he was actually quite impressed with his work and even quite fond of him. He was similarly harsh to Gant, possibly with fatal consequences. His behaviour towards Jeanie after they split up, and particularly after he found out she was HIV positive, was utterly contemptible. And yet, he was fascinating to watch - partly because of the considerable skills of Eriq la Salle, who subtly conveyed the emotions that were going on beneath the stoney façade. In the fourth series fatherhood, but much more importantly the appearance on the scene of Elizabeth Corday, have revealed a new dimension to his character: from that first, priceless date where she got him drunk on two glasses of Pimm's, Elizabeth has made more progress in turning the 'ice-man' into a human being than anyone could have thought possible. His reaction to the departure of Morgenstern, and to Corday's assurance that he must have known the respect Peter had for him, also hinted once again that Benton's long-lost relationship with his father may have a strong part to play in forming his personality. Despite all that, though, there is still enough of an edge to Benton's character to give him a great deal of potential for the future, with or without (but preferably with) Corday.]

SECTION TWO

Personnel File Extracts
[Secondary Characters]

Doctors
(Second-year residents and above)

Donald Anspaugh   *[John Aylward]*

Neil Bernstein   *[David Spielburg]*

Janet Coburn   *[Amy Aquino]*

Div Cvetic   *[John Terry]*

Greg Fischer   *[Harry J Lennix]*

Angela Hicks   *[CCH Pounder]*

Jack Kayson   *[Sam Anderson]*

Abby Keaton   *[Glenne Headly]*

Sarah Langworthy   *[Tyra Ferrell]*

David Morgenstern   *[William H Macy]*

Nina Pomerantz   *[Jamie Gertz]*

Robert 'Rocket' Romano   *[Paul McCrane]*

William Swift   *[Michael Ironside]*

John 'Tag' Taglieri   *[Rick Rossovich]*

Carl Vucelich   *[Ron Rifkin]*

Medical students and interns

Debra Chen   *[Ming-Na Wen]*

Anna Del Amico	*[Maria Bello]*
Margaret 'Maggie' Doyle	*[Jorjan Fox]*
Dale Edson	*[Matthew Glave]*
Dennis Gant	*[Omar Epps]*
George Henry	*[Chad Lowe]*
Harper Tracy	*[Christine Elise]*

Nursing staff

Haleh Adams	*[Yvette Freeman]*
E Ray Bozman	*[Charles Noland]*
Lydia Garbarsky	*[Ellen Crawford]*
Wendy Goldman	*[Vanessa Marquez]*
Chuni Marquez	*[Laura Ceron]*
Malik McGrath	*[Deezer D]*
Conni Oligario	*[Conni Marie Brazleton]*
Yosh Takada	*[Gedde Watanabe]*

Emergency Medical Technicians (Paramedics)

Allison Beaumont	*[Michele Morgan]*
Raul Melendez	*[Carlos Gomez]*
Doris Pickman	*[Emily Wagner]*
Ray 'Shep' Shepherd	*[Ron Eldard]*

Reception staff and aides

Randi Fronczak	*[Kristin Minter]*

Cynthia Hooper	*[Mariska Hargitay]*
Jerry Markovic	*[Abraham Benrubi]*
Bogdanalivetsky 'Bob' Romansky	*[Malgoscha Gebel]*

DOCTORS
(SECOND-YEAR RESIDENTS AND ABOVE)
DONALD ANSPAUGH

POSITION: **Hospital chief of staff.**

Accomplished surgeon and hospital manager, formerly chief of staff at Southside. Innovative theoretician of hospital practices (gave lecture on 'Modern architecture for emergency medicine management'); pioneered the health-mobile project at Southside. Appointed Chief of Staff County General following closure of Southside and amalgamation of personnel. Instituted new efficiency standards in ER on arrival; test studies carried out thanks to shared outlook and strong working relationship with Dr Kerry Weaver. Admirable caution in organizing departmental decisions re HIV-positive health-care workers *[episodes 3-9 and 3-10]*. Has mediated in several cases of staff training and promotion: Dr Benton's aborted transfer to Dr Kenner for a second paediatrics rotation; concerns of Dr Gant about Dr Benton's teaching methods *[episode 3-11]*; tenure review and recommendation of Dr Greene *[episodes 3-13 and 3-18]*. Headed investigation into mental state of Dennis Gant following tragic death. Granted Dr Carter's request to leave County surgical program.

Note: Reputation for being "completely lumpy" and "a crackpot": inefficient doctors are made to wax his car. Much admired by Dr Weaver.

Note: Recommended Dr Greene for tenure over Dr Weaver because of his better people skills despite being Weaver's "intellectual inferior".

Note: Before Dr Carter's request made, had considerable clashes with

Anspaugh: Anspaugh missed diagnosis of atriol fibrillation; case of Mr Bartok; case of Mr Lensky. Told Carter he had often wondered over the years whether he made the right decision in becoming a surgeon.

Family background: Widower; one son (Scott, born 1986, died of cancer 1998); one daughter (Yvette). Scott Anspaugh received chemotherapy at County; Jeanie Boulet acted as private duty care giver (see also Personnel file of Jeanie Boulet).

[Trivia: Once member of the US Army, and shared rooms with Schwartzkopf at West Point. Drives a black Cadillac Seville with burgundy interior. Member of prestigious Fair Oaks golf course and consequently on good terms with some of Chicago's most influential businessmen. He is, to quote Elizabeth Corday, "a bit of an Anglophile", having worked with British surgeons on joint NATO exercises in 1974. His English accent leaves a lot to be desired, however. He is a big fan of dinosaur pencils!

From his arrival at the beginning of the third series, Anspaugh has become one of the series' most interesting, amusing, and imposing regular characters. His quick sarcastic wit is used brilliantly to put down interns and attendings alike. His reaction to his son Scott's illness and death was suitably understated, with the few words he exchanged with Jeanie speaking volumes about his love for his son, and his gratitude to her for supporting him in his last few months.]

NEIL BERNSTEIN

POSITION: **Head of paediatrics.**

Running complaint with Morgenstern about activities of Dr Ross, holder of ER paediatrics fellowship (paid for by paediatrics dept). Ross on permanent duty in ER, dismissive of Bernstein's authority and abusive to his physicians. Confrontation re mistake of County paediatrics clinic resident in prescribing incorrect AIDS pills to Chia-Chia Loh and later Ross's admit of boy with head trauma for overnight observation against Bernstein's wishes. Refusal to renew Ross's fellowship, November/December 1995. Following Ben Larkin rescue *[episode 2-7]*, Ross reinstated and given award for outstanding community service. Board unimpressed with decision of Bernstein to sack Ross. With Dr Morgenstern, drew up new arrangement for Dr Ross in which funding underwritten by ER.

See also: Personnel file on Dr Douglas Ross.

Note: Ross continues to regard Bernstein as "an idiot". Reputed to have denounced Bernstein in first draft of award acceptance speech.

JANET COBURN

POSITION: **Attending physician, obstetrics (OB) department.**

Expressed serious concern over the conduct of Dr Mark Greene in the Jodi O'Brien case. Offered help to Dr Greene as soon as eclampsia was, belatedly, diagnosed in Mrs O'Brien. Greene decided to go ahead with labour; patient consequently died *[episode 1-18]*. Coburn was leading voice against Greene at conference presenting the case *[episode 1-20]*. However, later satisfied with Greene's performance when ER temporarily took over OB duties: eight healthy mothers and nine healthy newborns, a good ratio *[episode 2-15]*.

Also, with Dr Bernstein, one of the critics of Dr Douglas Ross; argued for non-renewal of fellowship *[episode 2-1]*.

Carla Rees, girlfriend of Dr Peter Benton, was Coburn's patient. Coburn delivered baby two months prematurely in summer 1997 *[episode 3-21]*.

Coburn to Greene, during Greene's treatment of Jodi O'Brien: "I've never seen such a chain of errors of judgement."

Note: Coburn not popular at County - Dr Anna Castigliano, who gave birth in ER, specifically requested not to have her supervise the delivery!
See also: Personnel file on Dr Mark Greene.

DIV CVETIC

POSITION: **Former head of psychiatric department; left County in November 1994 [between** *episodes 1-8* **and** *1-9*]. **Worked in psychiatric medicine for 15 years.**

Harsh attitude towards patients and colleagues noted throughout late 1994. Relationship with Dr Susan Lewis began April or May 1994. Manifested symptoms of clinical depression prior to leaving County; also left apartment, and Dr Lewis, without her knowledge. Latest information (supplied by patient running dating service): Dr Cvetic living with woman who owns a chain of mortuaries.

"After fifteen years, not one week has gone by without being bitten, spat, puked or peed on." (Div Cvetic).

"You try to find ways not to hate them. You feel nothing. Every drop of pleasure has drained from your life." (Div Cvetic, confessing his own feelings into a dictaphone.
[Though quite understated, Div Cvetic's slide into depression is one of the most disturbing storylines of the first series, particularly in his last episode [1-8] - which begins with his confession into the dictaphone and ends with a shot of him standing in the middle of a stream of traffic, and in pouring rain. The news about his new partner was an odd coda, but at least gave us a hint that he might have found happiness after leaving County, and probably leaving psychiatry too.]

See also: Personnel file on Dr Susan Lewis.

GREG FISCHER

POSITION: **Virologist, County General Infectious Diseases. Virology consult to the ER.**

Dr Fischer ran successful private practice but discontinued when business partner died of AIDS-related illness. Well respected for treatment of HIV-positive patients; personal physician in case of Jeanie Boulet, PA. Involved in new AIDS treatment study, County infectious diseases dept (Al Boulet is one candidate). Consult to ER on cases of malaria *[episode 3-12]*, neuro-syphyllis *[episode 3-13]*, and staphylococcus outbreak *[episode 3-14]*. Also tragic case of Suzanne Alner, overdosed on AIDS pills *[episode 3-18]*. Brief relationship with Jeanie Boulet ended when Boulet returned to her husband.

Note: "One of the most eligible bachelors in Chicago" (Dr Weaver)

*[**Trivia:** Amateur astronomer who held frequent comet watches during appearance of the Hale-Bopp comet. Lukewarm feeling about opera. Having been accused by Jeanie of being unromantic and lacking spontaneity, he organized a picnic in sub-zero temperatures.]*

See also: Personnel file on Jeanie Boulet, PA.

ANGELA HICKS

POSITION: **Attending surgeon, County General. Leader: surgical 'red' team.**

Formerly ER attending physician *[episode 1-9]*, currently responsible for training surgical residents and medical students, including allocation of surgical sub-internships. Panellist on admissions board for surgical interns: has noted increased pressures may result from intention to rank all interns on procedures for purposes of deselecting. Has brought two disciplinary points against Dr John Carter: recommended expulsion from surgical program, April 1997 *[episode 3-18]*. Nevertheless regards Carter highly: he currently works with Hicks on 'red' team with Dr Benton. Continues to enjoy excellent working relationship with Dr Peter Benton.

Note: Reprimanded Benton re failure to confirm donation of organs before informing recipient hospitals, December 1994. Has once let Benton's enthusiasm cloud her judgement.

"It's not about ambition... It's about healing people." (Dr Hicks to Dr Benton)

Hicks to Carter (following admission of denied surgical candidate to OR): "'John Carter is not a law unto himself.' I hope you learn that. You won't get another chance."

Note: Hicks reputedly received negative assessment of Dr Benton's tutelage from John Carter but original assessment never attached to Benton personnel file.

Note: Dr Ross mistook Hicks for a nurse on arrival and assigned her to bed-pan duty.

See also: Personnel files on Dr Peter Benton and Dr John Carter.

[Hicks is the perfect foil to Peter Benton and one of the few people of whom he takes any notice, though at times he has been resistant to her orders. Here we have one of the best examples of a convincing work relationship within the series, with Hicks showing equal concern for Benton's professional and personal failings. Hicks should be Benton's role model, having the skills and knowledge of a great surgeon with the added ability to work within a team. She also has a wonderful wry sense of humour, dropping to Carter during surgery that Benton once accidentally sawed off an appendix and later rescheduling Carter's operations to enable him to perform Benton's appendectomy!]

JACK KAYSON

POSITION: **Head of cardiology.**

Clashed with Dr Susan Lewis on several occasions during the second half of 1994 *[episodes 1-2 to 1-13]*; later treated by Lewis for a heart attack, January 1995 *[episode 1-13]*.

With Dr Mark Greene and Dr Maggie Doyle, argued for a place on the heart transplant waiting list for Louise Cupertino, a 35-year old woman with Down's Syndrome who was refused by the transplant committee following the recommendation of Dr Nina Pomerantz, spring 1997 *[episode 3-16]*.

Led questioning of Dr Morgenstern at resident review committee's enquiry re Lyle Swanson, May 1998 *[episode 4-19]*.

See also: Personnel file on Dr Susan Lewis.

ABBY KEATON

POSITION: **Paediatric surgeon. Left County General for placement in Pakistan, January 1997.**

One of the most highly regarded paediatric surgeons in the country, certainly the best in Chicago. Awards include Paediatric Surgeon of the Year, 1995, and Price Award, 1996. Transfer from Southside Hospital after its closure in October 1996. Supervized Dr Peter Benton for one rotation, but refused to recommend him for second rotation. Brief but intense relationship with Dr John Carter.

Note: Benton and Carter had both followed Keaton's work before her arrival at County.

Benton on Keaton: "She's a great surgeon but she's not much of a teacher. All that psychobabble...She doesn't say what she wants. She's soft. She doesn't act like a surgeon."

See also: Personnel files on Dr Peter Benton and Dr John Carter.

*[**Trivia:** Enjoys deep dish pizza with pepperoni and anchovies. Wears size 7^1/$_2$ surgical gloves, with no powder.*

Possibly the all-round best doctor seen on the show and certainly one of the most likeable characters, combining brilliant surgical skills with an obvious affinity for dealing with patients' and parents' emotional needs, and having a sense of humour too. Often seen wearing one of her selection of patterned showercaps, and on one occasion a pair of novelty cat's ears, to put her patients at ease. With her girlish voice, gentle manner and huge technical powers, who could wish for a better person finally to put Benton in his place?]

SARAH LANGWORTHY

POSITION: **Former surgical resident.**

Won Starzl fellowship November 1994 *[episode 1-7]* after competing against Dr Peter Benton. She was then a third-year resident, while Benton was in his second year. Intended to return in Spring 1995.

At one time romantically interested in Benton; her attentions were harshly refused.

See also: Personnel file of Dr Peter Benton.

DAVID MORGENSTERN

POSITION: **Former head of ER.**

"Give me a good sick body that needs a little slicing, and I'm a happy man." (Morgenstern)

Morgenstern's comment to Weaver following appointment of Donald Anspaugh as County's Chief of Staff: "Funny how life is so like surgery. Sometimes you can make that incision in the right lower quadrant, and then there are those days when your bowel ruptures and spills into your peritaneum, and all you're left with is intense pain and sepsis."

Easy-going manner concealed dedication and skill in surgery, and ability to make tough decisions as ER chief. Personally taught almost half of County's ER residents. Had great respect for Doctors Greene and Weaver particularly: responsible for appointment of former as attending physician and latter as chief ER resident. Regarded Dr Ross as disposable until rescue of Ben Larkin, December 1995 *[episode 2-7]*. Expressed concern re Dr Lewis's self-confidence and commitment to the job, especially request to turn part-time. Admiration for Dr Benton's surgical skills, if not his attitude.

Left County for six months to set up emergency medicine training program at Brigham, Harvard (program never passed committee stage). Returned September 1995.

Suffered heart attack [myocardial infarction - MI] in ER during visit of filming crew, September 1997 *[episode 4-1]*. Absent for 197 days while Weaver deputized. Concern expressed during absence re extent of ER's budget deficit: $1.7m over budget when Dr Weaver took over. On return, Dr Morgenstern said MI had given him new outlook: more concerned re patients' individual backgrounds and stories. Concern expressed (eg Elizabeth Corday) re Morgenstern's competence as a surgeon after his return; Weaver expressed opinion that Morgenstern had returned too early.

Morgenstern to Weaver, on the job of ER chief (while drugged up on morphine!): "I don't mind telling you, sometimes I've felt like a sheriff with no posse, like a general with no grunts in the field, like a lone shepherd, high up on a hill with no sheep dog . . . Everywhere you look there's sheep, sheep, sheep . . ."

May 1998, performed surgery with Dr Benton on Dr L. Swanson: a pathologist, aged 71, with torsion of stomach. (Morgenstern took histology from Swanson; he inspired Morgenstern to become a surgeon.) During surgery Morgenstern accidentally cut gastric artery; unable to control bleeding; Benton pushed Morgenstern aside and attempted to save Swanson, but unsuccessfully. Initially Dr Morgenstern did not accept Benton's word; claimed Swanson died from ruptured varices. At enquiry of residents review committee, Morgenstern's version preferred; Benton suspended from surgical rotation. (See also Personnel file of Dr Peter Benton.) Dr Morgenstern then viewed video of surgery and agreed Benton's version correct; resigned from County General and reinstated Benton *[episode 4-19]*.

Morgenstern to Weaver: "I've let this situation get completely out of hand . . . I was covering my own ass."

Morgenstern, after resignation: "Smell that: the smell of spring. All green and full of possibilities."

FAMILY BACKGROUND

Russian Jew on father's side, full-blooded Highland Scot on mother's. "Pa Morgenstern worked at the local tannery; ma was a taxidermist." Decided to go into medicine as a child while living in a farm house in North Dakota, when he attempted to save the life of a baby mole.

Note: arrived in ER on 25th January 1995 (Burns Night) wearing a kilt; injured himself tossing the caber. "I conked myself, the buffet table, and Great Aunt Jean Ferguson." Relatives arrived later in department;

Morgenstern cut haggis there. (Nurse Hathaway thought Morgenstern was dressed in Catholic school-girl's outfit - frilly blouse, slippers, knee-socks!)

*[**Trivia:** Morgenstern was invited to present one of his cases at a conference in Miami when he was a resident, but left his visual aids on the plane! Sent Carter a congratulatory basket of muffins on hearing he would be staying on as a resident. Once asked Weaver out to dinner and a movie, which she accepted, but no sign of any romance as yet! Has driven the same route to work for three years on the Eisenhower expressway.*

William H Macy as Morgenstern was the calm centre at the eye of the storm, always present in the background with his quirky manner and sometimes hilarious lines of dialogue. His appearance in the ER on Burns night with members of his 'clan' was a crowning glory, marred only by the most appalling Scottish accents ever heard on television! His dramatic and emotional departure in series four, easily his most important storyline, has sadly deprived us of one of the show's best characters.]

NINA POMERANTZ

POSITION: **Psychiatric consult and staff counsellor, County General Hospital.**

Divorced with one daughter, Emma, aged six. Saw Dr Dennis Gant on a few occasions when he was settling in. Provided counselling for Dr Carter for survivor's guilt over death of Gant. Turned down application of Louise Cupertino for heart transplant because unlikely to cope with post-operative treatment regime, against wishes of Dr Kayson. Decision later revoked following actions of Dr Greene. Consult to the ER re Mr Pappion *[episode 3-14]*, Iva Blender *[episode 3-18]* and 'Mr and Mrs Smythe' *[episode 3-19]*. Noted concern for Dr Greene following results of brutal attack, Summer 1997. Dated Dr Greene for a short period *[episodes 3-14 to 3-21]:* break-up may have been connected to Greene's feelings after his assault *[episode 3-20]*.

Nina (having heard Hilary Clinton may be interested in Greene's technique to break vacuum seal): "Well, if she ever gets her ass stuck in

89

a bucket, she'll know who to call."

*[**Trivia**: Boasts about her bowling skills. Was at school with Polly Mackenzie, much to Mark Greene's dismay. Claimed to have used electro-shock therapy to stop her daughter wetting the bed.]*

See also: Personnel file on Dr Mark Greene.

ROBERT 'ROCKET' ROMANO

POSITION: **Surgical attending.**

"A weird little dude" (Randi Fronczak).

Romano to Greene: "A hell of a job you ER docs have . . . scout all the territory, then call in the big boys to go in for the kill, huh?"

Expert in highly technological procedures (often using robotics), especially tib-fib transplant surgery. Ten months out of the year works in Europe and so rarely seen in County until 1997. Worked in United Kingdom where he met Dr Elizabeth Corday. Sponsored Dr Corday's 'BTA' ('been to America') and supervized much of her work in County. High profile figure: one operation covered by Channel 5 news *[episode 4-6]*. Surgical team included Corday and Benton.

Note: Benton initially reluctant to join Romano's team. Wanted to challenge his surgical skills not be dazzled by technology. Volunteered services in response to competition with Corday but following run in with Romano believed he had lost opportunity to join the team.

Note: Believed to have had unrequited feelings for Dr Corday.

*[**Trivia**: Romano doesn't perform head or neck surgery, yet went to a conference on the subject in the Caribbean during the winter months! He plays golf.]*

(See also: Personnel files of Dr Peter Benton and Elizabeth Corday.)

WILLIAM SWIFT

POSITION: **Former head of ER.**

Note: Popularly known as 'Wild Willie'!

Stood in for Morgenstern during his absence, February to September 1995 *[episodes 1-18 to 1-24]*. Began by summoning all medical staff on call on first night to false emergency: drill to test response time and to enable first meeting with staff. Dr Greene hours late. Relationship with Dr Greene turbulent; Swift regarded Greene as having developed attitude problems after experience with Jodi O'Brien case and during marriage problems. However, eventually supported Dr Greene's candidacy as attending ER physician. Has worked with Synergix Physicians Group as an attending since mid-1996 *[episode 4-11]*.

Note: Swift often calls drill on his first day in a new hospital - never popular.

Note: Has been known to enjoy menacing drunks in the ER with use of a New Guinea tribal mask, obtained summer 1994.

Note: Swift told Greene he was having "the time of his life" working for Synergix.

*[**Trivia:** Swift went to school with Taglieri (Ohio State) - the two of them played football together. This is where the 'Wild Willie' nickname was developed.]*

JOHN 'TAG' TAGLIERI

POSITION **Orthopaedic surgeon.**

PERSONAL INFORMATION

Nicknamed 'Tag'. Ex professional footballer. Attended Ohio State College concurrent with William Swift. Engaged to Charge Nurse Carol Hathaway early 1994 to May 1995. Wedding ceremony 18th May 1995 abandoned last moment *[episode 1-24]*. See Personnel file of Carol Hathaway.

Note: Benton claimed Taglieri looked like King Kong.

[Would seem to have disappeared after his non-wedding to Carol, while actor Rick Rossovich went on to star in 'Pacific Blue.']

CARL VUCELICH

POSITION: **Senior cardio-vascular surgeon.**

Extremely prominent and influential surgeon, bringing in millions of dollars worth of investment on the back of his own reputation and accomplishments. Obtained grant for aortic aneurism study: use of 'clamp and run' technique. Test for drug 'lazarol' (named by Vucelich in October/November 1995): helps prevent transverse myopathy from lack of oxygen to spinal cord. Rival parallel study undertaken by Norwegian surgeons. Dr Benton, third year resident, joined study in December 1995, made research associate but left one month later. Study published summer 1996, with addendum detailing omitted patients. Paper delivered in Paris (originally intended to be by Dr Benton).

Note: Dr Benton left study under confused circumstances, early February 1996. Reputed to have written letter to ethics committee at end of April 1996: denied by Dr Bradley. Nevertheless, was for some time regarded as "Carl's new chosen one" and successfully recommended Benton for position as 'Resident of the Year', 1996.

Susan Lewis joked she had heard Vucelich was "an easy-going kind of guy".

Vucelich to Benton re rival study: "We don't want the Vikings to steal our thunder."

Vucelich to Benton: "You're arrogant as hell - I like that!"

Note: Vucelich regards medicine first and foremost as challenge: admits plenty of drudgery but interested in the impossible and unlikely.

See also: Personnel file on Dr Peter Benton.

*[**Trivia:** Vucelich is very keen on the use of metaphors to make patients want his surgery. When Benton refused port and a cigar, Vucelich regarded him as conspiring in the downfall of civilized society. Gave Carter a glowing recommendation for position as resident; Hicks noted this was 'usual' for Vucelich. His office is cluttered with photographs of hundreds of his former patients: "You wouldn't believe the Christmas presents." Married to Marion, who intensely dislikes having spare places at her dinner table.]*

Interns and Medical Students

DEBRA CHEN

Position: Former medical student *[series one]*.

First class student of Dr Peter Benton. Superior presentation skills. Well organized. Photographic memory. First day in ER less promising: attempted rectal examination without lubricant; rendered Dr Carter unconscious with fibrillation paddles *[episode 1-12]*. First patient soon after: discovered rare allegic reaction to grenola and poppy seeds *[episode 1-13]*. Expected to take trauma sub-I from September 1995, but left County, and medical training, April 1995 after failed attempt at central line nearly resulted in patient's death *[episode 1-20]*. See also Personnel file on Dr John Carter.

Chen to Carter, after leaving County: "I really didn't care about the patient; I wanted the procedure...I like the science but the patients, the sickness, scares me."

Note: Mother is chief of surgery at St Bart's.

Note: Unwittingly took LSD in patient's spiked chocolates.

MARGARET 'MAGGIE' DOYLE

Position: Resident (beginning third year).

Student at St Monica's school. Took pre-med night school course at Malcolm X college. Thrown out of nursing college. Completed medical school and became intern at Southside; transferred to County General after hospital amalgamation in 1996. Notified police in case of woman who attempted to abort her baby in latest stage of pregnancy through intake of alcohol and tried to press charges for murder *[episode 3-8]*. Highly competitive, especially with Dr Carter *[episode 3-11]*. Reprimanded by Dr Greene for angry outbursts in case of Louise Cupertino *[episode 3-16]*. Difficult working relationship with Charge Nurse Hathaway *[episode 3-18]*. Supervized Carter's procedures when Carter downgraded to emergency medicine intern status. Advised PA Boulet on unfair dismissal claim *[episode 4-8]*.

Doyle to Hathaway: "I am the doctor, and you are the nurse. Keep that straight." Hathaway to Ross: "We grew up in the same neighbourhood and now she's a doctor. I'm a nurse and I gotta take orders from her all day long and I hate it."

Maggie to Carol: "I was never very good at following orders."

Doyle re case of pregnant woman: "Tell you what, if I get to testify against the bitch, I'll do it on my own time."

*[**Trivia:** Maggie flunked chemistry at St Monica's and had the same teacher as Carol Hathaway. She has an older sister who was in the same history class with Carol, and a brother, Jimmy, who has Down's syndrome. Her mother is a nurse, her father is a policeman (third generation). Consequently she has a great knowledge of firearms as well as a large collection of 'armaments' including a stun gun and mace spray. She hides a 357 magnum under the driver's seat in her red BMW and once used it to frighten a mugger at a drive through. Her cousin, Kenny, was convicted for breaking and entering and is now a locksmith. She has insisted that surgery is too cut-throat and wouldn't like to do it. Secret smoker who stores beer at the back of the staff room fridge. Her ex-girlfriend was Amy Elliott, a policewoman who is "jealous as hell".*

Throughout the third series Maggie Doyle was shaping up as one of the show's most likeable, interesting characters, with her own strong views and a good working relationship with Carter. Then in series four, something very odd happened. Though seen in the background and referred to on a maddeningly frequent basis, Doyle hardly had anything to say all year, with never a sign of the writers giving her a storyline of her own. Much of the role she played in series three - as a foil for Carter, and a moral voice against the more dubious practices of the hospital - was given to Anna instead. The relegation of such a promising character to background status is frustrating enough in itself, but it also effectively meant the disappearance of one of the very few openly homosexual role models in mainstream TV drama. At the time of writing it looks as if Doyle's role in series five will be much the same and though we may be used to it by now, it still needs to be said that this undervaluing of one of ER's best characters is profoundly irritating.]

DALE EDSON

POSITION: **Surgical resident (beginning third year).**

Harvard graduate. Had already taken out his first appendix before taking trauma sub-internship at County ER. Completed six weeks thoracic elective at Hopkins. Started residency in June 1996. Disagreed with Dr Carter over need for psych consult in the case of Mr Percy *[episode 3-7]*. Mr Gunderson: Dr Edson administered post-operative antibiotic resulting in allergic reaction leading to further confrontation with Dr Carter. In 1997-98 was allowed to scrub in and assist on a number of Dr Romano's surgical procedures.

Note: Abby Keaton broke up fight between Edson and Carter over Percy. Edson reputed to have falsified Gunderson's case history (unproven). Carter to Edson: "If you do anything like this again, I'll bury you."

*[**Trivia**: Dale was at college with Harper Tracy: they had a one night stand. Both Gant and Carter had experienced Dale passing his work on to them. Benton thinks that Dale is a "weasel" and that Carter is twice the surgeon Edson will ever be.]*

See also: Personnel file on Dr John Carter.

DENNIS GANT (DECEASED)

POSITION: **Surgical intern.**

MEDICAL TRAINING: Studied at LSU medical school. Internship at County supervised by Dr Peter Benton.

Arrived hours early for second day to assist Dr Carter on night shift *[episode 3-1]*. Covered ER in Carter's absence *[episode 3-2]*. Reported exclusion, with Carter, from surgical procedures in OR. Assisted Dr Simon on appendectomy, criticized by Dr Benton *[episode 3-3]*. Further criticisms on alleged lack of speed, lack of preparation, negative attitude. Mediocre initial evaluation from Dr Benton. Later, more positive evaluation from Benton written but never received. Dr Gant performed initial trauma assessment and assisted in surgery on Megan Herlihy, November 1996 *[episode 3-6]*.

Note: Dr Carter stayed at Dr Gant's home for a time.

Gant (on being told Dr Benton's reputation): "Benton can't be that bad, can he?"

Gant to Dr Benton: "I bust my ass and you give me a mediocre evaluation."

Gant to Dr Benton: "You're a real prick, you know that?"

Severe overwork: at one point in December 1996 *[episode 3-9]* dealing with 20 surgical patients at once. Worked longer and longer hours including 34-hour shift *[episode 3-10]*. Personal problems with girlfriend Monique. Friendship with Dr Carter faltered as Carter spent more time with Dr Keaton. Carter cancelled Christmas dinner invitation to Dr Gant. Gant requested two days' leave to attend to relationship problems; Dr Benton refused. Severely criticized by Benton for failure to monitor critically ill patient; Dr Carter did not support Dr Gant when challenged by Doctors Benton and Anspaugh.

Gant to Carter: "Benton wants me to pull my weight, I'm damn well gonna pull it. I'm not letting him get another shot at me."

Benton to Gant: "If you can't do the job, or you don't want to do the job, then you don't need to be here."

Dr Gant died in ER after being found severely maimed by train, January 1997 *[episode 3-11]*. Fell, jumped, or was pushed onto track. Coroner's verdict: accidental death. Dr Carter and others believed Dr Gant committed suicide, in part due to harsh teaching methods of Dr Benton. See also Personnel files on Dr Peter Benton and Dr John Carter.

Carter to Benton: "You can be sure that he never received any encouraging or supporting word from you... All he ever got from you was harping and criticism - and now he's dead, and you're going to have to face it."

Benton to Hicks: "I wish I could tell you that it was all intentional, that it was part of some masterplan I had going on but... truthfully, I never even thought about Gant. I mean, he was just an intern, and I was more involved about my career, my ambitions..."

[Omar Epps made Gant such a likeable character that we all expected him to become more prominent, perhaps become a regular - but instead, his death gave us one of the series' most dramatic moments. Benton's harsh treatment of him - partly because he was black, and Benton believed he should work twice as hard to convince others he was not a product of positive discrimination - contributed to his suicide, assuming that is what it was. But Carter's preoccupation with Abby Keaton also meant that he neglected Gant's friendship, among other things failing to listen to his problems with Monique, and leaving him alone over Christmas.]

GEORGE HENRY

POSITION: **Medical student, 1997.**

Engaged in four-year research degree (MD PhD) on 'happy puppet's disease' (causes patient to laugh inappropriately and flap hands like puppet on a string). No practical medical training before joining Dr John Carter for emergency medicine rotation in County ER. Report from Dr Carter contained numerous U/Es (unable to evaluate). Henry required to return to ER. Passed emergency medicine: 24th December 1997.

Note: Henry allergic to latex. Had to be resuscitated by Doctors Carter and Del Amico following near fatal reaction [episode 4-8].

*[**Trivia:** Henry constantly complained about his allergies, which are numerous. He had an out of body experience during his latex reaction episode. Finally passed his ER rotation by intubating a dead man - Carter wouldn't risk him on live patients.]*

HARPER TRACY

POSITION: **Third year medical student, 1995/1996.**

Exceptional high school academic record though evidence of social problems. Recruited by US Air Force while at college: Air Force paid medical school fees; Tracy to give four years service after residency. Traumatized by treatment of Chia-Chia Loh: possible involvement with Dr Ross *[episode 2-5]*. Noted for her compassionate care for Molly Phillips who died from rupture of mesenteric artery *[episode 2-7]*. Reprimanded for drinking on duty following celebration of Dr Carter's match as resident at County *[episode 2-17]*. Relationship with Dr John Carter. Left County General 2nd May 1996 to pursue OB rotation at Parkland, Dallas *[episode 2-20]*.

Note: following Chia-Chia Loh incident, rumoured to have slept with Ross. However, Greene staying with Ross at the time and no official complaint logged.

Note: Harper dumped by Carter following his excessive competitiveness and 'sucking up' to the surgeons.

*[**Trivia:** Harper did a lot of drugs as a kid and believes she didn't do well in high school, although she came 15th in a class of 2,000. Wanted more direction in her life - during college, with Dale Edson, realized she wanted to be a fighter pilot and a doctor - and signed up with the air force. She also wants to be an astronaut. Briefly involved with Edson while at college. Carter helped her practice procedures by giving him several IV's and taking his blood sample. Might have a pierced navel. Harper read* Now We Are Six *to Chia-Chia: her favourite character in* 'Winnie the Pooh' *is Tigger. She was told by her medical school professors that County was full of burn-outs who didn't care. Harper, having reconciled two parents, said she had a lot of practise on her own family.]*

See also: Personnel file of Dr John Carter.

Nursing Staff

HALEH ADAMS

Position: Senior nurse, ER.

More than 20 years' experience in emergency medicine. Temporary Charge Nurse replacing Carol Hathaway for eight weeks following attempted suicide in March 1994 and again during Hathaway's suspension in Spring 1997. Infamously failed to realize supplies were ordered by the gross not individually, resulting in over-supply of ER stocks. Was familiar with Mookie James and arranged for his placement in the ER and supervision by Dr Peter Benton. Principal member of nurses' union in the ER.

Also principal organizer of nurses' social functions.

[Trivia: Haleh knew Mark Greene when he joined County: he had blond hair and was the "best scut puppy I ever had". Haleh raised four children. Haleh is relentlessly pursued by Pablo, a homeless man who made a point only to attend Carol's free clinic if Haleh would be there. Pablo turns up every Thursday to see Haleh.]

E RAY BOZMAN

Position: Trainee nurse and receptionist.

"I'm a nurturer, I like helping people. So nursing seemed like the next logical step in my life progression." (E Ray Bozman)

Joined County November 1995 *[episode 2-5]* as nurse trainee in 'mid-life career shift'. Previous jobs include: UPS delivery man, short order cook, rodeo clown. Mid 1980s joined 'human potential' movement, giving lectures, inspirational speeches. Later decided to supplement nurse trainee stipend with "occasional footmanship" on reception *[episode 2-13]*. Highly qualified in information technology. Also licensed day care worker. Teaches yoga classes, Malcolm X Community College Thursday nights.

Note: Looked after Rachel Greene when brought into ER, showing her pictures of skin lesions. E Ray considered that "children benefit from confronting their fears in nurturing environment". Rachel thought pictures "cool".

[E Ray seems to have left the ER by the fourth series, which is of course appropriate to his restless character, but it was still a shame to see him go.]

WENDY GOLDMAN

POSITION: **Junior nurse**

Wrote a cover story for *Nursing News* about Dr Mark Greene *[episode 2-3]*. With Jeanie Boulet and Jerry Markovic, helped to save life of Heidi, genetically engineered mouse *[episode 3-19]*. Enjoys roller-blading *[episode 1-9]* and making candy *[episode 3-7]*. Helped Dr Weaver with her study of the effect of exercise on circadian rhythms of night-shift workers *[episode 3-11]*.

[Wendy too has been missing from the ER during season four, and her absence has not been mentioned. Has she left County altogether, been transferred somewhere else, or perhaps just been working different shifts?]

LYDIA GRABARSKY

POSITION: **Senior nurse, ER.**

Maiden name: Wright. First married name: Woodward. Married Al Grabarsky in ER on day of Dr Lewis's departure.

[Trivia: Lydia had a poem in Good Housekeeping *once. She used to date a technician at a Milwaukee hospital. The only present she ever received from her ex-husband was a vacuum cleaner. She gave up smoking [episode 1-11]. Lydia has been accidentally stuck with a needle nine times and never even had the flu. She met Al Grabarsky on Valentine's Day 1995. They were engaged on October 24th 1996 but Al infuriated her by appearing to delay their marriage. She always wins the 'guess the blood alcohol level' game. At the 1997 ER banquet, Lydia*

101

passed out and ripped her dress in the parking lot. Though she is married to Grabarsky, Carter still calls her Lydia Wright. She has at least one sister, who has children.]

MALIK McGRATH

POSITION: Junior nurse.

Expressed concern about Dr Greene's handling of Kenny Law case *[episode 3-17]*, alleging racist attitudes in unnecessarily searching Mr Law for needles, weapons. Dr Greene admitted McGrath correct, racist assumptions made though Dr Greene tried not to act on them.

Note: Also argued with Shepherd re balancing responsibilities of society and disadvantaged parents.

Note: Attended Carol Hathaway's wedding where he was first to start eating the food!

CHUNI MARQUEZ

POSITION: Junior Nurse, ER.

[Trivia: Mexican by birth. She and Mark Greene have sex in the time it takes to burn fried eggs! Drives a motorbike, or at least likes them - says she's a "motorbike chick". Her last ten relationships before Mark Greene indicated that she shouldn't plan for the future. According to E Ray her relationship with Mark was astrologically doomed. The ER staff raised a betting pool as to how long Mark and Chuni would see each other: Ross predicted they would stay together one week longer than they did. In Chuni's family, if a man sends flowers twice in one week it's tantamount to a marriage proposal! One of Chuni's five brothers, Julio, "packs a .45". Chuni was shot at in the health-mobile.]

CONNI OLIGARIO

POSITION: Junior nurse.

Three children; third born late February 1996. Helped look after baby Suzie Lewis while in ER. October 1994: persuaded Dr Ross to allow drug tests for father and sister of young Kanesha Freeman, suffering from cocaine overdose: Ross assumed Mr Freeman responsible and was aggressive towards him, but Mr Freeman tested negative; sister positive. Nurse Oligario noted possible racist assumption on Ross's part *[episode 1-5.]*

YOSH TAKADA

POSITION: Junior nurse.

Transferred to ER November 1997 *[episode 4-8]*.

Note: Yosh's appointment made Jeanie realize there was no freeze on hiring nursing staff, and to suspect her dismissal may not have been economically necessary.

EMERGENCY MEDICAL TECHNICIANS (PARAMEDICS)

ALLISON BEAUMONT

POSITION: Trainee Paramedic/EMT, spring 1998 *[episode 4-18]*.

Former patient (see Personnel file of Elizabeth Corday).

RAUL MELENDEZ (Deceased)

POSITION: Paramedic/EMT.

Drove Unit 47 with Shepherd. Charge Nurse Hathaway joined him and Shepherd for paramedic run in September 1995. Died following daring rescue of children from burning building. Suffered more than 90 per cent third degree burns.

DORIS PICKMAN

POSITION: Paramedic/EMT.

[Doris appeared regularly since the pilot episode, but was only named as Doris in the fourth series: until then, she was only referred to by fans as 'the cute paramedic who looks a bit like Lewis'. The writers have been giving her more lines lately, and she features more prominently in series five.]

RAY 'SHEP' SHEPHERD

POSITION: Paramedic/EMT.

Drove Unit 47 with Melendez and later Reilly. Following summer paramedic run with Charge Nurse Hathaway, began dating her. Led Raul into burning building to rescue several children. Children recovered but Melendez suffered more than 90 per cent burns and died at County ER. Following Raul's death, became increasingly embittered and blamed himself. Resented Reilly: believed fire department were punishing him for death of Melendez by giving him a rookie. Almost killed one homeless man as well as assaulting one drunk (stopped short of attacking Charge Nurse Hathaway). Subject of incident report logged by EMT Reilly re assault of Vietnamese boy. Subsequent investigation by David Haskall vindicated actions of Shepherd following statements of Charge Nurse Hathaway.

Note: suffered nervous breakdown following death of Melendez. Refusal of psychiatric help reputed to be cause of separation from Hathaway.

*[**Trivia:** When his parents moved out of his childhood home, he carved his name in every closet. As a child, he fell off the banister and broke his collar bone. The house has a crawl-space where he and his brothers used to hide their copies of* Playboy.*]*

Reception staff and aides

E RAY BOZMAN

See Nursing Staff.

RANDI FRONCZAK

Position: Reception clerk, ER.

*[**Trivia:** Randi has a parole officer and a criminal record for "Malicious mischief, assault, battery, carrying a concealed weapon, and aggravated maim." She suggested Carol's resolution to the nursing budget problem - it eventually resulted in unofficial strike action. Randi never wears her lab coat because it doesn't fit. She knows a couple of guys who can track down a repo man instantly. Randi designed her own brand of clothing and was set to meet investors to launch "Randi-wear". Took an accounting course for her fashion line. Randi says she has bypassed security and passed through the front door of the White House. She has been attracted to both Jerry Markovic and Raul Melendez but instantly gave Doug Ross a withering look.]*

CYNTHIA HOOPER

Position: Former Reception clerk, ER.

Hired by Dr Greene, October 1997 despite poor interview performance. Appointment opposed by RN Hathaway. Competence questioned by several parties. Advertized free clinic one week earlier than planned *[episode 4-8]*.

Relationship with Dr Mark Greene lasted six months. Colleagues noted her "needy" character at odds with Greene's casual approach. Suggested moving in with Mark when her landlord raised rent to $500/month, but Mark agreed to help with rent instead. Broke up in San Diego when Greene admitted he was not in love with her. Cynthia left Chicago soon afterwards. (See also Personnel file of Dr Mark Greene.) Now working at law firm as administrative assistant, and looking after son, Jason, aged five (broke up with father when Jason born; Cynthia had not seen Jason since aged two; raised by boyfriend's parents in a trailer in Kankakee).

[**Trivia**: *Cynthia was originally from Joliet, and lived in Virginia for a while before moving to Chicago. Both her parents are dead, and she has no brothers and sisters. Previous jobs included processing bills as a cashier at a Ford dealership, and telemarketing of vitamins. She was dismissed from the latter job because she refused to sell to the elderly, claiming it was "too late for them". At school she appeared in a production of 'Death of a Salesman', apparently because her teacher wanted to see her in pants. She is an expert at massage, and frequently used her talents on Mark to relax him. Mistakenly received Doug's letter to Carol, marked only 'CH', and assumed it was from Mark. (Sample line: "I dream of the taste of your neck and the smell of your hair on my pillow".) When first met Rachel (Mark's daughter), took her out shopping and, to Mark's astonishment, helped her have her hair dyed purple!]*

JERRY MARKOVIC

POSITION: **Supervizing emergency service co-ordinator.**

Note: Promoted to 'supervizing' October 1995, involving no extra money, benefits or responsibility but requiring him to wear a tie!

Has worked in ER for eight years, and has a sterling attendance record: rarely takes leave. Qualifications with merit in information technology following nightschool courses at Midwest Business Academy, 1993. Accidentally fired patient's grenade launcher into ambulance bay, October 1997 *[episode 4-3]*. Put on night duty for four months as disciplinary measure. Single. Formerly lived with mother in Cortez Street, West Town Ukrainian Village; now has own apartment.

Note: Known for money-making schemes including pyramid investment scheme, and attempt to capture genetically engineered mouse for $5,000 reward, using humane traps which drew attention of Physician's Assistant Jeanie Boulet. Attempted to sell sperm to Cryogen Labs, posing as medical doctor with IQ 145; scheme foiled by Dr Weaver. Took multiple-choice IQ test legitimately and scored 15 (less than expected *score for random answers).*

Note: Responsible for staphlyococcus outbreak due to lax personal hygiene.

Note: Co-organized ER banquet 1998 with Dr Greene. Jerry's mother handled catering, a Swedish smorgasbord, much of which turned out to be frozen!

*[**Trivia:** Vegetarian. Joined theatre group: first role, male lead in Romeo and Juliet, episode 1-19. Staffed drive-through window at MacDonald's for two summers.]*

BOGDANALIVETSKY 'BOB' ROMANSKY

POSITION: Former ER aide.

Note: Named 'Bob' by Dr Ross!

Vascular surgeon in her native Poland, discovered when intervened to save patient of Dr Susan Lewis, December 1994 *[episode 1-9]*. Feared her intervention might prevent taking of board exam to practise in USA.

['Bob' continued to be seen as an ER aide until the early second series, although her surgical skills were never again referred to or used, and the storyline of her intention to qualify in America was never continued. Some ER fans now use the word 'Bobbed' to refer to any characters who are introduced with interesting backgrounds but are later dropped for no apparent reason.]

SECTION THREE

The ER Files
[An Episode Guide]

Pilot Episode (1994)
*["24 Hours", "The Beginning",
or "ER: The Movie"]*

It's 5.00 am on the morning of March 17th, 1994. In the Emergency Room (ER) of County General, a busy Chicago hospital, a doctor lies sleeping in an empty lab. "Dr Greene?" calls a nurse, Lydia, as she opens the door. She wants the doctor to deal with a drunk and disorderly man who has come into the ER, but Mark Greene is reluctant - until he's told that the man in question is his colleague, Dr Doug Ross. Wearily, he gives his friend aspirin as Doug drawls on about a woman he has been with tonight, and asks about Mark's intention to leave the hospital and his problems with Jennifer, his wife. Another nurse, Wendy, assists Greene and asks if Ross is always like this. "Only on his nights off," Greene replies...

Greene/
Ross

At the admissions desk, receptionist Timmy and others watch as the TV news reports the collapse of a nearby building: two people are dead, and twelve are injured. Head nurse Carol Hathaway arrives for work, as does Dr Peter Benton, who sees the news report and wryly comments: "Good day for us surgeons..." Before long, though, he shows an angrier side when a senior doctor tells him he is not allowed to re-attach a patient's hand: Benton is only a resident, and years away from a case like this. He takes out his anger on Carol in the staff room, when he realizes that the nurses have drunk all the coffee. Carol tells him to make his own, and Benton replies: "We work thirty-six hours on, eighteen off, which is ninety hours a week, fifty-two weeks a year. For that we are paid $23,739 before taxes - and we also have to

Carol/
Benton

109

make the coffee?" Carol is unimpressed: "My heart bleeds," she says sarcastically.

Greene/ Lewis   Mark Greene meets his wife in the hospital canteen, with their seven-year-old daughter, Rachel. Jennifer is concerned that between her studying for Bar exams next month and Mark's gruelling hospital schedule, they hardly see each other. She persuades him to go and see a Dr Harris, who has a private practice. Meanwhile Dr Susan Lewis, a medical resident, puts herself through the emotionally draining experience of telling a 40-year-old patient, Mr Parker, that he may have cancer. Mr Parker is shocked and scared: he has responsibilities, a mortgage, a family. Susan is honest with him about the risks he is facing, but says that in her job she has learned that nothing in this life - good or bad - is certain.

Carter/ Benton   John Carter, a surgical student in his third year, arrives in the ER for the start of his 'hands-on' training. On seeing him, Greene's first reaction is to comment: "That's the first tailored white coat I've ever seen. Do you think he knows anything?" But it's Benton who will have the opportunity to find out: Carter is his student. He gives Carter a lightning tour, starting with the admitting desk and briefly introducing Carol ("She's terrific, isn't she?") before moving past the medical examining rooms - "where the pill-pushers kill their victims" - and on to the surgical room. "This is where the real action is," he smiles, just as a man walks up to them whom Benton introduces as David Morgenstern, head of the ER. Morgenstern tells Carter that Benton is one of the best residents they have. "You learn everything you can from him - except attitude." Benton laughs off the comment, and shows Carter to the suture room, where he will "sew people up" - and probably spend most of his time. His head reeling, Carter admits that he hasn't yet done any suturing, or put in an IV, and can't even put on surgical gloves. Benton gives him an impatient look: he has a lot of work to do...

Ross/ Carol   Ross's student is a young woman, Tracy Young. He clearly finds her attractive and instantly turns on the charm, telling her they'll be working closely together for the next few days. Not that closely, she tells him. A little dispirited, he leaves her with a patient and goes to ask Carol Hathaway for some supplies. Doug and Carol were once lovers and he seems interested in renewing their romance, but Carol is now going out with an orthopod and ex-footballer, John 'Tag' Taglieri. He had his chance, she tells him.

Greene has to rush out in the snow to meet a woman who is going into labour, and Carter helps him deliver the baby boy - much to the annoyance of Benton, who reminds him that he's on the surgical, not the medical, service. Carter is delighted with the birth, however, which also seems to brighten Greene's day. When Greene finally pays a visit to Dr Harris and is offered a job at his practice, he doesn't seem enthusiastic - despite a $120,000 salary plus bonuses and perks. Later, back in the ER, he surprises a patient by suddenly exclaiming: "I can't give this up!"

Greene

By now it is late evening: Carol Hathaway, Wendy and others have gone home, and Jerry Markovic has replaced Timmy on reception. While Carter treats a woman who has crashed her father's Cadillac and Ross reassures the mother of a boy who has swallowed their house-key, Benton argues with Dr Steve Flint in radiology about an injury Benton believes is a gun-shot wound. Suddenly, the confident routine of the ER and its staff is shattered dramatically as the paramedics push their next patient through the doors: the unconscious woman lying on the gurney is Carol Hathaway, who has taken an overdose of pills. The nurses and doctors are stunned, but none more so than Doug Ross. "How could this happen, to her of all people?" he asks, devastated. Lydia asks Carol's flatmate why Carol did it, but she doesn't have any idea - Carol only moved in three weeks ago - and Greene tells her they don't need to know. "We don't ask that about any other OD that comes through these doors, and we don't ask it about this one," he says. Pulling the curtain across to block the views of the

Carol/
Ross

assembled staff, Greene works to try to save Carol, but the situation looks desperate: Carol took a combination of fast-acting drugs; she knew exactly what she was doing.

Benton   Benton takes charge of Mr Harvey, a patient who has a ruptured aneurism bleeding into his stomach. With all the senior surgeons busy, Benton is the only man capable of saving his life, and he calls down a team from the OR (Operating Room) upstairs to help him. As he starts the complex surgery, it looks as if Benton is out of his depth - but before long, and with the help of another doctor who joins him at the last minute, he manages to save the man's life. In the final stages of the operation, Morgenstern arrives and takes over; his first comment to Benton is that he has made an ugly incision, but then adds, almost as an afterthought, that he has done a good job. "You were lucky as hell, but you were right to open him up. Good work," he tells him, and Benton leaves the room with a triumphant grin on his face.

Greene/   Feeling sick during emergency surgery on a knife- wound
Carter   victim, Carter rushes outside to get some fresh air. As Greene joins him, Carter says he's afraid to go back and face Benton after backing out like that, but Greene offers some reassurance. There are two kinds of doctors, he tells him - those who get rid of their feelings, and those who keep them. "If you're going to keep your feelings, you're going to get sick from time to time." For good measure, he adds that as a medical student, Benton used to get sick all the time.

Ross   Still shaken by Carol's attempted suicide, Ross is angered about the condition of a baby boy who has been brought in by his child-minder. The boy has multiple contusions, having "fallen out of his cot", and also has burn marks on his legs. When the mother arrives, Ross shouts at her with obvious fury, convinced that the child is being battered. He then takes his anger out on Tracy Young, his student, yelling at her about a lost chart - but undeterred, she asks him if he'd like to go for a coffee.

Greene   As the night draws on, Greene treats a rather flirtatious
            college student, Liz, who has burned her legs - avoiding
            her obvious advances with the help of Lydia, who
            obligingly 'stands guard' by the door. Carol Hathaway is
            still in a critical condition, and isn't expected to live, but
            Greene tells Morgenstern that they are still holding out
            for a miracle - for the sake of staff morale if nothing else.
            Exhausted, and with the clock reading 5.00 am, he closes
            his eyes for a short sleep. But before he knows it, it's 6.30
            again, and he is woken for another hectic day...

*[The ER TV movie is where it all began, and it still makes absorbing
viewing - partly because it's easily as good as the best regular episodes,
and partly to see the differences between this and the more recent series.
It's not just George Clooney's big hair, or how very young Noah Wyle
looks as Carter, but the differences in the characters too. Amazingly,
Benton is seen joking and smiling like a regular guy, and when he
introduces Carter to Carol Hathaway he even comments, "She's terrific,
isn't she?", once she's out of earshot. (He still doesn't get on with her,
though.) Designed to be able to stand alone, the TV movie still manages
to set up some of the storylines that would become more important later,
such as Greene's marriage troubles and Ross's attitude towards abusive
parents. The clearest evidence that this is separate from the regular series,
however, is the fact that Carol Hathaway is very definitely killed off.
Informed medical opinion has it that for her to survive her overdose, after
the condition she was in at the end of the pilot, would be nothing short of
a miracle. Bringing the character back was perhaps the biggest medical
mistake the show ever made; but thank goodness they went ahead and
did it anyway.]*

Series One (1994/5)

1-1: "Day One"

Carter   Carter enjoys a very mixed day. It begins with him
            making rectal examinations on a group of German
            tourists, who have food poisoning from eating at a burger
            bar, but takes a turn for the better when a flirtatious
            female college student, Liz *[see the pilot episode]* is
            brought in complaining of a rash on her buttocks. Carter

volunteers to look at it - after all, he has recently done his dermatology rotation...

Benton   Four victims of a car accident are brought in by helicopter: a mother, father and daughter, and the driver of the car that hit them. Greene and Ross take the daughter, who is suffering from internal bleeding, and manage to stabilize her for sending up to the OR. Benton takes the mother, whose condition is more serious. The father, who is relatively unhurt, waits to hear about their progress. Lewis, meanwhile, looks after the other driver, who has nothing more than minor injuries - but insists on complaining about them anyway. By all accounts, it seems that the accident was his fault. Later, Benton has to tell the father that although his daughter will be fine, having had successful surgery on her spleen, his wife has a spinal fracture and internal bleeding; she is going to die. Benton immediately asks whether the couple ever discussed organ donation, but the husband's only response is to break down in tears. A little taken aback, Benton puts his arm around him in an attempt to give him some comfort.

Ross/   A pair of newlyweds and 60 of their wedding guests
Greene   arrive complaining of stomach pains: it seems they have been to the same burger bar as the poisoned Germans! However, they continue the reception in the waiting room. Meanwhile Ross and Greene treat an 86-year-old woman, Mrs Franks, who has impending respiratory failure. While she is unconscious her husband makes the difficult decision to put her on a respirator, but when the woman wakes, she tells the doctors she doesn't want to be kept alive. As she slips away Mr Franks sings to her softly, with the sounds of the wedding reception going on in the background - and many of the surrounding staff, including Doug, are moved to tears.

Greene   Jennifer arrives at the hospital, telling Greene that she has passed her Bar exam. They celebrate by making out in one of the examination rooms, but embarrassment follows when they are discovered - because Greene has

114

been leaning on an emergency call button! Later, Greene arrives home and Jenn wants to make love, but Greene's next shift begins in two hours and he has to go. "You're never going to leave, are you?" Jenn asks him. "I don't know," he answers. Jenn insists that she needs him.

Carter assists Benton with liquor store owner, Ivan Gregor, who was shot in a hold-up, and later a man complaining of abdominal pains. Carter makes an attempt at a diagnosis, but Benton insists he has thrombosis as a result of an operation on his leg. However, when the man's GP arrives, it transpires that he had nothing more than a urinary infection; the GP tells Benton to stop trying to show off to his medical students. Embarrassed, Carter tries to tell Benton that he thinks Benton was right, but he brushes it off with a sarcastic comment. Later Benton is woken and told that the man now has a ruptured bowel: it seems he was right after all. Meanwhile in the car park, Carter is intercepted on the way to his car by Liz, the college student he treated earlier. She is now very definitely coming on to him and suggests they go to her place.

Carter/
Benton

It is eight weeks after Carol Hathaway's attempted suicide but Ross still hasn't paid her a visit. He tells Greene he's driven round to her mother's house a couple of times, but didn't get out of the car. Greene offers to go with him if it will help. "It's not your fault, Doug. You've got to forgive yourself sooner or later." Ross seems unconvinced, but that evening drives round to Carol's mother's house again. This time he gets to the front door, but is almost turned away by Carol's mother. Carol comes to the door though, and Ross asks her awkwardly how she is. She's fine, she says. Ross doesn't have much more to say than that, but at least he's made the effort.

Ross/
Carol

Lewis spends much of her day dealing with Victor, a man with senile dementia. She treats his injuries, but requires support from psychiatrics which Dr Div Cvetic is unwilling to give. The man has to be discharged, and is later found wandering naked around town. Lewis decides

Lewis

to sign him in to the psychiatric service herself, provoking an angry response from Cvetic, who tells her never to do anything like this again. Exhausted after a long and exasperating day, Susan Lewis gets into bed, with her partner - Div Cvetic.

1-2: "Going Home"

Carol

Carol at last feels she is ready to go back to work, although her mother isn't sure. Once there, Carol is perturbed by the thought that not long ago, she herself was an ER patient. Ross has told every member of staff to be "sensitive" around her, but Carol is the first person to make jokes at her own expense. Greene is glad to see her: "You may have doubts about being back, but none of us do," he tells her. Thankfully, it's a slow Monday, but it seems Carol still can't find the time to talk to Ross, spurning his lunch invitation: instead she goes to lunch with her fiancé, John 'Tag' Taglieri.

Benton/
Lewis

Ivan, the liquor-store owner *[episode 1-1]*, is brought in for a second time: again he has been shot during a hold-up, and again it is Benton who restores him to health. Meanwhile Lewis clashes with attending cardiologist Dr Kayson when he disagrees with her decision to give drug therapy to Mr Flannigan who has suffered a heart attack, arguing that surgery is needed. At a conference later, Susan has to defend her decision before Morgenstern, Kayson and others. She hopes for Greene's support but he arrives late, having been concerned with a domestic abuse case, and, to her horror, supports Kayson's stand. Nevertheless, it transpires that Lewis's drug therapy was successful, and no surgery was necessary.

Carter

A mysterious woman found wandering around Chicago by the police has been brought in to the ER; she disturbs some and delights others with her constant singing! Carter tries to ask her some questions designed to test her mental state, but it is Div Cvetic who makes the breakthrough when he talks to her about music, and discovers she believes it's 1948 and that she's still a child:

he diagnoses Alzheimer's. Later, another patient recognizes her as Mary Kavanagh, a famous singer, and her granddaughter is contacted to take her home - but not before Mary has befriended Carter.

Lewis and Hathaway treat an elderly woman with leukaemia, Mrs Packer, who has slipped and fallen in her kitchen. She has severe anaemia and needs a blood transfusion, but initially refuses to have it, saying she wants to be able to make it to her granddaughter's christening. Later, though, she collapses and reluctantly agrees to the transfusion, although she will leave straight afterwards to attend the christening. "Life might be giving up on me, but I'm not giving up on it," she tells Carol.

Carol/
Lewis

Ross confides to Greene that he regrets breaking up with Carol, and later manages to grab a coffee with her. He tells her he wants to see her again, but Carol thinks he just feels guilty, and assures him that she didn't attempt suicide because of him. She's happy with Taglieri now, she says: he was there for her before her overdose, and since. Ross makes one last plea: "What we had... is it worth another chance?" "You thought what we had didn't work, remember?" Carol replies.

Ross/
Carol

1-3: "Hit and Run"

Jennifer Greene has left town for Detroit for five days to attend a job interview. Ross teases Greene about "other, more immediate temptations" - referring to Susan Lewis - but Greene says they are just friends. But when he later hears of her relationship with Cvetic, he does seem to be a little jealous.

Lewis/
Greene

A mother brings her son, Ozzie, in to see Ross, saying that he can't hear certain things. These turn out to be imaginary voices in her own head. The boy knows that his mother is disturbed but wants them to stay together, and Ross tells him they will. However, Div Cvetic says she will have to be admitted to the hospital, having come

Ross/
Carol

117

off her medication for schizophrenia. The boy will have to go into a home. Carol befriends the boy and is angry with Ross for not telling him the truth: "You told him what he wanted to hear because you didn't want a big emotional scene, which is something you can't handle and avoid at all costs," she says.

Greene   A man and a woman are brought in, partially clothed and handcuffed to each other: he has had a heart attack, but they cannot be separated because they have lost the keys! The man's wife then arrives, and despite the attempts of Greene and the nurses, she discovers the woman - who is her secretary. "I suppose you all think this is very, very funny," she says...

Benton   Benton is competing for the coveted Starzl fellowship, and one of his rivals is Dr Sarah Langworthy - a young woman who is a year ahead of him. Their rivalry is such that both make prolonged attempts to revive a patient brought in with gun-shot wounds, although he is effectively dead on arrival. Benton also meets with his brother-in-law, Walt - who lives with Benton's mother and his sister Jackie - and promises to sit with his mother this evening so that Walt and Jackie can celebrate their tenth wedding anniversary. But when the time comes, he forgets. "Funny how that happens when it comes to your family," Walt says acidly.

Carter   Carter must identify Benton's GSW victim from his high school yearbook. Having done so he calls the boy's parents, but when they arrive it appears that Carter has made a serious mistake: the dead boy isn't their son! Mortified, he corrects his error and this time calls the right parents, having to go through the difficult business of breaking the bad news all over again.

Lewis   Susan Lewis treats Harry Stopac, a stressed-out photocopier salesman who is constantly making and receiving calls on his mobile phone while she sees him. She tells him he probably has irritable bowel syndrome, but needs to reduce the amount of stress in his life;

however, he is impatient with her.

Benton has to admit that he turned down a woman for surgery who Morgenstern has now sent up to the OR for an appendectomy. Morgenstern says a lot of surgeons make similar mistakes, because they don't listen to their patients. Good surgeons do, he tells Benton. Meanwhile, Carter finds an unoccupied electric wheelchair that seems to have a mind of its own - the chair, and a woman's fibrillator which sends shocks through her at random, are controlled by signals from Stopac's phone! Greene angrily tells him to take it out of the hospital.

Benton

Ross pays a visit to Carol's flat that evening, carrying a bunch of flowers - but the door is answered by Tag, who is obviously staying overnight. Ross quickly walks back to the station, but Carol chases after him. "What were you thinking?" she yells at him. "I will not let you do this to me again... "

Ross/ Carol

Carter tells Jerry that he's fed up with his work, after his mistake earlier and having learnt that Benton told his adviser that he was doing "a generally adequate job". However, at that moment, a car pulls up outside the hospital containing a pregnant woman about to give birth. With some support from Lewis he manages to deliver it, and as mother and child are taken into the hospital he shouts, "Yes!" into the night air.

Carter

1-4: "Into That Good Night"

4.00 pm. Ross is on a double shift, with Lewis, as two car-crash victims are brought into the ER. One of them is a pregnant woman, who goes into labour over two months early. The other victim is a teenage girl who had stolen the car she was driving - and Benton suspects she's on drugs. After unsuccessful attempts to halt the labour, Ross delivers the baby - and despite initial lung problems, she'll be fine. Benton's patient later dies after surgery.

Ross/ Benton

119

Greene   Jennifer Greene tells her husband that she has been offered her dream job, as clerk to a federal judge - but it's in Milwaukee, two hours away by train. She's determined to do the job and Mark tries to be pleased for her, but he can't hide his anxiety. He agrees to make some phone calls to Milwaukee hospitals to see what jobs are available.

Carter   Carter worriedly approaches Ross with a 'hypothetical' question about sexually transmitted diseases, which Ross correctly deduces is really about Liz. Ross belatedly (and hypocritically) advises him not to "dip his pen in the company ink". Later, as Carter receives the results of the tests he has had done, he is disturbed to see Liz arriving at reception complaining of new ailments, and this time accepting an eager offer of help from Dr Kayson...

Greene   Later in the evening, Greene and Carol treat a man, Sam Gasner, who is plagued by heart problems. He has been waiting for a transplant for months, but now his situation is critical and they must find one tonight. At 4 am they are still waiting for a suitable heart - a type 'A' - and as Sam's distraught wife and daughter arrive, he tells Greene that he knows he's going to die, but that he's not ready: his family needs him. As Greene and Carol leave them to be alone together, Carol says, "Don't say it - I should be grateful to be alive." Greene shakes his head: "That's not what I was thinking." Later, when Sam dies, Greene has to comfort Sam's young daughter, Sarah, who wants to know why the doctors couldn't 'fix' her father. "We can't fix everything," he admits.

Benton/   For a third time, Ivan is brought in with a gun-shot
Lewis   wound - but this time he is his own victim, having shot himself in the foot with a newly-acquired gun. Again, it's Benton's job to treat him. Meanwhile, Lewis tells Div she is worried because Dr Kayson is on her review board: she'll need his recommendation to continue working at County General.

Greene   Ross finds Greene outside the hospital, practising basketball shots. He notes that Greene has stayed very late - his shift was meant to end at midnight - and tells him to go home. It's 7.30 am before he finally gets home though, and he's obviously been thinking all day. If Jenn wants him to go to Milwaukee, he tells her, he'll go. "You'll hate it," Jenn answers. "It's not a big deal. It's only two hours away." They leave it at that, but when Rachel comes into their bedroom she knows that something's wrong. "Nothing's wrong," Greene tries to tell her, but he doesn't believe it himself.

1-5: "Chicago Heat"

It's the hottest day in October, and the air-conditioning in the ER is down. What's more, Mercy is closed to trauma and Lakeside's power is down, so County General has a bigger workload than usual. The ER staff have a further problem when a pizza delivery man suffering from a stab-wound arrives in reception - having crashed his car right through the doors! Ironically, the 'stab-wound' turns out to be little more than a scratch.

Ross and Greene try to help a five-year-old girl, Kanesha, suffering from respiratory distress, who may have a heart problem. She develops a fever, and Ross discovers the reason for her condition is really an overdose of cocaine. Once the immediate danger is dealt with Ross wants the girl admitted to the hospital, but Greene thinks she should be sent home. The girl's father, Mr Freeman, comes in for heavy criticism from Ross who thinks she must have found his drug supplies, but Conni argues that Ross should give the father a chance. Ross then orders drug tests for him and for the girl's older sister. Freeman turns out to be clean, but the sister tests positive, and Ross apologizes to the father, offering to help in any way he can.

Ross

A report comes through from the police: there's been a shooting at Ivan's liquor store, and it looks bad. Benton is surprised to discover that the victim is a 14-year-old boy

Benton

who's been shot by Ivan. The store-owner claims that this is the boy who has attacked him before, but the police inform him that the boy was unarmed, and that he was shot in the back. Ivan is obviously sorry about what he's done, but it's too late: the boy dies. Benton admits to a detective from the serious crimes unit that Ivan told him he had shot the boy.

Ross/
Carol
Ross finds himself in an awkward situation when he shares an elevator with John Taglieri. Hathaway later tells Tag that Doug is "a little kid - he always wants what he can't have". Tag says he wants Carol to move back in with him. Later on Linda Farrell, a representative of Novell Pharmaceuticals, arrives promoting her company's products. Ross is impressed - but more by her appearance than her sales pitch!

Greene
Greene's daughter Rachel comes to the ER for the first time, but Greene doesn't have much time to spend with her. Instead Wendy reads to her, but Rachel also sees something of the harsh reality of the ER, including Benton's 14-year-old patient. Later she asks Benton whether he made the boy better, and Greene decides to tell her the truth - that he died. "Are you sad?" she asks, and Benton nods. "If you're sad, then why aren't you crying?" "I am," Benton says, "right here." He points to her heart. Later Greene comforts his daughter as she starts asking difficult questions: if she was sick, she wants to know, would her father let her die?

Lewis
Susan's sister, Chloe Lewis, arrives in the hospital. Chloe has lost her apartment and run out of money, despite the fact that Susan sent her $500 recently: Susan is clearly frustrated by her sister, but reluctantly agrees to let her stay at her apartment "for a couple of days". She later finds that Chloe has stolen money and credit cards from Susan's locker. Susan suggests to Div Cvetic that he might 'talk' to her sister with a view to trying to sort out her psychological problems, but Div thinks this is a bad idea. When Susan gets home in the evening, she finds the apartment in disarray and her stereo stolen.

['Chicago Heat' *is a fairly routine episode, but probably the best so far, helped by the fact that the* ER *is so busy throughout. For the first time, we see Doug make a serious error by misjudging the OD girl's father, and it's strongly implied that he's made a racist assumption about him: an issue that recurs a lot during the series, although later it applies more directly to Greene with the case of Kenny Law. The episode also introduces a couple of recurring characters: Linda Farrell, who features right up to the beginning of series two, and Susan's troublesome sister Chloe. The highlight of the episode, though, is Rachel bringing a child's perspective to the doctors' work - especially Benton's very sensitive reply when she asks him why he isn't crying, which suggests some well-hidden depth to his character.]*

1-6: "Another Perfect Day"

Arriving for work, Ross is surprised to find a large, friendly man he doesn't recognize on the ER reception, spinning happily on the swivel-chair and answering the phone with: "No this is not the ER, this is Patrick!" He deduces that Patrick is not a new staff member but a patient, and sends him to see Carol about his injured elbow. Carol befriends him, while Patrick entertains with a knock-knock joke ("Who's there?" "Patrick." "Patrick who?" "Me, Patrick!") and a minimalist card-trick (Carol picks a card - and that's it). When Carol has finished she gives Patrick the X-ray, much to his delight. Meanwhile, a group of police officers brings in a patient, it's not the first time this week, but on this occasion a particular officer, Al Grabarsky, catches Lydia's eye.

It's Susan's birthday, which is common knowledge among the staff, but Lewis is more concerned to hear that everyone knows about her relationship with Div Cvetic. It also seems to be widely known that Div has asked her to wear a particular black dress for dinner this evening, in which she apparently looks fabulous! She confronts Div, who says he didn't tell everyone - just Doug Ross. Susan sighs: doesn't Div know that Doug is the biggest gossip-merchant in the hospital? | Lewis

Carter is looking for a one-bedroom apartment: he's | Carter moving out of his father's place. Jerry advises him to keep a look-out for accommodation becoming available after patients die, but Lydia also knows of a couple of spare apartments in her block. Later, he performs his first lumbar puncture successfully and Greene gives him a bottle of champagne: it looks like a perfect day.

Benton   Benton tries not to show that he is nervous about an interview with Dr Morgenstern and Dr Bradley regarding the Starzl fellowship, scheduled for this afternoon. Meanwhile a teenage boy, Mookie James, is brought in with severe lacerations after a gang fight - and Haleh is anxious that Benton should see him. She's known the boy since he was four, and thinks Benton might encourage him to start dealing with his problems. But Benton fails to make the time for him. Later Haleh tells him that she's secured a voluntary job for Mookie in the ER - and Benton will be his supervisor. When the time comes for Benton's Starzl interview, it's brief and not very promising. His rival Sarah Langworthy, on the other hand, seems to have done well.

Carol/   Tag is getting impatient with Carol: it's two weeks since
Ross   he asked her to move in with him, and still no answer. She tells him she has to be sure - not about him, but about herself. Then, after Carol and Doug successfully save a child injured in a boating accident, she finds herself looking into Doug's eyes - and they kiss. At first she offers no resistance, but then realizes what she's doing and pulls away.

Greene/   Greene finds time to meet with Jennifer, who is finding
Ross   her new job challenging. She has to re-write an opinion for the judge, which will take time; given their workload, it looks like they have very little opportunity to see each other. Doug, meanwhile, has been waiting for a visit from Linda Farrell, but she later cancels, promising to make it up to him at the weekend. But Doug appears to have lost interest. "She's a bit perky for me," he tells Greene, who says he thought that's what Ross liked. "Lately I've been attracted to sullen, withdrawn and

confused." Greene jokes that Ross should try going out with him! Later, Carol finds Doug and tells him that she's moving in with Tag. What happened earlier, she says, was an accident. "There are no accidents," Doug insists.

The staff decide to surprise Susan with a small party in the ER - but then Chloe arrives, drunk, wanting to go to a nightclub. Susan is worried about her but Chloe tells her to shut up: Susan's just like their mother; she hates everything that Chloe does. Their argument soon becomes a fierce, blazing row, ending with Chloe smashing her hand into the glass partition at the reception desk. As Benton fixes her hand, Div finally talks to Chloe, offering to listen to her if she wants. Susan, meanwhile, is exhausted, and calls off their dinner date. Carter later finds her sitting quietly up on the hospital roof, and they share Carter's bottle of champagne.

Benton

1-7: "9½ Hours"

Greene has called in sick, and Ross is having trouble standing in as chief resident: paperwork isn't really his forté. He calls Mark pleading with him to come in despite his flu, but realizes from the background noise that his illness is feigned: he's really spending the day with his wife.

Div Cvetic is tense, snapping at Jerry and then at Susan for "wasting his time", and causing Susan to be concerned for his state of mind. But Susan has troubles of her own: her car has broken down, thanks to Chloe. Carter offers to help her out, in return for her help in getting him into the OR: he calls a mechanic to fix the problem and when the substantial bill arrives, he pays it. "She'd better be worth it," the mechanic comments, and doesn't believe Carter when he replies that she's just a friend.

Lewis/
Carter

As Mark and Jenn enjoy their day at home, making love

Greene

125

in almost every room of the house, Jenn asks Mark if he isn't beginning to "itch" after nearly seven years of marriage - and suggests that Susan Lewis might be more than just a friend. Mark brushes off the suggestion, and asks if Jenn's "projecting"; maybe she's the one with the itch?

Benton   Benton is even more prickly than usual today, awaiting the announcement about the Starzl fellowship. When his mother is brought in, with a sprained ankle, he is annoyed that she befriends Carter, especially when she comments on his name: she knows of a Carter family in Tennessee, and tells Benton, "I think his people used to own our people... " Nevertheless she invites Carter over for Thanksgiving dinner. Benton puts his mother into Carter's care, by this time clearly furious, but Carter in turn is angry that Benton has abandoned her. Passing by the reception desk, Benton learns that the Starzl fellowship has gone to Sarah Langworthy; he tells his assembled colleagues that he didn't expect to get it anyway. Later, there's an awkward moment between him and Sarah, with her suggesting that his real problem with her is that he wants to sleep with her. Benton viciously retorts: "Not only don't I want to sleep with you, I've never even fantasized about it. Obviously you have."

Lewis   A new ER aide arrives: a Polish woman named Bogdanalivetsky Romansky; Ross decides she will have to be called 'Bob'. Meanwhile the police bring in a drunken man; his head is covered in blood and he is shouting maniacally about his wife and child who were killed in a car crash. Div Cvetic is unsympathetic, and when the man tries to hit him, has him committed for 72 hours. Seeing this and thinking that Div has obviously gone too far, possibly to the detriment of his career, Susan later goes to release the man, who has calmed down substantially now that he's sober.

Greene   Carol treats a woman named Jamie, who claims she has been raped by a friend of her boyfriend. She is clearly uncertain about her story, and tests reveal that she has actually had sex with three men: who turn out to be her boyfriend and two of his friends. While no-one is looking she leaves the hospital, but Carol catches up with her outside later on. Her boyfriend doesn't want her to come home, not believing she tried to resist. Maybe she should have fought harder, she says. But she said no, and Carol insists that's enough. She leads her back to the hospital so that she can finish her tests and give evidence against her attacker. "You've got to take care of things," she tells her. "If you don't, they come back. They always do."

Doug Ross treats a young boy with a sore throat, who suddenly stops breathing. Ross diagnoses epiglottitis and starts treating him - but then Benton intervenes, having seen Ross's patient from the next room where he had just finished with another patient. Ignoring Ross's protests, Benton operates, cutting a hole in the boy's throat to hyperventilate him. After Ross has finished treating the boy, he rushes out of the hospital and challenges Benton with trying to prove something after losing the fellowship. Benton apologizes, and tells Ross he feels he made a fool out of himself at the interview. "You saved two lives in five minutes," Ross says. "That's not a bad day." Later, Benton confides his worries to brother-in-law Walt. "It's hard to lose," he tells him. "Yeah, well most of us are used to it," Walt replies.

Benton/
Ross

1-8: "ER Confidential"

Susan wakes in the middle of the night, but Div is not in bed beside her. She finds him in the living room, confessing his worries into a dictaphone. He says that he is making notes on a patient's file, but she knows it's evidence of his own depressive state. When she discusses her worries with Greene, though, he seems more concerned with Cvetic's ability to deal with his patients.

Lewis

Benton is astonished to find that Carter has taken his mother's invitation to Thanksgiving dinner at face value, and intends to accept. Together they treat a Miss Carlton, who was injured when her car crashed into a

Carter/
Benton

127

bridge, but Carter is ill at ease when he discovers that 'Miss Carlton' is actually a male transvestite. He completes the necessary stitching in silence while Carlton tries to talk to him, clearly depressed, but it is only later that he realizes the extent of that depression when he finds that his patient has disappeared. Carlton is on the roof of the hospital and ready to jump. A panic-stricken Carter is relieved when Div Cvetic arrives, but Div doesn't have the chance to say anything before Carlton jumps, and dies. Utterly crushed by the experience, Carter is consoled by Benton who says that he should have realized the truth about Carlton: the car 'accident' was really a suicide attempt. In an attempt to cheer him up a little, Benton relents on his earlier decision and tells Carter to come over for dinner after all.

Carol   Two victims of a road traffic accident are brought in, but one of them, Larry, dies in trauma. The other, Andy, confides to Carol while he is being taken to the OR that he was the driver - but after his operation, she overhears him telling Larry's mother that it was her son who was driving the car. Lydia thinks Carol should tell the police - but Carol says it's not appropriate to reveal things told to her in confidence. When Larry's mother comes to her, though, crying over the death of her son but saying that she's angry with him for causing the accident, Carol decides to intervene. She goes to Andy and puts the pressure on: "I've kept things from people, and it makes you hate yourself," she says. Later, she tells Tag that she slept with Doug while Tag and she were going out, well before her overdose - and that two weeks ago, he kissed her and she let him. Tag reacts badly, demanding to know what more she wants from him. "I've been patient, I've been faithful... Should I treat you like garbage, like Doug Ross? Is that what you want?" She tries to tell him that she loves him, but he doesn't want to talk any more - and tells her to go to hell.

An animal rights campaigner is brought in having been attacked by a turkey he was trying to rescue from an early grave. Ironically, during the struggle he had to kill

the bird, and Tag takes great delight in plucking it so that
the ER staff can eat it later. The man admits that he took
some satisfaction in killing the bird, and is later seen
tucking into the staff's turkey buffet.

Greene, Benton and Sarah Langworthy work together on
a patient who requires an urgent heart operation, as none
of the cardiology specialists are available. Sarah takes the
lead, but allows Benton to perform the complex
operation, saying she will back him up if needed.
Although at first it looks as if Benton has made a serious
mistake, Sarah helps him through it and the patient is
saved. Later, Benton thanks her for allowing him to help,
but she's dismissive: this is a teaching hospital, after all.
She tells him that she's leaving tomorrow, and Benton
says an awkward goodbye.

Benton

Susan and Div are meant to be having dinner at Susan's
apartment with Chloe and her new boyfriend, but Div is
nowhere to be found. Susan waits at her apartment and
phones Div repeatedly, but he isn't at home: he's
standing somewhere in the streets of Chicago, drenched
in rain, in the middle of a flow of traffic.

Lewis

1-9: "Blizzard"

Seventeen shopping days left to Christmas, and the
streets are covered in nine inches of snow. It's a slow day
in the ER, with not a single patient being treated there so
far, and the staff are taking advantage: Wendy is roller-
blading through the corridors; Malik is rapping to a tape
playing over the loudspeakers; and, while Carter takes a
few hours' sleep, Greene and Lewis playfully put a cast
on his leg.

Hathaway reluctantly shows off the expensive
engagement ring Tag has bought her, but the assembled
nurses fall quiet as Ross enters with Linda Farrell, having
returned from their long weekend in the Bahamas. When
Ross hears Carol is getting married, for a moment he's
lost for words, then quietly says: "That's great.

Carol/
Ross

Congratulations." Linda seems to have been frustrated by Doug's lack of enthusiasm for wind-surfing and snorkelling, saying "Doug's idea of a perfect vacation is to lie in a deck-chair for a week." Carol says it sounds pretty good to her...

Greene   Greene receives a call from a Mr Blinker, whose wife is about to give birth. Rather than drive her through the snow to the ER though, they have decided she will deliver at home - and Greene reluctantly agrees, telling him to call if they hit trouble.

Just as the staff get stuck into playing polo on their swivel-chairs, Carol takes a call on the radio. There's been a 32-vehicle pile-up on the Kennedy expressway, with between 50 and 100 people injured. Communication and access for rescue vehicles are being inhibited by the weather, and the power is down at neighbouring Mercy hospital. All the victims are coming to County General.

After some speedy preparation, the ER staff are ready - and the flow of patients starts to come in thick and fast. Coloured tags are assigned to each patient as they come in: green for non-urgent; yellow for urgent; red for critical; and black for dead on arrival. Linda helps out on the phones, while Benton asks Mookie to put his hand on a tourniquet as he operates on someone's leg, saying he'll make a surgeon out of Mookie yet. In the midst of the chaos, Patrick arrives to see his new friend Carol, and makes himself useful by straightening out the Christmas decorations. Meanwhile Ross greets new attending ER physician Dr Hicks by mistaking her for a nurse and assigning her to bed-pan duty! Instead she goes to help Benton, whose patient Dex appears to be known to him. Dex's leg has been completely severed, but Hicks decides that they can re-attach it in the ER. "The vascular team will swoop down when they smell the glory," she tells Benton, who grins: "Now we're talking!"

130

While operating on Dex, Greene gets another call from Mr Blinker over the loud-speaker, and he gives him instructions for delivering the baby. Carter does his best to work with the cast still on his leg, and is terrified when a patient offers to remove it with an electric saw. Ross tries desperately to revive a man who has suffered a heart attack, but fails. He tells Greene he feels responsible, having green-tagged the patient when he came through the door. And Ross is still waiting for Div Cvetic to arrive and deal with a woman complaining of pain from the alien implants in her nose.

Linda admires Carol's ring, saying she reckons it's worth around $12,000. Carol is uncomfortable when she starts talking about Doug, especially when she asks speculatively if Carol thinks there's one perfect love for every person. "I don't know; why?" she asks hesitantly. "Because for Doug," Linda says, "it's you."

Carol

One of Lewis's patients from the pile-up suffers an unexpected seizure while she is gone, which Lydia and Wendy are unable to deal with. At the last moment, Bob intervenes and makes an incision, messily but successfully performing the life-saving operation. Lewis arrives on the scene late and is astonished at Bob, who quickly throws down the surgical gloves and runs out of the building. Later Morgenstern compliments Lewis on what he assumes is her work. Outside the hospital, Carter finds Bob sitting on the sidewalk, crying. "Now I will never be a doctor here," she says. She was a vascular surgeon in Poland, but fears she won't be able to take the board exam to practise in the States now that she has operated on a patient without permission. Carter tells Bob she'll be all right, and promises to help her with her English for the exam. Meanwhile, as Greene leaves, the Blinkers drop by to thank him for his help: "God bless you, Dr Greene."

Lewis/
Carter

[The first of two Christmas episodes this year, and the first time a single event - in this case, the 32-vehicle pile-up - dominates much of the action. In some ways the staff's quietly efficient, lightning-speed

preparation before the victims start to arrive is as impressive as the way they eventually treat the patients, and the shot of them all standing by the doors waiting for the ambulances to arrive - the proverbial calm before the storm - is a powerful one. We also get the first hint of Div's disappearance, and find out that 'Bob' was once a surgeon - a really interesting storyline which unfortunately goes nowhere, despite Bob's continued presence in the background until she vanishes early in the second series.]

1-10: "The Gift"

Greene/ Carter
It's 10.00 am on Christmas eve, and Greene still hasn't bought a present for his wife. Lewis agrees to cover for him for an hour while he goes out to find one, but on his way out he is stopped by a man whose son, Murray, has fallen into the water while they were ice-fishing together. Greene and Ross attempt to raise the boy's body temperature; they may have to perform a cardiopulmonary bypass. Meanwhile, Carter wakes a man dressed as Santa Claus who is sleeping in the waiting room, having come in to the ER complaining of dizziness. He leaves, saying he is feeling all right now.

Benton
Benton and Carter go up to the helipad to receive a 25-year-old man, Teddy Powell, who has been injured in a snowmobiling accident. Carter diagnoses a haematoma on the right side of the brain, but Benton is reluctant to perform surgery yet. Then, Carter notices cerebral spinal fluid draining from the man's ear: Benton soon establishes that he is brain dead. Hicks tells Benton to keep his heart going and find his family, so that they can get consent for organ donation. Benton searches the computer for nearby hospitals that are in need of organs, and finds two that are suitable. He tells them to expect the organs soon - but when the man's wife arrives, she refuses to allow the donation. Seeing her husband on a respirator, she can't believe that he is dead, and demands a second opinion.

Carol
The staff discuss Carol's engagement party, but Doug says he is not invited: anyway he's committed to a dinner

organized by Linda's parents. Carol deals with Patrick, who arrives having cut his head. She finds him a replacement for the helmet he usually wears, but he wants to stay a little longer. No one is answering the phone at his home. Meanwhile Mary Kavanagh wanders into the ER again, telling Carter she would like a suite with a view of the lake.

Murray recovers consciousness after the operation, but Greene is concerned that there may be brain damage because Murray has not uttered a word. Meanwhile the situation with Teddy Powell is becoming desperate: Benton has only an hour left before the organs begin to deteriorate, and transplant surgeons from the other hospitals are rushing to County General now. Hicks is astonished that Benton has committed himself before obtaining consent, and Benton admits that he has made a mistake: he was not expecting Mrs Powell to refuse, and Teddy's driving licence shows he would have been willing to donate his organs. He asks Greene for help and he tries to persuade Mrs Powell, but it is only when Benton finally gives up that she relents and signs the form.

Benton

Overhearing Greene's problems with Jenn's Christmas present, Linda offers to help - and returns later having bought some sexy lingerie. As Greene inspects the present in the lounge, Lydia compliments him on his good taste! Meanwhile Carter's Santa Claus has suffered respiratory arrest, and attempts made to revive him are unsuccessful. As they search in vain for a wallet or a driver's licence, Carter is in shock. "Oh God - I killed Santa." At midnight, Murray properly recovers and starts to talk: his father tells Greene this is the best Christmas present he could wish for.

Greene/
Carter

In the lounge, Greene talks to Ross as he pulls his tuxedo from his locker, ready for the party organized by Linda's parents. He doesn't express much enthusiasm, and Greene asks if he's all right. "I thought I was," he answers; he thinks about Carol all the time. "Did you ever tell her that?" Greene asks. He didn't, he says, and now it's too

Ross

late; but as Greene points out: "She's not married yet... "

Ross/
Carol

Ross takes a taxi to the venue for his slap-up dinner, but instead of going in he walks across town to Carol's engagement party. He manages to say a few words to her before she throws him out of the restaurant. "I love you," he pleads. Tag follows the two of them out, and punches him in the face, telling him to go. As Doug picks himself off the floor, Carol tells him, one last time, and out of Tag's range of hearing: "Stay out of my life, Doug."

Lewis/
Carter

Lewis is frustrated because she can't get in touch with Div, although she's been paging him for hours. Malik is surprised: didn't she know that Cvetic had quit? Susan asks Carter for a lift to Div's apartment. There, she finds it empty and abandoned: Div has moved out. Carter takes Susan home where she opens his Christmas present - a perfectly made music box. At her front door she thanks him for being a really good friend, and kisses him on the cheek. "Are you sure you're going to be okay?" he asks her. "Because I could come in for a while - keep you company... " He moves in for a kiss, but Susan pulls away, saying she doesn't think it's a good idea. Carter feels awkward and says he's sorry, but Susan says there's no need, and smiles as she bids him goodnight. Inside her apartment, she is greeted by Chloe, who tells her excitedly that she is pregnant...

1-11: "Happy New Year"

Carter

As Carter arrives for the beginning of his shift, he finds the victim of a gang shooting in the street outside. Passing him on to Greene, he is allowed to take part in Greene's surgery, given the task of intubating the man. He does well, but at that moment Benton arrives and takes over, preparing the patient to be taken up to the OR. "I'm the one who found him," Carter protests. "Yeah, well, you probably saved his life," is Benton's curt reply.

Lewis

Lewis is having trouble getting hold of Dr Kayson,

whose signature she needs before she can discharge one of her patients. When she does catch up with him, he chastises her for not trying harder to contact him - and Chloe chooses that exact moment to turn up and embarrass her. Over coffee, Chloe tells Susan her plans to move to Texas - today - with Ronnie, the father of her child. Susan has strong misgivings, but knows she can't stop her.

Carter learns that the gun-shot wound victim he brought in earlier died ten minutes into surgery. Angrily, he tells Benton that he's sick of doing nothing but "scut-work" - this is supposed to be his surgical rotation - but Benton says it's Carter's job to make his teacher's life easier. Carter then confides in Greene that he doesn't think Benton is interested in supervizing him, but Greene advises him that there are worse residents around. "My advice? Get used to it."

Carter

Unusually, Benton takes a break for lunch - and has coffee with his sister, Jackie. They talk about their mother, who has needed special care since having a stroke eight months previously. Jackie says that she and Walt can't look after her any more - both now have full-time jobs, and they have two children - which means that she will have to go into a nursing home. Benton refuses to accept that there's no alternative, suggesting that her neighbour Mrs Luki could look after her.

Benton

Hathaway comes to Greene, needing someone to treat a car crash victim with abdominal trauma being brought in on the helicopter. Benton isn't back from lunch and the others are busy, so Greene gives Carter the job. On their way down to a trauma room, Benton arrives back and is ready to take over, but after a little prompting from Greene, he lets Carter do most of the work. When Morgenstern arrives in trauma, he is impressed by the young student. Benton tells Carter he's welcome to scrub in on a gall-bladder operation he and Morgenstern are doing later, and Carter is delighted. But in the event, Carter doesn't see very much: after gowning up, he

Carter

135

inadvertently contaminates himself by putting his hand on Benton's shoulder, and is made to stand, dunce-like, in the corner for most of the operation!

Ross   Ross treats an elderly couple who are brought in suffering from carbon monoxide poisoning from kerosene heaters. They have been married for decades, and Ross is touched by their dedication to each other. Later, in bed, he mentions them to Linda Farrell, but she sees no possible comparison with their relationship. "You'll forget my name," she says. "You're assuming it won't last," Ross counters, and she agrees: it won't.

Lewis   Lewis has another patient, Mr Vennerbeck, with chest pains, and again needs to run some tests by Kayson. Eventually, Kayson gives her the all-clear, glancing at the file impatiently and paying little attention to what Lewis says. Mr Vennerbeck is discharged, but later returns to the ER having arrested. Kayson is called down to deal with it - giving Lewis a cutting look as he takes him to the OR. Later, Kayson angrily informs Lewis that Vennerbeck has died. His history of back pain, shown from previous admissions to the ER, could have alerted Kayson to the danger he was in - but Lewis didn't mention it to him. She protests that it was on his chart, and that Kayson never gave her a chance to volunteer information. But Kayson is determined to report Lewis's handling of the case to Morgenstern, and says he will ask for a full case review.

1-12: Luck of the Draw

Carol   Carol tells Lydia about her weekend away with Tag as they start to undress and wash a homeless man. And suddenly Carol finds a syringe sticking into her hand. The syringe is sent for HIV testing, but the chances of infection are small - around 1 in 250 - even if the patient has the virus. Lydia says she's been stuck with a needle nine times and never had so much as the flu; this is Carol's fifth time. Meanwhile, Carol is frustrated that everyone keeps asking whether she and Tag have set a date for the wedding; she tells Lydia she's not certain about whether she wants to get married at all.

As they arrive in the car park, Greene and Lewis discuss Kayson's demand for a full review on the Vennerbeck case. Susan is worried about her meeting with Morgenstern this afternoon, but Mark tells her not to worry - "Kayson's just covering his ass" - just as they pass Kayson himself locking up his car! At the meeting, Morgenstern tells Lewis that the specifics of the case don't worry him as much as Lewis's inability to stand up to Kayson: she has to be more assertive if she wants to stay in the ER. Later, Lewis discovers that Greene has been co-signing all her charts. Greene says Morgenstern has told him to, but as Lewis challenges him to support her, it transpires that Morgenstern's worries about her assertiveness were prompted by Greene himself. Susan can hardly believe she has been betrayed by her friend.

Lewis/ Greene

Benton has a new student, Debra Chen. He puts her into the care of Carter, who gives her the same induction Benton gave him on his first day, and tells her she can start her work with a rectal exam. She attempts the procedure without a lubricant, with painful results for the patient, and later adds to her mistakes by accidentally hitting Carter with the defibrillation paddles, causing him to fall and hit his head. He recovers after a while, but Deb and Haleh play a trick on him by pretending to have undertaken a very thorough examination of him while he was unconscious!

Carter

Ross treats a young boy, Ben Gather, suffering from respiratory failure due to septic shock. Once Ben is stabilized and sleeping, his father tells Ross that Ben suffered brain damage when hit by a car two years ago, and has needed constant care ever since. As he regains consciousness, Wendy hands Ross a DNR [do not resuscitate] order for the boy - signed by his father. Ross confronts the man, saying Ben will die if he's not put on a ventilator. He takes Ben to intensive care, while his father goes to a job interview. When he returns, he tells Ross

Ross

that he's been offered the job, in Detroit. "Coming back, I just couldn't help thinking how much easier it would be if Ben were dead... What kind of a father thinks like that?" He breaks down in tears, but Ross offers no sympathy, standing before him in silence.

Carol/
Lewis

Susan and Carol treat a man, Alan, suffering from shortness of breath, who is living in a home for the emotionally disabled. Alan seems obsessed with colours, and carries a folder containing all his medical information, however slight, in colour-coded sections. He is dressed entirely in blue - "because it's Monday", he tells Carol - and refuses to enter a room that is decorated in green. An X-ray reveals that he has a cancerous tumour, but it is not news to Alan: he did not tell Susan or Carol because he has been trying to ignore it, and his aversion to the colour green is explained by the fact that information about his cancer is contained in the green section of his folder. But as Carol talks to him, Alan seems to overcome some of his fears and seems ready to undergo treatment - and to move to a flat he has been looking at with a friend, despite its green bathroom. "Sometimes you've got to take the plunge," he says.

Benton

In the middle of surgery with Morgenstern, Benton receives a phone message from Walt: his mother is missing. As he meets up with Walt, Benton is critical of Mrs Luki, who is looking after her, and then of Walt and Jackie: in short, everyone but himself. He still won't consider putting his mother into a home. When he finds her wandering in the city, Benton gently sounds her out about going into a home, but she doesn't want to go.

Lewis

A girl is brought in having suffered a gun-shot wound: the bullet has gone into her heart and as Susan tries to operate, Kayson arrives and starts to question her competence. Greene takes over and deals with the patient, finding the bullet and removing it. Susan meanwhile is showing signs of losing her grip on the job, and Carol later finds her crying in the washroom. Greene later tries to apologize to her for not being more up-front

about his concerns, but she won't accept his apology. As
a peace offering he asks her to come to Doc Magoo's
after work, the cafe across the road from the ER, where
many of the staff have arranged to meet tonight.

A man is brought in with various minor injuries, the
result multiple assaults. Asked why he seems to be so
unpopular, he reveals that he's a sociologist from the
University of Chicago, researching the hostility levels of
different people. His method is to ask each of his subjects
two questions, and then to insult them using the
information he gets. Trying this method on the unwitting
Carol - he asks about her engagement ring, and why she
hasn't set a date for the wedding - he is assaulted within
seconds, and puts her in the top percentile of his
'hostility index'! Annoyed at being a research subject,
Carol later gets her revenge when a heavyweight boxer is
brought in as a patient: she puts him in the bed next to
the sociologist, and is pleased to see a knockout blow
within minutes!

Carol

After work, most of the ER staff meet in Doc Magoo's -
even Benton, who tries in vain to order health food. The
nurses lament the fact that none of them have won the
lottery this week: the chances of winning a prize are one
in 250. "Sounds familiar," says Carol, who chooses her
moment to announce the date of her wedding: May 18th.
Ross proposes a toast to her: "May your upcoming
marriage bring you laughter and happiness, and kids, and
most of all love. God knows, you deserve all of those
things." Outside the cafe, Lewis hesitates for a moment
but decides not to go in, and instead heads her car for
home.

Carol/
Lewis

['Luck of the Draw' *is a brilliant episode by the show's best writer, Paul
Manning. It tells several really funny stories, including that of the
sociologist who makes his living insulting people - who says his insurance
company charges him the same premiums as cab drivers! - and Carter
being accidentally knocked out by Deb. The story of Alan, the man
obsessed with colours, is one of the most moving for a patient who appears
in only one episode. Add to this our first visit to Doc Magoo's, and the*

139

clever theme of taking chances (the needle, the lottery ticket, perhaps even Carol 'taking the plunge' and naming her wedding date), and you have easily the most satisfying episode so far, and one of the best of the series.]

1-13: "Long Day's Journey"

A 36-year-old woman, Mrs Horne, is brought in to the ER suffering from respiratory arrest, having supposedly fallen from a ladder. Her children watch as Ross and Benton struggle to help her and as they wait for the husband to arrive, the daughter Mandy receives treatment for a hand injury sustained during her mother's 'fall'. Looking at Mrs Horne's file, Carol sees that she has been to the ER several times before for similar injuries: she suspects domestic violence. Ross confronts Mandy and her brother, David, asking who has been hurting their mother. David replies that Mandy hits her.

Carter arrives in the ER looking groggy and tired, having stayed up all night preparing for a presentation. Deb on the other hand is bright and breezy, and has already checked the files of all of Benton's patients before Carter can get to them. Later, they are both are called out to the car park to examine a family's Uncle Ed, who is sitting very stiffly in their car with his eyes closed. The diagnosis doesn't take long: Uncle Ed has been dead for hours!

Carter

A pregnant woman, who has attempted suicide by taking a drug overdose, is brought in by her friend - who is also clutching the pregnant woman's child. Greene attempts to revive her while her husband looks on anxiously and reads his wife's suicide note. Haleh talks to Carol, saying it must be hard for her, but Carol says she tries not to think about her own suicide too much. "Did you leave a note?" Haleh asks. "No," replies Carol. "I couldn't figure out what to say."

Carol

Susan is to face the review board at 3.00, and remains hostile towards Greene throughout the day. At the review however, despite continuing hostility from Kayson, Lewis is vindicated: the board accepts Lewis's admission

Lewis

that she should have considered Vennerbeck's back pain more carefully, and lets the matter drop. Later, Lewis is called upon to deal with a man brought in with chest pains, and is shocked to see that it's Dr Kayson, who has suffered a heart attack. She decides to treat him with tPA [a drug which breaks up blood clots during a heart attack] and he nods his agreement, but when he is taken up to the OR another doctor, Steinman, tries to give him angioplasty instead. Lewis is firm, threatening Steinman with a review committee if he doesn't do what she wants.

Ross treats a boy, Zach, whose leg has been broken by his over-enthusiastic PT instructor. He calls for the assistance of a Dr Nelson rather than the 'ortho' on call - who happens to be John Taglieri. But Nelson is unavailable and when Tag arrives, he berates Ross: "It's not personal, it's professional," he tells him. Later, Ross consoles the child of the woman who had taken the overdose: despite Greene's efforts, the woman has died, but Ross tries to tell her child that it will be all right. Meanwhile, Zach's X-ray has revealed a mass in his leg, but his parents cannot bring themselves to tell him he may have cancer. Eventually they let Ross tell him, and he sits with Zach as Tag performs the biopsy.

Ross

Benton is trying to find someone to look after his mother a few days a week, and Haleh suggest Jeanie Boulet - who works part-time in the physical therapy department of County. "You'll like her," she assures him, adding, "as much as you like anyone." Benton goes up to see her and she agrees to help, for a fee, though as a physical therapist she feels she's over-qualified for house-sitting. Unusually for Benton, he makes a point of thanking her.

Benton/ Jeanie

Greene sees a pregnant woman, Mrs Chang, who is suffering from nausea and orders several tests before discovering the truth: she is ill as a result of taking a herbal drink which is reputed to induce labour. The Changs are anxious that their child should be born before the Chinese new year: if born in the Year of the Pig, apparently, their child will turn out to be lazy.

Greene

141

Greene is sceptical and refuses to induce labour, but the couple eventually obtain co-operation from the aptly-named Dr Noble.

Carter   Carter and Deb examine a patient with acute stomach pain, and Deb immediately spots the cause of the problem - an allergic reaction to poppy seeds and granola. Deb remembers the allergy from a textbook: it appears she has a photographic memory. Carter reports her diagnosis to Benton who agrees with it; next time, however, Deb should present her own findings. To Carter's amazement, he hands the patient over to her.

Benton   Outside the hospital, Benton meets Jackie, who has chosen a nursing home for their mother. Benton refuses: he can look after his mother two days a week, with Jeanie doing three days a week; he won't have his mother's savings eaten up in nursing home fees. Jackie points out that some of those savings were spent on Peter, but Benton brushes it off, saying he's up to his ass in debt.

Ross   Practising basketball shots outside to relieve his melancholy, Doug meets a young boy, Jake, who plays - quite successfully - against him before being collected by his mother, Diane Leeds, who works for County in risk management. Before Doug can chat her up, she stops him: her friend is an ex-girlfriend of his, and she knows all about him! After a long day and with Tag and Carol setting off for a weekend away, this is the last thing Doug wants to hear.

1-14: "Feb 5, '95"

Carter   Carter and Deb have a trauma presentation to do later, but neither has prepared properly and Benton refuses them more time. Managing to grab half an hour during the day, Carter reckons his is ready - but when the time comes, his brief efforts are overshadowed by Deb's immaculate presentation, complete with slide-show and computer graphics! When Carter later expresses his annoyance to Deb, she takes issue with his ambition to go into surgery. "It doesn't seem like you," she says. And Carter's insecurity grows when he learns that Deb's mother is chief of surgery at St Bart's.

Haleh angers Benton by suggesting a course of treatment for a patient. After a confrontation she makes a point of taking written instructions only during the day, and forcing Benton to do tedious procedures himself. When Benton complains to Carol she suggests he make an effort to get on with her: "Step off that pedestal you put yourself on and you'll see the nurses make this place work, not you." Meanwhile, Carol has acquired some new crash carts for the ER - only to have one of them go missing later in the day. The cart has been 'stolen' by the cardiology department, and Carol, Lydia, Bob, Conni, Ross and Carter sneak up to steal it back.

Ross

Greene and Lewis clash over a patient with chest pains, with Greene disagreeing with Susan's diagnosis of heart problems. When the argument is over, Lewis acidly requests that Greene refrain from contradicting her in front of other staff members, asking bitterly that he show her at least a little respect.

Lewis/
Greene

Benton and Carter treat a 12-year-old boy who has been the victim of a gang-related shooting. As they struggle to save his life, another boy of a similar age walks furtively through the corridors of the ER and when Bob confronts him and asks where he is going, he draws a gun on her. As staff and patients make way for him, he walks purposefully to the trauma room, and levels the gun at the boy on the operating table but as Benton says, he's too late: the patient has died already. The boy briefly turns the gun on Benton, then turns and flees the hospital, leaving the nurses and doctors stunned. Carter speaks for them all as he mutters, "It's madness... "

Benton/
Carter

A woman named Grace, who has breast cancer, is brought in, suffering the latter stages of her disease. Greene does what he can to relieve the pain but can do very little else, and Grace tells him she wants him to let

Greene/
Lewis

143

her die. As her respiration falls dangerously low, he has to stop giving her morphine, but he can't help her end her life. He tries to share his frustration with Susan but she is short with him, still angry about their professional disputes. It shouldn't affect their friendship, he says. "We're not married; we work together," she replies. "Professional is personal." Mark looks sullen. "I miss you," he tells her. Later in the evening, she finds him standing silently by the window, looking out into the rain: Grace has died, and he is more depressed than ever. Susan finally relents, and suggests dinner. Mark can't - Jenn and Rachel are in town - but he's grateful for the offer.

Ross   Ross goes up to Diane Leeds's office, supposedly looking for Jake. Diane says he can play hoops with Jake so long as he doesn't pass on any hatred of women to him, and Ross learns that Diane split up with Jake's father long ago. Meanwhile, the staff's business is hampered by the presence of a runaway tree snake somewhere in the ER. It is eventually found by Carter in a wall-mounted cupboard!

Greene   Morgenstern tells Greene he is impressed with his work, and asks him his plans for next year, after his residency is over. Greene says that he has sent out some letters applying for jobs, and is delighted when Morgenstern asks him to think about joining the staff at the ER as an attending physician. But when Greene later tells Jenn about the offer, she makes it clear to him that her career is important too: if she's offered the chance to clerk for the federal judge in Milwaukee again next year, she'd like to take it.

Benton/   Benton arrives back at his mother's house two hours late
Jeanie   - much to Jeanie's annoyance, although she has enjoyed his mother's company, and her stories about 'little Petey'! Jeanie also tells Benton she's concerned about his mother: she has limited use of her left arm and leg, and is suffering from incontinence. Benton agrees to let Jeanie try some physiotherapy, but in the longer term, she will

144

need more care than either of them can give.

1-15: "Make of Two Hearts"

It's February 14th, and Carter has a large number of Valentine's cards; Susan also has one or two. Benton is storing some flowers and chocolates in the fridge, and Ross refuses to believe his claim that they are for his mother. Doug himself is working tonight: he always works the night-shift on Valentine's Day, to avoid possible dating conflicts - he tells Mark he has learnt that lesson the hard way!

Policeman Al Grabarsky rushes panic-stricken into the ER, clutching a stray dog which he has hit with his car. Greene and Lewis manage to save it - with the help of some mouth-to-mouth resuscitation from Carter! - and Grabarsky thanks the doctors and nurses enthusiastically, hugging the doctors and surprising Lydia by kissing her on the lips. He decides to adopt the dog, and names it Bill.

A young Russian girl is brought in by her adoptive   Carol
mother, Mrs Hall, suffering from coughing and a fever. Mrs Hall soon departs however, leaving a false phone number, and Carol befriends the girl, whose name is Tatiana - using the few words of Russian she has learnt from her mother. Tatiana is comforted by the presence of Grabarsky's dog, Bill, but four hours later Mrs Hall has not come back and after a full day, she will have to go to a foster home. Later, tests confirm that Tatiana has pneumonia - and AIDS. Carol is frustrated that the hospital can do nothing more for her. She's glad Tatiana can't understand what's happening to her - but then, neither can Carol.

Greene bemoans the fact that Valentine's Day brings its share of "nutcases" to the ER, as he deals with a group of cheerleaders who have been given chocolates spiked with LSD by a college friend. Unfortunately Deb is unaware of this, and passing the open box of chocolates on her

145

way somewhere, she gives in to temptation and takes two or three! Later, various staff members are bemused to see her wander around the ER in a daze, but no-one works out the reason why...

Ross   Jake arrives to see Ross, complaining of stomach pains. Ross calls his mother down to the ER, who says Jake is faking it - hoping to set Diane up with Doug. "How do we deal with it?" Doug asks, and Diane gives a vicious smile: "Let's cut him open!"

Carol   Carol is surprised to see Mrs Hall back in the ER, checking up on Tatiana's progress. Carol tells her she is very ill, and won't be able to go home tonight: in fact, Mrs Hall might not be allowed to take her home ever. But, Mrs Hall doesn't intend to: she found out Tatiana had AIDS after adopting her ten days ago in St Petersburg, and doesn't want to let herself get close enough to be hurt by the girl's death. She leaves the hospital again without saying goodbye to her adopted daughter.

Lewis/   Dr Kayson pays a visit to Susan Lewis, telling her that
Greene   his heart attack has given him a new perspective. He'd be happy to be her mentor if she wants to go into cardiology, he says, and insists she call him Jack. When he invites her to dinner that night, Susan has to make an excuse: she tells him she's going out with Greene tonight! Later, Greene and Lewis save a patient together and Greene suggests they do something this evening: she wouldn't want Kayson to think she was lying, after all. The two of them go ice-skating after work, and he tells her about his problems with the job offer and Jennifer. Mark's skill at skating leaves a lot to be desired, but he and Susan enjoy themselves and the chance to talk.

1-16: "The Birthday Party"

Ross/   Ross wakes at 4 am in the bed of a woman named
Carol   Pamela - although he calls her Natalie by mistake! - and makes his way through the snow-covered streets to the

ER. It's a slow night, but Carol is still there after the end of her shift, waiting for Tatiana to be picked up and taken to Sunshine House, a hospice. She gratefully accepts Doug's offer to look after the Russian girl while Carol catches some sleep.

Benton wakes up at 6.30, having spent the night on a sofa in his mother's house. Jackie wearily reminds him that he ought to be home this evening for his mother's birthday party, and Benton says he'll be there. At the ER, however, no-one is willing to swap shifts with him - he has asked too many favours of his colleagues recently. In fact, as Hicks notes, Benton has swapped shifts four times lately: it's not something she wants to encourage. If his mother's health problems are interfering with Benton's work, says Hicks, he should consider taking a break and rejoining the hospital next year. Benton says that won't be necessary. | Benton

Deb is astonished to hear that Carter hasn't yet applied for his sub-I [sub-internship] for next year: doesn't he realize how competitive they are? Twelve requests have been received so far for a trauma placement in the ER, and Deb is confident that she has already got it, having made her request to Benton very early on. When Carter asks Benton what his chances would be if he joined the 12 current candidates for the post, Benton answers dryly that he should think his chances would be one in 13. | Carter

Tag takes Carol to see one of the churches they are considering for the wedding, but she hates it - much to Tag's annoyance. She explains that she's worried about Tatiana, then says she's been thinking about adopting her. Tag is shocked by the idea: he doesn't relish the prospect of spending years watching an adopted daughter die of AIDS. Later, though, Hathaway visits Tatiana in the hospice. She is lonely there without other Russian speakers, and is pleased to see Carol again. | Carol

Carter overhears Benton talking on the phone about a birthday party, and jumps to the conclusion that it's | Benton

Benton's birthday. The news soon gets round, and Lydia and Carter organise a surprise for the 'birthday boy': two exotic belly dancers, masquerading as patients. Several of the staff enjoy the show, as the women dance provocatively around a severely embarrassed Dr Benton! Meanwhile, it's Rachel Greene's birthday party as well, but Mark fails to leave in time to for her party. Jackie makes repeated calls to the ER to find out where her brother is, but he ignores them all.

Ross   While treating a young girl who has fallen 15 feet from a balcony, Ross notices the imprint of a large booted foot on her back. It seems she was kicked from the balcony by her father, who is sitting in the waiting room as Ross storms in and lunges for him, punching him repeatedly. Ross is pulled away before he can do any lasting damage, and Greene later tells him the father won't sue - he's too busy talking to detectives from domestic violence - but in any case, Ross has been stupid, and will probably have to face the resident review committee for his actions. Meanwhile, Diane Leeds is waiting for him at reception, supposedly to talk to him about Jake: she says she'll come back tomorrow.

Benton/   Police officers wheel in an unconscious white man
Jeanie   suffering from stab-wounds, and as Benton attends to his injuries he finds racist tattoos on the man's arms. One of the police officers explains that the man "took a crowbar to a black kid on West Avenue; another brother jumped him with a knife". Ironically he is saved by the efforts of Benton, Malik, Conni and Lily in the trauma room, then Drs Hicks and Benton in the OR. Benton is professional throughout, and only lets out his anger when he arrives back at his mother's house, after the party is over, telling Jeanie: "I couldn't be at my mother's birthday party, because I had to save a man with 'Die, Nigger, Die' tattooed on his forearm." She understands, but they don't have time to talk: her husband's car has pulled up outside, ready to take her home.

1-17: "Sleepless In Chicago"

To make up for the time he took off last week, Benton has been working for 48 hours, and with only one of his students to help him, Deb has called in sick. Hicks is angry that Benton has been trading shifts again, and they argue bitterly about Benton's drive to do as many procedures as possible, and whether he is currently fit for work - ending with Hicks ordering him to get at least two hours' sleep.

Benton

At the hospice where Tatiana lives, Carol receives the news that she has passed her adoption test with flying colours - and she tells Tatiana that she can come to live with her. She tells Lydia the news but she is sceptical, saying it's a tough way to start a marriage.

Carol/ Ross

Ross treats a young girl, Bonnie, with mysterious star-shaped burns on her hands: checking up, he discovers that she has previously been treated at another hospital for similar injuries. The girl's mother confides the truth to Carol, on the understanding that she doesn't tell Ross: she has branded her daughter, with a star-shaped paperweight left on the stove, as punishment for "touching herself - down there". It's no big deal, she says; her mother did it to her, too. She shows Carol the star-shaped mark on her own hand. Carol promptly tells Ross, who calls the police, and through a trick they separate the mother from her child. The woman manages to scratch Ross's neck, though. As Carol attends to it they discuss Tatiana: Doug tells her he thinks it's a wonderful thing that she's doing.

Carol/ Ross

Joseph, an elderly man with congestive heart failure is brought into the ER and treated by Lewis, Carter and - to Hicks's dismay - Benton. Unfortunately they cannot find out much from the patient, who has no voice box, and it is only when the doctors have stabilized his condition that Carter finds a note on his file: the man has terminal cancer, and last time he was in the ER signed a document instructing that no heroic measures be taken to prolong his life. Later, and with difficulty, Carter tries to

Carter

talk to him, eventually persuading him to write down the name of a relative - Roger, Joseph's son, who lives in Bloomington. Carter has no luck tracing him, though, and learns from Joseph that the two haven't made contact for 20 years.

Greene/ Lewis

Between patients, Greene and Lewis bump into a Dr John Koch, a researcher from MIT who is writing a study on 're-conceptualizing the hospital'. Overhearing Greene's woes about being separated from Jenn, he suggests that the couple move to Kenosha, midway between Milwaukee and Chicago. He also succeeds in impressing Susan with his rational, innovative ideas of how hospitals could be reformed - until the warders from his mental home catch up with him to take him back!

Benton/ Jeanie

Carter finds Benton lying in a darkened room, but he isn't sleeping, merely staying out of Hicks's way. He tells Carter to alert him if a surgical case comes through the doors - although normally he should wait until called for a surgical consult. When, a little later, one of Greene's patients looks like needing surgery, Carter calls his teacher and he comes running, taking over the case - which severely angers Greene.

Carter

Conni tells Carter that Joseph won't live through the night, and Carter decides to spend some time with him. Learning that he used to teach English, he brings him some books down from the library, and reads to him. Benton demands to know why Carter is "wasting time" on Joseph Klein, but Carter replies forcefully that there's more to patient care than just cutting them open.

Benton

Ross, Greene and Hicks operate on a 16-year-old boy with a gun-shot wound to the neck, and as she thinks Benton has had his two hours' sleep, Hicks lets Ross call for his help. Benton arrives having had no more than a short nap, but nevertheless proceeds to save the patient with incredible skill. "Looks like that rest did you some good," Hicks says, and Benton allows himself a smile.

Following Doug's assault of one abusive parent, and his injury at the hands of another, Diane Leeds has had to write up two separate reports for Ross as part of her duties in risk management. Doug takes the opportunity to ask her to dinner - after some prompting from Greene - but Diane refuses the invitation. Later, though, she comes back to the ER and suggests dinner on Friday evening. "If it means that much to you, OK," Doug smiles.

Carol

Morgenstern tells Greene that he's leaving the hospital to take over Brigham's residency program at Harvard. He has recommended Greene for the attending post and considers it "almost a lock", but the appointment will have to be approved by Morgenstern's replacement when he arrives...

Greene

Benton catches Carter writing up his notes, well after the end of his shift. "That's what you get when you spend too much time on one patient," Benton says. Carter, a little shaken, says he thinks it was time well spent: Joseph died ten minutes ago. Benton says Carter is wasting his time going into surgery, because he doesn't think like a surgeon. "Why - because I don't think like you?" Carter retorts.

Carter/ Brenton

Returning to Tatiana's hospice after work, Carol is devastated by the news that the girl cannot be placed with her after all - because Carol's attempted suicide has been discovered during the course of a background check. Later in the night, she goes to Doug's flat and cries in his arms. Doug was the only one who believed she could do it, she says. "Well," Doug says, "I love you." She looks deep into his eyes, and asks if she can stay the night. But Doug decides instead to drive her home.

Carol/ Ross

Mark Greene gets home and talks to Jenn about the idea of living in Kenosha, but Jenn is against it. She's tired of making sacrifices for Mark, and feels he's never given anything up for her. Mark protests, but Jenn has made her decision. "I don't think we're going to make it, Mark. I'm leaving you. I'm sorry."

Greene

Carol   Benton gets home on time for once, but he is due to wake at six to look after his mother for the day. Exhausted, he falls asleep instantly - and fails to wake up when the alarm goes off in the morning. Upstairs, his mother calls for her medicine, and struggling to get up on her own, she falls on the stairs. Benton wakes with a start, and, seeing that her hip is badly damaged, wastes no time in getting her to the ER. There, Greene and Lewis ask him repeatedly, "What happened?" But Benton can't bring himself to say a thing.

[Destined to be forgotten in the shadow of 'Love's Labor Lost', *which follows it,* 'Sleepless in Chicago' *is a* tour de force, *effectively playing on our expectations of Benton's complex character. We know he's increasingly worried about his mother, but at the same time determined to work harder and with better results than anyone else. His argument with Hicks is very revealing, showing how competitive he feels about his work and hinting that he blames the resident evaluation system, and his superiors, for making him work so hard. Then, of course, he puts the same pressure onto Carter - who makes his most impassioned defence of the more sensitive approach, making more time for his patients. When Benton manages a very difficult piece of surgery despite not having slept for days, we almost want him to fail. Dramatically, he does at the end of the episode, when he fails to prevent his mother's fall - a mistake for which he will be paying for a long time to come.]*

1-18: "Love's Labour Lost"

Greene/   As Greene and Ross throw a football around outside the
Benton   hospital, Ross is nearly hit by a car which speeds past, pausing briefly for its passengers to throw out a man with a gun-shot wound. They bring the man in and Greene performs CPR, managing to raise a faint pulse. In the next room, Benton is one of the team trying to help his mother. He calls a senior orthopaedic surgeon to operate on her and tries to take part in the surgery himself, but is told that he's way out of line and has to wait outside. Jackie and her children join him later, but contrary to Benton's expectations, Jackie isn't interested in blaming him.

Carter and Deb join Greene as he reassures Jodi O'Brien, a young woman 38 weeks into her pregnancy, that her stomach pains and constant need to urinate are merely the symptoms of cystitis. Her blood pressure is high at first, but soon falls to a more normal level. Greene checks the weight of her baby, which he calculates as five or six pounds: it's small, but he reasons this is because Jodi has miscalculated the baby's due date, and he releases her with some antibiotics. Jodi and her husband, Sean, thank him for his help, but before they can get into their car to go home, Jodi has a seizure. A panic-stricken Sean carries her into the ER at 7.15 pm.

Greene

Greene makes a rapid change to his diagnosis: Jodi has eclampsia, a rare disorder of late pregnancy in which the blood vessels go into spasm, causing a lack of oxygen to the brain. He sedates her and orders hyperventilation, as well as a foetal monitor - which indicates that at this stage, the baby's heart rate is strong. Lewis offers to take over from Greene as it's the end of his shift, but Greene feels responsible for not spotting the eclampsia earlier: the high blood pressure and traces of protein in her urine sample ought to have alerted him. He'd feel better, he says, if he saw it through.

Greene

At 9 pm, Greene decides that Jodi should begin labour, now that the eclampsia is under control; they can start in the ER and then move up to OB. He dismisses the doubts of OB attending Dr Coburn about his ability to deliver the child, telling her he's delivered about 200 babies in his time. The labour starts well, with help from Lewis, Carter and Hathaway, but as it progresses Lewis and Greene become more and more concerned about the baby's falling heart-rate. At 2.30 am Greene decides it's time that Jodi went up to OB, and pages Coburn - but they are still waiting to hear from her at 3.15. Obviously feeling out of his depth, Greene orders Carter to drag Drake, the OB resident, down to the ER, and Hathaway to fetch a baby-warmer and a new-born resuscitation unit. At 4.13, there's still no sign of Drake, and Greene attempts a forceps delivery, but the baby's shoulders are

Greene

jammed into Jodi's pelvic bone. With Carter, Greene tries a difficult manoeuvre to try to free the child, but he fails. All he can do now is push the baby back into the uterine canal, and attempt an emergency Caesarean. Sean, distraught, doesn't know if he wants to consent - Greene admits he's never done it before - but makes up his mind when Greene tells him if they wait five more minutes, the baby will be brain-dead. Sean waits outside as they rush to trauma one, where Greene - still calling for help from OB - administers a local anaesthetic and with Jodi's blood pressure rising, carefully begins the incision. In no time, Jodi is bleeding profusely from a placental abruption. Trying to act fast before mother and child both die, Greene gets the baby out, but its blood pressure is high, it is much larger than expected - and it is not breathing.

Greene   While Carter presses down on Jodi's aorta, Lewis and Greene intubate the baby. He performs CPR, hyperventilates the baby and then tries an umbilical line - eventually, Lewis says it's "pinking up". Meanwhile, Dr Coburn arrives and takes over Jodi's care, lamenting Greene's messy attempt at a C-section. "You should have let me know you were in over your head," she tells him. By 5.30, the baby's condition has improved, and Greene tells Sean that his son will be fine. But Coburn is scathing about Greene's handling of the case: "I have never seen such a chain of errors of judgement," she tells him. At that moment, Deb rushes in to tell Greene that Jodi is crashing. Mark starts an arterial line and tries desperately to replace the lost blood, but her pulse is lost and despite three attempts to shock her and an external heart massage, Mark can't bring Jodi back. Coburn calls time of death, but Greene is still trying - though it's thirty minutes past too late. Finally, breathless, he has to give up and almost runs from the room, immediately taking the lift upstairs to give the news to Sean O'Brien. He finds Sean sitting in OB, with his baby son in his arms.

Greene   Later, Carter discovers Greene standing silently by Jodi's body. Cautious but sincere, he says to Mark: "I just wanted to tell you that I felt what you did was a heroic thing." Greene just stares, dumbstruck. Walking to the station he refuses Susan's offer of company, and gets straight on to the train that will take him home. Once he is alone, he stares out of the carriage window, and breaks down in tears.

[This is one of the episodes that everyone remembers, and a tremendously draining experience to watch. Towards the end it seems that everything possible is going wrong, and we can feel Greene's desperation as he makes every attempt to reverse the relentless effects of his mistakes. The episode is a masterpiece of pacing, starting with subtle hints that Greene is missing something as soon as Jodi O'Brien arrives, but concentrating on other storylines until she is brought back in; from then on, it relentlessly follows every stage of Greene's struggle. The fact that the medical details are correct makes it all the more frightening, although it's unlikely that the ER would be kept waiting for so long without a representative from obstetrics.]

1-19: "Full Moon, Saturday Night"

In the trauma room where Jodi O'Brien died, Susan finds Mark standing silently, alone with his thoughts. Worried for him, she tells him to take tonight off 'sick', and promises she'll cover for him. He gratefully accepts, but instead of going home sits by himself in Doc Magoo's. He orders a bagel, and ignores a man's attempt to make conversation - not realizing that the man is Dr William Swift, the new head of the ER...

Greene

Benton is reluctant to leave his mother, who is recuperating after her hip operation, although he is obviously in need of sleep. Jeanie reassures him that she will stay with her while he gets some rest, but Benton uses his time off to look at his mother's file on the computer. Angry at what he finds, he pages Taglieri, and demands to know why the hospital has decided Mrs Benton should be discharged. She needs more time to recuperate, Benton says, and then she can go home. Taglieri replies forcefully that she's not going home - she will need skilled nursing for the rest of her life - but Benton refuses to accept it.

Benton

Carter   Deb succeeds in making Carter even more nervous when she asks him whether he thinks he's done enough procedures to merit high honours. Carter hasn't been keeping count, but decides to start! Lewis gives them both a helping hand by allowing them to suture on one of her patients. They decide that whoever does the most stitches will get the credit for the procedure, and go on to race each other - while the patient looks on nervously.

Lewis/   As Lewis treats a student who has been hit by a car
Carol   whilst playing a drunken game of 'chicken', Swift arrives and introduces himself - but not before Lewis, assuming he is junior to her, tells him to "glove up and get your butt over here!" When he asks her later where he can find the chief resident, she tells him that Greene is off with flu. Meanwhile, Tag has brought Carol some copies of *Modern Bride* magazine, and surprises her when he recognizes Swift from his college days - though he knows Swift better as 'Wild Willie'!

Benton/   Benton returns to his mother to find that her wrists have
Jeanie   been strapped to her bed, against her will. He removes the restraints and confronts Jeanie angrily, demanding to know why she didn't try to stop whoever put them on. She replies that it was her suggestion: his mother had tried to get out of bed, and Jeanie was worried that she might hurt herself. Benton simply tells her to go, and not to bother coming back.

Lewis   Lewis tells Carter that there is usually an influx of weird cases - and patients - when there's a full moon on Saturday night. Sure enough, the flow has already started: a 22-year-old man on PCP, recently jilted by his girlfriend, is wandering around shouting "You cheating bitch!" with a gurney strapped to his back, and four bathers are brought in having been left in Lincoln Park wearing just their shoes and socks, suffering from possible frostbite "to all extremities." Later Carol treats a man with scratches to his face, who asks to be put in restraints until sunrise - because he's a werewolf...

In the middle of the night, a radio message alerts the ER to a disaster situation - a fire in which 15 to 20 people have been injured. The on-call staff are immediately paged: Benton is called away from his mother, and Ross has to get out of bed with Diane Leeds. Greene doesn't hear his page, as he's preoccupied playing loud arcade games - but the others get to the ER quickly, and are livid when they discover that the 'disaster' was a drill called by Swift. He proceeds to hold a long introductory meeting with the staff. Greene arrives just as the meeting draws to a close. "Doctor Bagel!" Swift greets him, and asks sarcastically whether he's over his 'flu'. Their professional relationship has got off to a bad start, but Swift has been impressed with Lewis's performance during the day. While Susan helps him unblock a sink, he asks her if she's thought of applying for chief resident, and is surprised when she tells him she's only second year. Swift says he's observed "a few kinks in the chain of command", and sets off to get a plumber's snake from Bob. Susan's good day at the ER is complete when the radio plays a dedication to her - 'Twist and Shout' - thanks to a request by Carter...

Greene/ Lewis

When Benton gets back to his mother after Swift's meeting, she has fallen out of bed. Thankfully her hip isn't damaged, but she has a couple of bruises. Later, Benton goes to see Jeanie - meeting her husband, Al, for the first time - and tells her what happened. "I can't do this by myself," he admits, and asks for her help in finding his mother a good nursing home.

Benton/ Jeanie

On the train back from work, Ross tries to talk to Greene to see if he's all right, but Greene isn't listening, and turns down an invitation to go round to Doug's place to talk. He gets off at his stop, and sits at the station until Jenn arrives in the morning. She reassures him that he did his best for Jodi, as he always does, but he's human. "I'm not supposed to be," Mark says. "You are," she replies. "You're the only one who doesn't know it." The two of them go for breakfast...

Greene

*['*Full Moon, Saturday Night' *is notable for one truly ER moment - the staff dancing to 'Twist and Shout' in a packed reception. Quirky, funny and irreverent - moments like this are addictive.]*

1-20: "House of Cards"

Benton   Mrs Benton is discharged from the hospital, to be moved to the Melville Home. Jeanie joins her and Jackie in the ambulance, after Benton has broken the news to his mother that she is not going home. "Do I have to go, Peter?" she pleads. "Yeah, ma. You do," he says sadly.

Greene   Treating a man with stomach pains, Greene orders an ultrasound to rule out appendicitis - but Swift cancels it, saying the man's pain is obviously just due to gas. Greene tells Lewis he thinks Swift has already made up his mind about whether to make Greene an attending physician next year. When a pregnant woman is brought into the ER, Swift is disturbed to see Greene refuse to treat her, instead passing her on to Lewis. They discuss Jodi O'Brien, and Swift tells Greene he's arranged for him to present the case at a conference at 2.00. Later, Greene and Carter examine a Mrs Salizar, who has been coughing for one or two weeks - and her daughter is apparently sick as well. Greene suspects tuberculosis, and persuades Mrs Salizar to take a test, but she won't have her children tested - possibly because she fears their status as illegal immigrants will be discovered. Greene becomes very concerned that the disease will spread quickly and when Mrs Salizar's test comes back positive, he demands angrily that she bring her children in. Lewis gently reminds him that screaming at her will do no good, but Greene is obviously nervous about the imminent conference - especially when he hears that due to the numbers of people interested, it's been moved to the auditorium.

Carter   Deb is horrified when Benton tells her and Carter that he needs their procedure books today to start their sub-I evaluations. This gives Carter the edge because he's been there longer, but Deb is determined to make up time. She tries to sweet-talk Haleh into giving her the particular procedures she still needs, but instead she gets to help Wendy with an IV on a drug-user. When neither of them can find a suitable vein, Deb sees the opportunity to do a central line. It goes well until Deb loses the guide wire, and Swift has to take over as she runs out in panic. The wire is retrieved, but the hospital may be sued for the error...

At the conference, Greene presents the Jodi O'Brien case before a large audience - which includes Lewis, Carter, Swift, and Dr Coburn. Greene defends himself well and shows the wide extent of his knowledge, while also admitting that he made a mistake in assuming that he could handle the delivery of Jodi's baby. Coburn is his harshest critic, repeatedly questioning his qualifications. Swift defends him - but Greene doesn't thank him for it afterwards, resenting the fact that Swift put him through it in the first place.

Greene

Diane is concerned when Ross gives Jake an expensive bike that he wanted - without consulting her. He can't get to her through her son, she says.

Ross

At the Chen household, Carter turns up during a dinner party in order to talk to Deb. She tells him she's decided to quit. "I really didn't care about the patient; I wanted the procedure," she says. That's the difference between them, she tells Carter: he cares about the patients as people.

Carter

Mark talks to Susan about Jenn, and she tells him to go to Milwaukee tomorrow: she will cover for him at work. Mark telephones Jenn, but she can't see him until the weekend. When Susan gets home, she finds Chloe - by now heavily pregnant - sitting by her front door. Ronnie has left her, having stolen Chloe's belongings, and she's scared. "Don't worry - we'll be okay," Susan tells her, but she doesn't seem so sure. Meanwhile, at the hospital, Mrs Salizar returns - with her children - for treatment.

Greene/
Lewis

1-21: "Men Plan, God Laughs"

Benton Benton tells a staff doctor at the Melville rest home that his mother needs more exercise and social contact - but the doctor replies that she is not ready for that yet. Frustrated, Benton arrives for work at the ER, and finds Ross and Carter asking for his help with a man whose leg has been caught in a metal press. Benton establishes that it's a dislocation, not a fracture, and neatly pops the leg back into place. "You saved his leg!" Carter says. "Well, legs are something I can save today," says Benton.

Greene/ Swift tells Greene that he needs him for two hours after
Carter today's shift, to deal with an important visit by the joint commission surveyors. But Mark has arranged to go to Jenn's in Milwaukee this evening, and has to get the 7.30 train. "Since when does a resident have a personal life?" Swift says when Greene tells him he can't make it. "I'm sorry; I do," Greene replies. Meanwhile, Carter mentions to Susan that he's waiting for the announcement of next year's surgical sub-I, and she suggests he could go for the ER sub-I as well, with Greene's recommendation. Greene later confirms that he will give Carter a recommendation, but points out that it might not be very useful at the moment.

Benton A girl called Samantha is brought in by one of her teachers, after having collapsed at school. She has very low blood pressure, and looks almost blue from a lack of oxygen in her blood, but Benton can't work out what is causing it. As he orders tests, Sam goes into v-fib and has to be shocked with 100 joules. Discovering very high glucose levels, Benton realises Sam is in a diabetic coma. Her teacher is shocked to realise Sam is diabetic. Benton orders potassium every 30 minutes, and although Sam is not a surgical patient, he asks to be kept informed.

Ross Diane Leeds tells Ross he's obliged to see the hospital psychiatrist, Alan Murphy, following his earlier assault on an abusive father *[episode 1-16]*. Ross agrees reluctantly. Jake later comes in to see him, and asks whether he can spare the time to be the assistant coach to Jake's baseball team at school. Doug reckons he could make most of the practice sessions, and says yes. But as they talk, Linda Farrell arrives and asks Doug to dinner to celebrate a large deal she's just closed. Awkwardly, Doug introduces her to Jake, and says he can't make it tonight. Jake realizes from their body language that there's something between them, but when Linda has gone Doug explains it's just flirting - something adults do all the time.

After a friendly conversation with Benton - during which she mentions that she's studying to become a physician's assistant - Jeanie invites him to dinner. He's hesitant - but it's just dinner, she says, and he agrees. Ross and Benton then treat a teenage boy, Charlie, who can't move his arm and leg on one side - which may be connected to the fact that he fell over his brother the other day. Benton is uncharacteristically pleasant ("Yeah, they can get in the way can't they?" he smiles) and as he leaves, the boy tells Ross, "He's really nice." Ross answers quietly, "Yeah, he's a prince." **Benton/ Jeanie**

Ross goes to see the hospital psychiatrist, but to his surprise all Dr Murphy says is that Doug is "a reasonably normal guy, with sloppy impulse control", and that he shouldn't do it again! Doug tries to tell him that he has been a little unhappy lately. "Join the club," Murphy says lightly. "Try therapy - might help." Later, Diane asks him, for Jake's sake, what the future of their relationship is going to be; Doug says he hopes they're together for a long time... **Ross**

Benton goes to see Sam, the diabetic girl, who has not been taking her insulin for days. She's tired of being sick, she says - she just wants to be like everyone else. "You have to accept the way things are," Benton tells her, gently: she is sick, and it won't do her any good to pretend otherwise. His kind but firm manner seems to have an effect on the girl, and also impresses Carter. **Benton**

Lewis   Chloe is due to have an ultrasound today - accompanied
          by Susan, who has been worrying about and cleaning up
          after her sister since she moved in. Chloe's casual attitude
          seems to change when she sees her unborn baby on the
          screen, and learns that it will be a girl. But she causes
          Susan further exasperation later when she returns from a
          shopping trip laden with hundreds of dollars' worth of
          baby clothes and toys - bought with Susan's credit card!

Benton/   In radiology, Dr Steve Flint shows Ross and Benton a
Jeanie   magnetic image which reveals the reason for Charlie's
          paralysis - a large aneurism in his brain which is pressing
          down on his spinal tract. The aneurism could blow at
          any minute, but to Ross and Benton's dismay Flint insists
          that Charlie will have to be moved to Mercy, where they
          have the right facilities for the operation. Benton rushes
          him to Mercy in Carter's car, and finds the surgeon
          himself: as Carter comments on his return, if Benton
          can't cure his own mother he'll compensate by curing
          everyone else. Later, Benton and Jeanie enjoy their
          dinner together, talking and joking with each other.
          Benton tells her he wouldn't be getting through his
          mother's illness if it weren't for Jeanie's help. "I
          think Peter Benton could get through just about
          anything," Jeanie says. "He used to think so," Peter
          admits...

Greene   At Jenn's home in Milwaukee, Rachel is overjoyed to see
          her father come home - but it is only temporary. Mark is
          desperate to talk, telling Jenn he's willing to move to
          Milwaukee and get a job there rather than take the
          Chicago job and lose his family. But Jenn is too tired to
          talk.

1-22: "Love Among The Ruins"

Carter   Swift tells Carter he's received his application for the ER
          sub-I - but is concerned that he hasn't bothered to get a
          recommendation from Benton. When Carter asks him,
          however, Benton tells Carter to write his own
          recommendation, and he'll sign it. Carter makes an

attempt, but when he brings it to Benton, Benton probes Carter on why he's making sub-I applications for both surgery and the ER. Realizing Benton is not going to support him, Carter rips up the signed recommendation.

Greene is annoyed to find that Swift is running the board on which patients are allocated to doctors. With Lewis, he examines a man, Donny, who has driven his car into a tree in an apparent suicide attempt, and orders an X-ray to check for possible spinal injuries - but Swift cancels it. Angrily, Greene leaves Swift and Lewis to deal with the patient. Later, he tells Ross he's given up on the attending job, but Ross reminds Mark he's been working towards it for seven years: "If you lose it over this petty crap, buddy, you're a fool." Eventually, Greene tells Swift he resents being treated like a med-student, but is told that he needs an attitude adjustment - and Susan later tells him that Swift is probably right. Meanwhile Donny's girlfriend, Amy, tells Susan she's afraid of the responsibility that comes with their relationship, and she leaves - giving Lewis a note to give to him. But later, as Susan's shift ends, she's surprised to see Amy back at Donny's bedside.

> Greene/
> Lewis

Carol endures an awkward moment with Tag and Diane Leeds in one of the elevators when it turns out that they know each other well - according to Diane, because she helped him beat a malpractice case a few years ago. Tag is alarmed when Carol invites her to the wedding: surely she'll bring Doug with her? Later, Tag is frustrated when Carol can't find the time to go through their wedding vows together. She's clearly nervous about the wedding, now two weeks away, and asks Lydia whether she ever had doubts: Lydia didn't, but her husband left her after four years. Tag won't do that, Lydia says; he's a terrific guy. Carol nods, but just a little too cautiously...

> Carol

Benton is perplexed to see Carter giving personal attention to a man who has just entered the ER suffering from nothing more than a cut hand - until Carter tells

> Carter/
> Benton

him it's Howard Davies, a wealthy benefactor to the hospital. Carter recognizes Davies because he went to school with Davies' son, and Davies asks him eagerly about his progress. Swift, meanwhile, begins fawning obviously over Davies, rather unnecessarily calling the chief of hand surgery and the head of plastics - just in case! Later, Benton's suspicions that Carter comes from a rich family are confirmed when Jerry finds an entry for his father in *Chicago Magazine's* 'rich-list': Roland Carter, net worth $178 million. Benton is resentful, having just received a call from his student loan company reminding him that his payments are three months overdue.

Carol   Ross and Carol have to deal with an entire nuns' netball team when one of them is brought in with meningitis. In case of infection, everyone must be tested - but because the procedure can be harmful to pregnant women, everyone must take a pregnancy test first. The netball coach, Sister Elizabeth, tells Carol there's a possibility she might be pregnant, but in the end the test comes back negative. She is relieved, but says that part of her wanted a positive result: she doesn't know whether to remain a nun or marry her boyfriend, and a pregnancy would have made that decision for her. Later, Carol finds Tag writing his marriage vows, and he reads her what he's written so far. It's beautiful, and shows that Tag is really committed to her: she's the only woman he has ever really loved. "So, do you feel the same way?" he asks her. "Of course," she says. But he's noticed that she hasn't seemed happy lately. "Tag, I love you and I want to marry you," she insists.

Ross   Ross acts as umpire at Jake's baseball game, but embarrasses him when he allows Jake a home run that ought to have been disallowed. Afterwards he tells Jake he's sorry: his old man would have done the same. The two of them meet up with Diane and go for dinner.

Benton/   Jeanie tells Benton she needs some help with a paper she
Jeanie   has to write for her course, and Benton says he'll see her

at the Melville nursing home tonight. But by the time he arrives, Jeanie has already left. Walt, who is still there, tells Benton he hopes he knows what he's doing, getting involved with a married woman. Benton tries to deny it, but Walt insists: "When she's around, you start talking like Barry White!" he says, and does an impromptu impression. Benton's veneer cracks for a moment, and he breaks into laughter.

When Susan gets home, she's angry to find that Chloe didn't have the check-up she was meant to have today, saying that they kept her in the waiting room for too long. She tells Chloe she'll need to get her own place when the baby's born: "I'm not going to let you guilt me into taking care of you again," she insists.   Lewis

After the long train journey from Chicago to Milwaukee, Greene gets back to Jenn's place. Jenn is already in bed, and beckons him in - but in minutes, Rachel arrives wanting to get in with them. "I'm glad you're home," she tells her father. "So am I," Mark says...   Greene

[All's fair in love and war but not in the ER. An intricate, sensitive relationship episode.]

1-23: "Motherhood"

Chloe wakes Susan with the alarming news that she is having contractions every two minutes. They rush to the hospital, carrying a tape-player and a bag of music tapes. While Susan reminds her to breathe properly, Chloe demands the Beatles' White Album, but despite a mad scramble through her bag Carter can't find it. They sing Chloe's favourite song instead - 'Blackbird' - as Susan delivers her own niece.   Lewis

Greene tells Carter that he has got the ER sub-I if he wants it - but he needs to know his decision by the end of the day. After some thought, Carter tells him he has to decline; he's holding out for the surgery sub-I. But then Hicks tells him that it's been awarded to someone else,   Carter

165

and Lewis tells him the ER sub-I has been accepted by another student - which leaves Carter with nowhere to go...

Lewis   Cookie Lewis, mother to Susan and Chloe, arrives at the hospital to see her new grandchild. As far as Susan's concerned, the plan is for Chloe to stay one more night at the hospital then go to her mother's house, but Cookie has other ideas: she tells Susan she can't take her, and it wasn't fair of her to ask. Later, Ross is alarmed to see Chloe carrying her new-born daughter around the hospital, and persuades her to give 'little Suzie' to Conni who will take her back to the nursery. Demoralized after her tour around the sick and injured of County General, Chloe confesses to Susan that she doesn't know if she'll be able to cope: "How do I keep the bad things from happening?" she asks her plaintively.

Ross   Diane tells Ross that she's being moved out of her apartment, so she and Jake are looking for a bigger place - one which Doug could move into if he wanted. This makes Ross extremely nervous, but he says that if they find a good place, he'll come and have a look. Later, Linda Farrell arrives and asks Doug if he has plans for Mother's Day - adding that she's been dumped by her latest boyfriend, Brian - but Ross says he's not interested. In the evening, Greene and Ross practise basketball shots and Greene asks whether Doug's lack of readiness to commit to Diane has anything to do with Carol getting married. He doesn't answer. "If I make this shot, you're ready," Greene announces - and fails to make it.

Benton   Benton gets a call from the Melville nursing home, and he rushes there at once - to be told by a staff doctor that his mother has suffered a fatal heart attack. "We used all of our capabilities," the doctor says, "but her heart was too weak, and she died. I'm sorry." Stunned, he goes to his mother's room, where Jackie is sitting with their mother's lifeless form. They hug, and Jackie cries for a moment before leaving her brother to mourn

alone. He sits, head bowed, holding his mother's hand for
a long time.

Diane arrives at Ross's flat - and finds him leaving it with   Ross
Linda Farrell. "It's not how it looks," he tries to protest,
but she knows better. Trying another tack, Doug admits
he was scared, he's stupid, and he's sorry; it won't happen
again. But Diane has had enough: "Yes it will." She drives
off.

At the Melville home, Jeanie finds Benton standing in the   Benton/
library, looking out of a window. "'All of our capabilities,'"   Julie
he says quietly. "I've said those words I don't know how
many times. I never actually heard them until today." He
thought he'd be more prepared, he tells her, but Jeanie
replies that no-one ever is. She holds him and kisses him
gently as he starts to cry.

*[The Tarantino episode. From the surreal sunglasses on-the-roof-scene to
the quintissential, moving birth of little Suzie to a Beatles soundtrack.]*

1-24: "Everything Old Is New Again"

Carter is called to deal with a child who has accidentally   Carter
shot himself in the head: an airway needs to be cut in his
throat to enable him to breathe and Carter isn't sure that
he can do it alone, but no-one else is available. At first
making a vain attempt to intubate him instead, Carter
eventually decides to cut - just as Benton arrives and
takes over. "Did I make the wrong decision?" Carter asks.
"No," Benton replies - but instead of thanking him, he
merely adds that since it's Carter's last day, he must
remember to hand in his lab-coat and ID before he
leaves.

It's also Carol Hathaway's wedding day, and as Carol   Carol/
tries on her veil at home, Susan Lewis gets ready to go to   Lewis
work - telling Chloe she'll be back home in the afternoon
to get changed for the big event. But Chloe is concerned
about caring for Suzie: "I don't think I'm going to be able
to make it," she says, to her sister's dismay. Later, when

Susan gets back to her flat, she finds Chloe gone - and little Suzie left behind...

Carter   Carter is delighted to hear that, now his training under Benton is over, he has to give an evaluation of his teacher. With Haleh's help, he completes the tick-box form - giving Benton a final mark of 16 out of a possible 40. Later, though, Benton tells him that the student who was offered the surgical sub-internship in the ER has pulled out, leaving a vacancy which Carter is overjoyed to accept. He rushes to Dr Hicks's office to retrieve the negative evaluation, but she has already read it. Benton's evaluation of Carter, by contrast, is glowing, calling him "one of the finest students I've ever had the opportunity to work with" and recommending high honours. Hicks hands the course evaluation form back to an embarrassed Carter, warning him not to overdo it...

Greene   Swift again challenges one of Greene's decisions - this time, to test for a possible pulmonary embolism in a patient who Swift claims has alcoholic cardiomyopathy. Greene, by now out of patience with Swift, orders the test anyway. When Swift later catches up with him having discovered this, his only response is: "Good work." But he adds that the hospital has been served a writ for malpractice this morning, relating to the Jodi O'Brien case, and tells Greene to see him later.

Benton   Lewis and Benton treat an end-stage AIDS patient, Thomas Allison, who is suffering from a fever, vomiting and low blood pressure. Lewis tells Mr Warner, Thomas's partner, that Thomas may need surgery to remove a bowel obstruction - but power of attorney rests with Thomas's mother, who is due to arrive at the hospital soon.

Carter   Ross and Carter attend to a young leukaemia patient, Caleb, who is suffering from a fever. Caleb is irritable - especially towards his sister, Sarah, who brought him in - but makes an attempt to calm down when he is told that the irritability might be a sign of meningitis, in which case he would have to have a spinal tap. As they prepare to run a series of tests, Carter keeps Caleb company and tells him that he shouldn't be so rough on his sister: when Carter was young his brother, Bobby, had leukaemia and used to take it out on him, too. "Did he make it?" Caleb asks. No, he died, Carter says, but adds that Bobby's form of cancer was harder to beat, and medicine wasn't as good back then. Caleb smiles bravely back at him, as Sarah - unseen by either of them - looks in through the door.

Swift tells Greene he's decided to take a chance, and will agree to Greene's appointment as attending physician next year. Greene replies that he will have to talk to his wife, and Swift says that's fine - but he'll expect a decision tomorrow.

Greene

Benton has lunch with Jeanie at Doc Magoo's. He tells her he wishes he could have said goodbye to his mother, and told her he loved her, but Jeanie says it's all right: she knew. She goes on to say that she's not sure whether their relationship should develop. "I like you, Peter," she tells him, "but I think this is about your mother." Maybe they'd both like to think that, Benton says...

Benton/
Jeanie

Susan arrives at the wedding in her bridesmaid's dress, with Suzie, and bags of diapers in tow. Haleh, Malik and Lydia are also there, along with members of Carol and Tag's families, and the bride herself: the only person missing is the groom. As time moves on, Carol goes looking for Tag - and finds him sitting on a bench in the church grounds, deep in thought. "I was thinking that maybe you don't want me enough... You really don't love me," he says. She protests that she does, but Tag tries to tell her how complete and passionate his love for her is, and how much she really means to him. If Carol cares at all about him at all, he says, she has to tell him whether she feels that strongly in return. She hesitates, completely torn. "No, I don't," she says at last. "But I do love you, Tag, and I want to be with you." Tag gives her a sincere and heartfelt smile. "Thank you," he says. And without

Carol

169

another word, the wedding is off.

Ross   Outside the hospital, Diane's son Jake arrives to see Ross,
            wanting to know if his mother split up with Doug
            because of something Jake did. "No, it was all me," Doug
            says. "I did something bad, and I hurt your mother." But
            Jake has already worked out that it has something to do
            with Linda Farrell.

Benton   Thomas Allison's mother arrives in the ER, and Benton
            finds her singing softly to her son. But she has refused
            permission for the emergency surgery which Thomas
            would need to save his life. As Warner tells Benton,
            Thomas wanted to die when the disease reached this
            stage. That was the reason why Thomas gave power of
            attorney to his mother, because Mr Warner would never
            be able to let him die. "We already said our goodbyes," he
            says, "but I guess you're never really ready." Later,
            Benton joins Thomas at his bedside, crying softly as he
            gently clasps Thomas's hand.

Carol/   The reception at Carol's 'wedding' is awkward, but
Ross   Greene and Malik decide to break the ice by starting to
            eat some of the food. Carol, meanwhile, is sitting alone in
            the church when Doug arrives and sits next to her.
            "What's wrong with me?" she asks. "Why can't I fall in
            love with a nice guy?" She tells him she just wants to be
            happy, and she's so afraid she never will be. Doug smiles
            at her. "You will," he says. They are soon giggling over
            some of Tag's duller traits. She goes out to join the
            wedding guests, who by this time are dancing along to
            the band as well as enjoying the food and drink. On top
            of everything, Carol's friends demand a speech! She
            doesn't know what to say at first, but looking around at
            her colleagues from the hospital she says that she feels
            lucky to be alive, and to have so many good friends who
            care for her. "It's been a wonderful year because of all of
            you," she says, to loud applause. As Doug looks at her
            with a wistful gaze, Carol joins her friends as they dance
            together.

Carter's day at the ER is over, and his training year there is finished. Sarah, Caleb's brother, stops him on his way out and thanks him for what he did earlier. "I hope that just once in my life I can make a difference in someone's life like that," she says. Filled with a warm glow of satisfaction, Carter finally leaves the hospital - but he'll be back again in September.

Carter

[As the last episode of the series, this is crammed with important storylines for all the characters, not least of which is Carter's last-minute acceptance into the ER surgical sub-internship. But the reason why this is one of the highlights of the year is, of course, Carol's wedding - or rather, the lack of it. Throughout the series it became more and more obvious that she shouldn't marry Tag, that she didn't love him enough, and to hear her say it was as much of a relief as it was poignant. Of course, what we all wanted was for Carol to admit that she was really still in love with Doug - but it was far too early for that, and we had to settle for Doug's heartfelt assurance to her that she would be happy, and that longing look on his face as he watched her dance.]

Series Two (1995/6)

2-1: "Welcome Back Carter!"

Carter, complete with tan, Hawaiian shirt and luggage, arrives at County more than two hours late. Discovering Benton is performing emergency surgery on a pregnant woman caught in a drive-by shooting, Carter quickly scrubs in and makes his apologies. Benton, however, is already maddened by Carter's lateness and tells him to leave. He is further angered by Carter's evident lack of preparation and knowledge: "You reflect on me now," he tells him. "You screw up, I screw up." He is also quick to remind the student that next year he will be a candidate for residency and should be trying his best. Despite meeting Harper Tracy, a new med student who Carter eagerly tries to impress, Carter's first day back proves traumatic. Having failed to answer Dr Hicks's questions in surgery, he is faced with a bloody emergency procedure on the drive-by shooter who has been shot in revenge. As the rib-spreader is used, Carter

Carter/
Benton

falls in a dead faint to the floor, much to Malik's amusement.

Greene   It's Greene's first day as an attending in the ER, and Morgenstern quickly makes Mark aware of the extent of his responsibilities. Problems between the ER and other departments, appointing a new chief resident, attending staff meetings, and welcoming four new third-year students now all fall within his purview - all this on top of his normal duties in the ER which today includes treating Loretta Sweet, a prostitute and mother of two, who has contact dermatitis.

Carol   Carol assists a drunken father whose young son, Noah, called 911. Having managed to stabilize the man, she speaks to Noah and discovers that father and son live together, the mother lives elsewhere, and this isn't the first time Noah has had to ring for an ambulance. Later, she speaks to the father who tries to leave. She asks him to stay and get himself sorted out - to give his son something to be proud of. The man just laughs. Carol has also discovered that she must complete a compulsory stint with the ambulance crew and arranges to join Unit 47, with firemen Raul and Shepherd, in the near future. 'Shep' accepts, and Doug senses he has his eye on Carol.

Greene/   Greene's first staff meeting proves a revelation. Dr
Ross   Bernstein, the head of paediatrics, threatens not to renew Ross's fellowship at the end of the year: though paid for by the paediatrics team and officially part of it, Doug is permanently in the ER - and persistently disrespectful towards Bernstein. Coburn is sympathetic to Bernstein's point and argues that Ross is a loose cannon. Meanwhile in the ER, Doug is preoccupied with a Scandinavian air-stewardess called Holda!

Greene/   The question of appointing a new chief resident is also
Weaver   raised. Though Lewis has recommended Jane Pratt, her ex-room mate, for the post of chief-resident, and Greene proposes her nomination, Morgenstern urges Mark to

consider instead Kerry Weaver, from Mount Sinai, whose strengths he feels support Mark's failings. Carol concurs but in the end Weaver virtually chooses herself, shamelessly asking Mark when she can start. Lewis and Ross, however, are less pleased with the decision.

Mark also finds three of the students (the fourth, Harper Tracy, is taking the case history of the jabbering Mrs Constantine) and gives them several heavy-weight text books to read. He is only reminded about them at the end of the day and quickly has to apologize for abandoning them before a last-minute dash to catch the train back home to Milwaukee.

Greene

Lewis returns home with baby Suzie and hands her to Chloe. Chloe is training at school and says she had a good day. Lewis looks at mother and daughter together a little sadly.

Lewis

In Benton's flat, Jeanie Boulet wakes and gets dressed. It's almost midnight and she has to get home: her husband, Al, returns from work in ten minutes. Benton asks her to stay but he knows she can't. She tells him she loves him, and leaves.

Benton

2-2: "Summer Run"

It's Kerry Weaver's first day and she manages to irritate almost every member of staff (with the exception of Benton, who has already worked with her.) Her main conflict is with Lewis, who is infuriated when Weaver calls time of death on a patient she was struggling to save. Later, Kerry tries to make an effort, but Susan finds her irritating and tells Greene as much.

Lewis/ Weaver

Later in the day, Susan is called to day care: little Suzie has a fever. When efforts are made to contact Chloe at the college, Susan discovers that her sister dropped out three weeks ago. Susan is preoccupied with Chloe's lie for the rest of the day and later confronts her at home. Chloe says she tried to tell her and thought that maybe

Lewis

this time she wouldn't screw up, but Susan's patience is clearly wearing thin.

Carol   Carol Hathaway has begun her ride with the Unit 47 paramedics, Shepherd and Raul. Their first call is to a shooting, where Carol manages to resuscitate a 14-year old boy and get him to the ER. Though Susan and Carol desperately try to save the boy, their best efforts are to no avail. Worse, Weaver asks Shep to tell Mrs Rodriguez of the fate of her son: Carol helps the fireman who is out of his depth. Carol returns to the ER periodically throughout the day, meeting Weaver and anticipating a bumpy ride in light of the new chief resident's ideas, and bringing in a sticky bag-lady covered in maple syrup! Hathaway enjoys her day on the paramedic run which ends with a trip on the ferris wheel at a funfair with Shepherd.

Ross/   It's not just Susan Lewis that Kerry Weaver manages to
Weaver   piss off. Doug Ross treats Byron Fields, a young boy who burnt his hand when he set his motel room on fire. The boy is disturbed and Ross calls for a child psychiatrist. Later, he finds that, on Weaver's orders, Byron is being treated by Dr Myers, a general psychiatrist rather than a specific child specialist. As he and Myers argue, Byron sets the examination room on fire and has to be saved by Ross. Ross confronts Weaver with her decision but she blames him for the fire because he left Byron alone and also for the child and mother's voluntary discharge because he wasn't handling the case properly. Ross storms out.

Carter   Carter is punished by Benton for oversleeping by having to hold the dead-weight of a man's arm for some time during surgery, but manages to save face later by alerting Benton to a hernia case, for which he is congratulated. Morgenstern too is impressed with Carter's work that day - as is Benton, though only vaguely. Carter spends some time taking an interest in Harper Tracy, allowing her to practise taking blood samples from him and inserting IVs. Benton is less than interested by this avenue of

Carter's extra-curricular activity.

Loretta Sweet *[episode 2-1]* returns to the ER doing the 'PID shuffle': Greene explains that pelvic inflammatory disease is an occupational hazard. He takes the opportunity to test Harper and another third-year, Berensky, on Loretta's problems but the patient is so familiar with her own problems that she orders the treatment more accurately and quickly than either of the med-students.

Greene

Later, Mark is alerted to a new patient shortly before he can leave. The hyperventilating youth has a bruised chest and Kerry Weaver accurately diagnoses that the boy has a pocket of blood around his heart which needs to be drawn to release the pressure on the heart. Greene and Carter observe Weaver's consummate skill as she performs the procedure but Mark suddenly has to run for his train. Despite a hard-fought race to Union Station, he arrives on the platform just as his ride home leaves.

Greene/
Weaver

Jeanie and Peter try to maintain the appearance of simple friendship at work and arrange to talk privately later. Jeanie makes excuses to Al so she can see Benton but her car breaks down and Al has to come to fix it. Later, Jeanie meets Benton on the steps outside his house. He tells her that he thought he could cope with the situation but that it's too hard: she has to tell Al.

Benton/
Jeanie

2-3: "Do One, Teach One, Kill One"

Having confronted Benton about not being assigned patients of his own, Carter is given the responsibility of performing a spinal tap on Ed Menke. Harper eagerly stays to observe the procedure, but all does not go well. Carter accidentally pierces Ed's liver requiring immediate surgery. In the OR, Carter's profuse apologies are dismissed by Hicks as just one of those things - Benton once accidentally sawed off an appendix! Hicks is more preoccupied with Ed who she has discovered would have

Carter

died anyway without surgery. Benton and Carter manage to reinvigorate the man's liver, but he arrests on the table and dies. Carter is dismayed: his first patient has died and he feels partly responsible. Benton insists: "It's how you learn. It'll make you a better doctor." Later, Harper asks about Ed and Carter shows her Ed's liver in a jar. They take it to Ed's local and give him a good send-off with a round of beers.

Carol   Carol, Shep and Raul are called to the flat of an eccentric, obese rabbit-lover called Mitchell. The man is clearly incapable and Carol insists, despite Shep's opposition, that they bring him in. At County they discover Mitchell is at risk from a cerebral haemorrhage. Mitchell is more worried about his rabbits, and Carol urges Shep to rescue them. Unfortunately animal control has been called to Mitchell's flat, and Shep only manages to save one rabbit. In the meantime, Mitchell has haemorrhaged and died. Later, Carol and Shep have more success as a team, managing to get an enraged fat man down from the roof of Shep's ambulance. "What is this, crazy fat guy day?" asks Carol. Shep asks Carol out for a drink and, though a little hesitant, she eventually accepts.

Lewis/   Lewis and Weaver come into conflict over Mr
Weaver   Holdhouse, a strange spiritual man who relaxes with the aid of a Tibetan singing bowl, and who is suffering from dizziness and nausea. Susan orders a head CT but Weaver demands that Susan fill in her charts and run all procedures by her first. Susan demands that Mark get Weaver to cut her some slack, but when Greene approaches Kerry she pre-empts him by expressing her own concerns about Susan. Later, they disagree again over the best way to treat a half-hearted suicide case, but to Susan's annoyance Mark agrees with Weaver's analysis. Eventually, Susan's horrified realization that Weaver has put her own voice on to the computer, complete with nagging message, persuades her to retire to the bathroom with Holdhouse's singing bowl.

Doug looks after a boy with AIDS, Chia-Chia, who has become unconscious after an overdose of his medication. He manages to stabilize the boy and is furious with his mother for not following the prescription. But he discovers that County General clinic was to blame for prescribing two effectively identical drugs, and makes an angry phone call to them. Later, Bernstein finds Ross and tells him not to shout at one of his residents again. Doug's job is hanging by a thread, insists Bernstein, and it will take more than Greene to save it for him. Ross returns to Chia-Chia, who is stable, and finds the mother, Mei-Sun, blaming herself for the overdose. He tries to comfort her, but she is utterly distraught.

Ross

Benton rings Jeanie's answerphone and asks to meet at the same spot later that day. Jeanie confirms, but is late for their appointment. He drives to her house and waits outside. When she arrives, she explains that she's not ready to walk out on Al. Benton is hurt but leaves it at that: he's not willing to carry on as they are. He tells her to take care of herself, and drives off.

Benton/
Jeanie

Having dropped out of her course at the college, Chloe is now going to the diesel mechanics academy. She goes to see Suzie at day care, but is evidently trying to avoid Susan. As Susan is getting into her car that evening, she sees Chloe through the fencing of the car park. Drunk, she tells Susan she is leaving with her new-found friend Ruth to make money on the flea markets. Susan desperately urges her to stay and not to abandon the baby, but Chloe quickly drives off with Ruth.

Lewis

[Another significant episode, signposting a number of the forthcoming storylines, but perhaps best remembered for its perfect balance between the traumatic Chia-Chia plot and a spate of amusing whimsy, courtesy of writer Paul Manning. Ross's treatment of Chia-Chia reveals much of his strengths and weaknesses: quick to anger, jumping to conclusions, and an undiplomatic bluntness all driven by his despair at Chia-Chia's condition. The character conflict is handled intelligently: Ross's showdown with Bernstein promises more to come, and the tension between Weaver and Lewis is not so condescending as to be a simple

choice between right and wrong. Carter's romance with Harper - as with that of Carol and Shep - is developed and pushed forward effortlessly. Much of the rest of the episode is treated with a lightness which makes it wonderfully entertaining, from the Weaver computer (nicknamed Hal by Jerry in the next episode) to Randi's arrival, which draws the doomed attention of Doug Ross.]

2-4: "What Life?"

Lewis — Susan doesn't believe that Chloe deserves another chance and is considering adoption for baby Suzie, but she has heard from an attorney that she will have to wait three months before she can claim abandonment. Ross suggests Dr Halloran and his wife who are looking to adopt, but he has misunderstood her: Lewis wants to adopt Suzie herself. Later Susan interviews a baby-sitter, who looks promising but is put off by the need to fit in with Lewis's irregular hours, alternating day- and night-shifts. Eventually, under pressure of work, she remembers Doug's suggestion and rings the Hallorans.

Benton/ Jeanie — Benton's day moves from bad to worse, as a brief fist-fight with an artificial limb salesman causes Peter to dislocate his index finger and effectively puts him out of surgery until it heals. Benton now has to pass all procedures to Carter. Much to his delight, Carter assists on a gastroplasty with Hicks while Benton is told to scrub and observe the unusual surgery. "There's a lot to be learned by watching," Hicks says as Benton quietly fumes, reduced to changing the background music.

Lewis — Chia-Chia *[episode 2-3]* is brought in to see Ross, and he puts the boy in a quiet room alone. When Weaver is about to place a boy with chicken pox in the same room, Ross quickly intercedes only to be reprimanded by Weaver and Greene for not putting the boy's name on the board.

Lewis/ Weaver — The conflict between Weaver and Lewis is reaching a crescendo. Susan finds partial solace in Ross's words as he takes her aside and says "If you're considering violence, count me in." Susan is overjoyed: "It's not just me!" Weaver questions Susan's handling of the case of a pregnant teenager and her mother and later accuses Susan of neglecting an obese patient when he was in respiratory arrest. Susan tells Weaver not to make excuses for her just because she is having problems coping with Suzie. As their argument blows up, Mark takes them aside and reprimands them both. He gives Kerry his full backing so long as no ruling prevents a resident from doing his or her best and tells them to get along. Later, despite apologies and sacrifices on both sides, it is clear that Lewis and Weaver still have a bumpy road ahead, and Weaver is clearly hurt when she finds Ross doing a cruel impersonation of her in the staff room. Mark, who is staying over at Doug's that evening, is looking forward to an evening of TV and beer, but Ross already has a date.

Shep drops Carol off at work in the morning, much to Ross's evident chagrin who later makes the off-hand comment that he had a dog called Shep! The fireman is clearly hung-up on Carol, checking in to County on the radio more frequently than usual. One such call is cut off with the sound of gunfire bombarding the ambulance and there are several heart-stopping minutes until Shep and Raul arrive with a young girl suffering from gun-shot wounds. A little later, the girl's uncle arrives but it becomes clear that he has come for the kilo of cocaine they find strapped to the girl's leg. Shep chases the possibly armed man through the ER, worrying Carol again, and eventually catching him. Later, Shep is overjoyed to find that she was worried about him!

Carol

2-5: "And Baby Makes Two"

Susan Lewis has taken a 'personal day' to meet the Hallorans *[episode 2-4]*- a pity, since it's also Weaver's day off and the nurses and receptionists are celebrating with cake, popcorn and plenty of music. The Hallorans, Kevin and Lisa, can't adopt for three months but would like to take Suzie home earlier so that she can settle with

Lewis

them. They are also willing to consider Susan remaining a part of Suzie's life as her aunt. It's a difficult situation for Susan: she doesn't think she can be a good enough mother and just wants Suzie to be happy, but needs to know all her options before putting Suzie up for adoption. She asks Mark to look into the possibility of continuing her residency part-time. Susan explains her thoughts to her parents. Her mother is horrified and uncooperative, but her father offers to take Suzie for three days a week, allowing Susan to adopt and continue working. Later, Mark drops by to see Susan: Morgenstern was not too impressed, but he agreed to present Susan's request to the residency committee.

Benton   With his finger still in a splint, Benton is reduced to taking a french fry out of a child's nose. He angrily removes the splint a day early and promptly injures his finger again while treating Vickie Mazovick, a badly-beaten woman rushed in to the ER. Benton discovers Vickie has been in three times before: the first time she said it was her husband, but on the other two she insisted she fell. Later, a social worker tells Benton to talk to Vickie and he asks her to speak to the police. Thinking his words have had no effect, he is pleased to see Vickie with a policeman but discovers that the officer is her husband. "What goes through your head when you're beating her?" he asks. "What a big man you are?" Officer Mazovick is hurriedly pulled away by his wife before he can hit Benton. Benton talks to the police and offers to testify, but they can do nothing without the wife's testimony. Later, the same officer brings in Officer Mazovick, brutally beaten, and explains to Benton that Mazovick was chasing a suspect and fell...

Ross   Chia-Chia, the four-year-old with AIDS, is brought to the ER again, suffering from flu symptoms. Ross and Harper perform a painful lumbar puncture on the boy to draw spinal fluid for testing. Harper finds the boy's struggles harrowing and is upset to find that they need to perform another, as a result of a laboratory error. The mother is similarly distressed but agrees to the second lumbar puncture. Ross discovers that Chia-Chia has cryptococcal meningitis - he is close to the end. Ross's proposed treatment is two doses of highly concentrated medicine per day injected through the spine puncture. Chia-Chia may not respond and would have to be hospitalized, but if he does respond he will be able to fight the AIDS. Mei-Sun cautiously agrees to the painful procedure but is later taken aside by Greene who explains that the side effects of the treatment are often more painful than the meningitis itself, and that realistically Chia-Chia has only days. He offers medicines which would allow her to take her son home, make him comfortable, and allow him to die in peace. Mei-Sun follows Mark's suggestion, which is backed up by Ross, but later the two doctors argue. Harper, herself having had a traumatic day looking after Chia-Chia, finds Ross and asks how he copes with days like this. "I tend to drink," he says, but adds that he's not the best role model. "I wouldn't mind a drink," Harper says...

Benton takes out his anger on Carter through a number of mundane procedures. There's a foreign body extraction, a boil to be drained, and a little suturing to be done. While Carter sees to a cut finger, he notices a large mole on the man's arm and discovers it to be a malignant melanoma. He eagerly tells Harper that he is to perform a limp node biopsy but she is less than impressed with Carter's eagerness for the procedure: "A 36-year-old has cancer and you get to do the biopsy - congratulations," she says sarcastically, her mind still plagued by thoughts of Chia-Chia.

Carter

Carol gives assistance to the newcomers throughout the day. First, she introduces Harper to the 'Turkey File': the hospital's index of drug-users who fake illnesses to get drugs like Demerol. Then, she welcomes the distinctly odd E Ray Bozman - one time rodeo clown, child-minder, and short-order cook - to the hospital as a new nurse trainee. Later, she tries to comfort the wife of a man who, following a hit and run, arrived in two pieces:

Carol

his arm is still in the back seat of their car. The arm is successfully reattached but the woman, Carrie, still seems on edge - especially about the number of days left on their medical policy. Carol and Haleh eventually find the woman in the bathroom high on morphine. In her delusional state, Carrie talks about cutting off her husband's arm with a blunt axe to claim on the policy. Sure enough, husband and wife are listed in the Turkey File, and Carol didn't spot them.

2-6: "Days Like This"

The ER is swamped with gun-shot wound cases, following some "serious gang-banging in the wee hours". Worse still, fights start to break out in the hospital. When one suspect lashes out at Weaver and Jeanie, knocking them both to the floor, new receptionist Randi picks up Weaver's crutch and knocks the man unconscious. She asks Weaver not to tell her parole officer, prompting the staff to take bets on what Randi did time for. Eventually, Weaver asks her. "Malicious mischief, assault, battery, carrying a concealed weapon, and aggravated maim," comes the answer, which transfixes the staff gathered around the admissions desk.

Ross/
Carter

Having left some paperwork at Doug's flat, Mark arrives only to discover that Ross and Harper have spent the night together, in violation of hospital rules. Ross could find himself in serious trouble, as could Mark for not reporting the incident, if the news becomes known. Harper spends much of the day trying to convince Carter that it was a momentary lapse: she was upset about Chia-Chia and needed to spend time with someone who shared that harrowing experience with her. Ross finds himself repeatedly dismissed by Greene during the day and is condemned by him for his carefree breaking of the rules. Ross tries to explain to Carter that he had no idea about the student's relationship with Harper Tracy. "I'm really happy you've both made your peace with this, but I'm going to need a little more time, if that's okay with everybody," Carter says pointedly.

Susan Lewis is annoyed to find that Benton is poaching one of her patients, Mr Lake, for Dr Vucelich's aortic aneurism study. She convinces him that, although a borderline case for surgery, Lake's condition can be treated medically. Vucelich, however, disagrees and convinces Lake of the necessity for surgery, much to the annoyance of Benton who is reprimanded for cancelling Vucelich's consult. Benton is further humiliated when it becomes clear in the OR that Carter has a wider knowledge of Vucelich's study and is aware of the drug being tested, Lazarol. Benton is cautious of the drug's effectiveness but Vucelich seems confident of its inevitable success.

Benton/
Carter

Carol Hathaway is buying a house and tries to find time to sign the necessary papers in the care of her notary, Abraham Zimble. Her duties consistently put obstacles in the way of her signing the papers. Worse still, Zimble collapses in the hospital cafeteria and is admitted. With only two pages left to sign, and a matter of minutes before the deadline for the signatures, Zimble arrests. As Susan and the nurses struggle to save the man, Carol quickly signs the papers, puts the stamp in Zimble's hand and authorizes them - just before the man dies! After work, Carol takes Shep to her new home - a broken-down house under the path of an elevated railway track.

Carol

It's Jeanie Boulet's first day as physician assistant in the ER, and Benton is not happy to see her. Not content with ignoring her in trauma situations, he even snaps at Carter for exchanging pleasantaries with Jeanie. When asked by Weaver to show Jeanie how to suture, Benton barks a complete list of orders in a matter of seconds and promptly leaves. "He's nothing if not thorough," Weaver notes. Jeanie's day proves to be thoroughly unenjoyable: she is assaulted in the corridor, is the target of projectile vomiting, and has to deal with an incontinent elderly man. Jeanie takes Peter aside and asks if he would at least try to be civil. Benton accepts, but the tone of his voice does not inspire much confidence from Jeanie.

Jeanie/
Benton

183

Ross   Ross consults Bernstein about a young boy who was knocked unconscious when he fell off his bike. Ross wants to keep the boy in observation for the next 24 hours, but Bernstein bombastically demands that the boy be discharged. Ross admits the boy anyway much to Bernstein's indignation who says that as of December 31st Ross will no longer work at County: his fellowship will be discontinued. Greene defends Ross to Bernstein, but paediatrics cannot afford to pay for a loose cannon like Ross out of their budget when he is on permanent secondment to the ER. Mark later asks Doug why he has pushed both him and Bernstein in recent days. Ross doesn't know, but has already told Carol he realizes he has to leave.

2-7: "Hell and High Water"

With Doug Ross at a job interview, Benton takes charge of treating Molly Phillips, a ten-year-old injured in a hit-and-run incident. The girl quickly connects with Harper, who comforts her until her parents arrive. The parents, however, are separated and launch into a series of heated arguments. Though the girl seems to be stable, and a plastic surgeon is ordered for her, it becomes clear that Molly has ruptured a mesenteric artery and is suffering from massive internal bleeding. She crashes on the table and Carter and Benton intubate her, but can get no pulse. Harper stands on as they try to save Molly, but it's too late and their best efforts are not enough.

Ross   Following his job interview at a private practice, Ross is offered the post. "Ninety grand a year and nobody dies," he tells his colleagues in the ER. Carol asks if this is really what he wants, but he thinks he has little choice in the matter. Later Linda Farrell arrives at the ER with a costume and strict reminder about that evening's fancy dress ball. Jerry, who just confiscated a bag of joints from an old lady, hands one to a reluctant Doug. On the way to the ball, Doug's car gets a flat tyre and he briefly gets out to check it in the torrential rain. He is just considering lighting the joint when suddenly a young boy, Joey, calls for Doug's help: he and his brother, Ben, were playing in an outlet tunnel when Ben got his foot trapped in a fence of metal railings. Now, with the rain water pouring through the pipe, he is in danger of drowning. Ross sends Joey to call for help and wades up to Ben, but can't free his leg. The boy is freezing in the cold water and Doug gets him to curl up to conserve heat as he leaves to check for another way to get to him, and gets his jack and crowbar from his car.

Having helped Joey find a telephone, Ross returns to Ben who is in serious danger of falling asleep. He gets the boy to talk to him about baseball while he breaks the grip of railings on Ben's leg with the jack. Ross frequently has to wake the boy and pull his head up as he starts to slip off to sleep and into the dark, gushing water. Eventually, he releases Ben's foot and tries to break the lock with the crowbar, but Ben falls under the water and Ross can't reach him. He desperately smashes at the lock until the grille breaks, washing him and Ben out of the tunnel. In the beam of a TV news helicopter search-light, Ross dives beneath the surface, eventually finding Ben and bringing him to dry land. The boy has arrested, and Ross has to perform CPR and an emergency tracheotomy with his pen-knife and ball point pen. After a long pause, Ben starts breathing again.

Ross

The news helicopter lands as an ambulance arrives. The paramedics want to take Ben to Mercy, but Ross says County has the necessary hypothermic care unit and suggests that the news helicopter can fly them there, even though it is not equipped for medical emergency. He accepts full responsibility for Ben, defying the paramedics; the TV reporter convinces the helicopter pilot to help them, saying it's a great story...

Ross

In the ER, Greene is absorbed in a game of networked Doom II with Mount Sinai ("I've had thoracotomies that were less bloody!"), when he is amazed to see Ross on Channel Five as they follow Ben's fight for life. He speaks to Ross on the radio and orders all possible

Ross

preparation for Doug's arrival. On the chopper, Ben has a run of abnormal heartbeats and Doug tries to stabilize his rhythm, but without success. The boy arrests and Ross has to get the reporter to help him. The picture from the helicopter is lost as the ER staff watch horrified.

Ross   Reporters decend on the ER, and Greene backs Ross's decision to bring the boy in with the helicopter as he takes the elevator to the roof. The chopper lands and the reporter begins relaying footage again. On the roof, Mark shocks Ben three times, then a fourth, a fifth and they still haven't got a rhythm - they decide to get him inside and try again. In trauma, they eventually get a faint pulse and begin to warm Ben up, but the process is too slow. A cardiac surgeon and profusionist is called to warm the blood directly. As before, Ross manages to convince Ben to hold on and the doctors are able to save his life.

Ross   Ross is met by Joey and the grateful parents, and has his cuts seen to personally by Greene. As Mark escorts Doug from the building, they are swamped by camera crews and reporters wanting to speak to the hero of the hour.

[It's going to take an incredibly strong episode to knock Hell and High Water *from its commanding position as the series' finest hour. Trouncing the competition in the ratings war, Doug Ross's desperate battle to save Ben's life was watched by 47 per cent of the American viewing public at the time. The unrelenting chaos of Doug's heroic rescue attempt, happening almost in real time, is peppered with a succession of traumatic medical crises and tough decisions. The appalling moment where it appears that Doug's decision to transport Ben in the helicopter has proved fatal is heart-rending. Equally the final scenes where Molly's grieving parents are mistaken for Ben's parents have a tragic irony. A great deal of the success of the second half of the episode comes from the use of the live news coverage, which cleverly accelerates the tension to tabloid feverpitch. And in the midst of Ross's conflicts with Greene and Bernstein, it's wonderful to see Mark Greene back Ross unconditionally - and still all those problems remain for the next day. Combined with yet another emotional kick to the gut for Harper and the amusing 'Doom II' sub-plot,* Hell and High Water *has a fluidity of style which makes it a sure-fire favourite.]*

2-8: "The Secret Sharer"

Doug Ross arrives late for a meeting with Greene, Morgenstern, and Bernstein. All three - with great reluctance in Bernstein's case - urge Ross to consider the renewal of his fellowship and to reject his job offer in private practice. Ross is a *bona fide* hero and has done wonders for hospital publicity: that evening, the hospital will present him with an award. After the meeting, Greene presses Doug on the question of his fellowship, but he is uncommunicative.

Ross

Susan now needs a baby-sitter urgently: Greene says the staff can't keep covering evening shifts for her indefinitely, and her parents are apparently unable to help her further. However when Susan treats Mrs Ransom, an elderly English child-minder, she appears to have found the perfect solution. Tragically, she discovers the woman has aplastic anaemia, a terminal blood disease requiring a bone marrow biopsy. Ransom refuses the test, explaining she has already had one, and would rather leave and hope for the best. Later, Susan finds her father in the day care with Suzie: "I'm here to apply for the job of night man," he says, though as Cookie still disagrees with the idea, he'll have to come to Susan's apartment.

Lewis

Shep brings in Julia, a teenager who has taken a drug overdose. Despite Julia's struggles, Carol and Malik manage to pump her stomach. Shep says that people who overdose on pills don't seriously mean to commit suicide, but is shocked to hear Carol say: "I meant it." Eventually, Julia's brother is found: he explains that their mother died in a car accident last May and their father, finding it difficult to cope, isn't around. Carol also discovers from test results that Julia is pregnant. The girl confides in her that her brother Kyle is the father: following their mother's death, Kyle was a mess and she only meant to hold him until the crying stopped - "and now I'm pregnant." Kyle quickly realizes that Julia has confided in Carol, and is worried that his father will literally kill him.

Carol

187

Ross/ Ross assists a young boy called Alan who is suffering an
Greene asthma attack. He manages to stabilize him, but is told
that another hospital wants the boy. Ross refuses to let
Alan be moved and falsifies the boy's chart to make his
condition appear more serious, even though Chuni
insists that the chart will read inconsistently. Sure
enough, Greene notices the problem and takes Ross
aside: "If you're going to stay here and work for me, this
cowboy crap has got to stop," he insists. Later, the two
disagree violently while treating two victims of a
motorcycle collision and Greene orders Ross to leave,
taking over Doug's patient and informing him that a
formal report will be made of his conduct.

Carol At the reception desk, Carol and Lydia discuss Julia
Kasler's pregnancy - and are overheard by Mr Kasler,
who is filling in some forms just yards away. Alarmed at
the breach of confidentiality, Greene alerts Julia and Kyle
and posts security, but Carol finds Mr Kasler in the
cafeteria and is terrified when he takes a gun from his
pocket. He gives it to her, to prevent himself from doing
something he would regret. Later, as Shep botches an
attempt to fix the roof of Carol's house, he apologizes for
his earlier comments. He tells her he's really glad that her
own suicide attempt didn't work. "Me too," replies Carol.

Carter Carter has his authority questioned when the mother of a
young boy suffering from Bell's palsy asks to see a real
doctor. Carter has his diagnosis confirmed by another
doctor and discharges Wilbur and his mother, though
she is still curt with Carter. Later, Doug notes from the
chart that Carter did not check if Wilbur's ears were
inflamed; he could be suffering from the more serious
Ramsay Hunt syndrome. Both Greene and Ross tell
Carter to get Wilbur back in and check, but he can't get
through to the mother on the phone. As a result, Carter
over-compensates on his next case, Mrs Briggs who has
a history of renal failure and lupus; he orders an extra
cardiac echo as well when he discovers she is Vucelich's
patient! Benton is annoyed by Carter's excessiveness and
is about to apologize to Vucelich on Carter's behalf,

when the older surgeon insists that congratulations are in order. Carter's scattergun approach has uncovered a serious blood disease and Briggs requires immediate surgery, for which Vucelich allows Carter to scrub in - to Benton's irritation. Later, Carter and Harper make a house call on Wilbur to check his ears. He's clear of Ramsay Hunt's though the mother's concerns about Carter seem confirmed in her eyes. As they walk away, Harper asks that they stop talking shop and instead they share a kiss.

Jeanie has to practise her suturing with the surgical consult in the ER - Benton. Both agree uncomfortably that it isn't a problem, and things do seem to be improving between them. A prolonged case of suturing a drunk who walked through a plate glass window gives them plenty of time to talk. When they have finished, Carter arrives, playfully implying that Benton and Jeanie should get together. Benton insists that she's married, but Carter says Jeanie has told him she's divorced. Later, Peter takes the opportunity to ask Jeanie what the situation is: she and Al have separated, but she explains that they had a lot of problems that had nothing to do with Benton.

Jeanie/
Benton

Greene tries to speak to Ross later but, surprisingly, Doug is called to speak to his father on the phone. Ross makes excuses, even though the two haven't spoken in over 20 years. Later that evening, Greene manages to speak to Ross in advance of the presentation. Ross previews his speech for Mark: a tirade against Morgenstern's sycophancy, Bernstein's idiocy and what he sees as Mark's self-righteousness. Greene asks if this is how Ross wants to end his career. Ross quotes his father: "If you're going to make a mistake, make it a big one." When the time comes for Mark to introduce his friend on stage, he does so in glowing terms and Doug looks about to go through with his speech - but in the end gives only a few words of thanks, and steps down. Later, Greene finds Ross on the roof of the building, just as he hurls his award away. Ross appears a little ashamed and has

Ross/
Greene

realized he's doing a pretty good imitation of his commitment-shy dad. He asks if he still has his job; Mark says he does if he wants it.

2-9: "Home"

Lewis   A young woman called Reba is brought in to the ER, having suffered a seizure after a head injury. Lewis manages to stabilize the young woman, but she again suffers a violent seizure. Susan suspects a case of lidocaine toxicity; Reba's case history, faxed over from St Anne's, confirms Susan's diagnosis. Weaver finds the case interesting and urges Susan to consider presenting it to a conference in Miami. Morgenstern is also alerted to the possibility by Kerry and tells Susan it's a terrific opportunity. To build her career Susan must take on more responsibility, but Susan already believes that she has. That day, she receives a Christmas card from Chloe addressed to Suzie containing three thousand dollars.

Benton   Vucelich is assembling residents for a research project but Benton has failed to sign up for the opportunity, refusing to believe that Vucelich would consider taking on a third-year resident. Carter, in between moments of heated passion with Harper, manages to cover for Benton's pessimism and arranges a meeting between his teacher and Vucelich. Benton suspects he is being set up, but makes the appointment anyway. Vucelich confirms Peter's suspicion that third-year residents were not automatically in the running for the research study, because they lack the necessary skills. Benton insists he has the skills. "You're arrogant as hell," says Vucelich. "I like that." He tells Benton to scrub in.

Ross   Doug Ross appears to be making an appointment for a date that evening but in fact joins his mother for a meal. He tells her that Ray, his father, has been in contact but that he told him to get lost. His mother suspects Ray just wants money and is up to something, but Ross reassures her: "He can't touch us - ever again."

Carol and Jeanie treat a young man calling himself 'Mr Sullivan' who has a superficial cut to his arm, but seems more interested in borrowing a pencil. Jeanie discovers the man is Joshua Schem, a diagnosed paranoid schizophrenic who has run away from his residential home for the third time. The home faxes a list of medications and insist they won't take him back again; meanwhile Josh uses the pencil to draw impressive architectural sketches. The psych consult insists Josh is no danger to himself or anyone else and should be allowed to leave, but Carol stalls him by talking to him about his sketches while they try to trace his mother. Josh discusses Carol's new house with her, and says that it should have a fireplace behind one wall. Josh's mother arrives and explains that Josh was going to be an architect but suffered a breakdown in college. They leave but Jeanie is perturbed: in rehabilitation they treat them for longer. Later, Carol finds Josh sleeping rough under Sullivan's arch, the subject of his sketches,and asks him if there's anything he needs; he replies that he can always use pencils. When Carol returns home,she finds that she does have an original fireplace in the precise place that Josh suggested she should look.

Carol/
Jeanie

Having dealt with a hit-and-run case where the culprit is revealed to be the victim's wife, Mark Greene is telephoned by a Milwaukee hospital and told that Jennifer and Rachel have been involved in a car accident. On arrival, he finds that Rachel is unhurt but Jenn has a compound tib-fib fracture and requires treatment. He is urged to wait outside and there meets Craig Simon and his daughter Amanda, who were also in the car. Craig insists on staying to hear about Jennifer. Everything goes well with Jenn and both Mark and Craig are relieved. Later, Mark goes to see Jenn and reassures her about the success of her operation. She asks if Craig is still there and he says yes. Mark asks if she has fallen in love with Craig. "I didn't mean to," she replies.

Greene

2-10: "A Miracle Happens Here"

Carol   Carol's house has no heating, only minimal plumbing, and a hole in the roof where the snow comes in. Despite this, she is still looking forward to her first Christmas at the house. In the ER, however, the same spirit is not in evidence. Having arranged for the staff to sing some carols in the recovery department later that afternoon, Hathaway soon finds that no-one is willing to join in the festive spirit. However, spending time treating the jolly, bearded Father Christmas look-a-like, Stan Calus, convinces Carol that she can't rely on others to spread the holiday spirit. Ignoring the ER 'bah-humbuggers', she gives her own strangled version of 'The Twelve Days of Christmas', only to be joined at the last moment by the ER staff. ("Ten tone-deaf doctors," sings Ross.)

Greene   Greene spends part of the morning making a deposition in the O'Brien case which is now reaching the settlement stage *[episode 1-18]*. Mark is concerned that a settlement will taint his record, but is advised that it is the best option available. When he returns to the ER, Ross notes that Greene is working both Christmas Eve and Christmas Day and offers to take those shifts, but Mark explains that Jennifer wants to keep Rachel in Dayton for a few extra days for a skating party. He'd rather have the time off when he can spend it with his daughter.

Benton/   The surgeons on Vucelich's research study ignore
Carter   Benton as they scrub in for a new 'clamp and run' procedure. Vucelich arrives and tells them not to panic: Mr Chamberlain has decided not to undergo surgery, but he and Benton will try to change his mind. Ultimately, however, it is Carter who changes Chamberlain's mind - or rather that of his wife, Macy, who had panicked and convinced her husband not to undergo surgery. Benton is irritated that Carter is now invited to join them in the OR. During the surgery, Benton accepts the challenge to finish the procedure in record time, but misses by a matter of seconds. "Pity: it would have been a nice way to ring out the year," says Vucelich.

Susan Lewis urgently administers to a priest who is brought in by some youths from his congregation suffering from a gun-shot wound. Despite Susan's reassurances, the priest is convinced he will die and urges to be allowed to speak with one of the young men. One of the boys is already talking of revenge, but the priest swears to God that the attacker was not from the hood. But the priest's condition worsens and despite frantic efforts he dies. Jeanie overhears the boy on the phone planning revenge and talks frankly to him: the priest would not have wished for endless recriminations for his death.

Lewis/ Jeanie

Benton is called to examine Mrs Rubadoux, an elderly woman suffering from a dissecting aneurism. He urgently alerts the OR and tells Carter, who had so much success with Macy Chamberlain, to convince Mr Rubadoux to sign his wife up for the clamp and run procedure. Vucelich also agrees that Rubadoux is a candidate for the new technique, although she is a high surgical risk. Carter explains the choice of surgical techniques, and their associated risks, to Rubadoux who asks for John's advice. After a little hesitation, he recommends the clamp and run and Mr Rubadoux agrees to sign.

Carter/ Benton

Mark treats Hannah Steiner, a concentration camp survivor who was pulled from her car at a stop light, and discovers that Hannah's baby granddaughter, Tiersa, may still be left in the abandoned vehicle. Greene convinces Steiner to submit to a head CT while they wait for news of Tiersa. Later, Greene tells her not to give up hope but realizes he doesn't have to tell her that. She explains that she has seen the worst and the best of people: she has tried not to let the evil she has seen own her. Today, she has prayed for the first time in many years, for the safety of her granddaughter, and she asks Greene to do the same. Ross and Greene are called to the arrival of Tiersa who has been found in the back of Hannah's car. The baby is crying but Hannah quickly realizes she is just hungry. Later, Mark (who calls himself

Greene

193

"the son of an agnostic Jew and a lapsed Catholic") joins the Steiner family, who have brought their celebrations to Hannah's bedside. The return of Tiersa is one miracle, but the fact that she and Dr Greene prayed for it is a miracle too. Later, Rachel rings Mark to ask if she can stay with Jenn for an extra few days. Convinced by the day's events not to take his problems out on his daughter, he agrees, and they arrange "the first annual Rachel and Dad post-Christmas, post-Hanukkah, pre-New Year's celebration".

Carol/   Carol's house has been commandeered for the staff
Benton   party. Benton arrives, introduced to all by Carter as the man who finished the clamp and run in record time. Benton moves aside and bumps into Jeanie. She hopes that his first Christmas without his mother isn't too hard. "I guess this is your first Christmas alone too, huh?" says Peter. "Well, have a good one." Meanwhile, in the kitchen, Shep tells Carol he loves her, and they sink to the floor with a passionate kiss.

[Every now and again ER *gives us moments of true purity and significance. The Hannukuh ritual at Hannah's bedside is beautifully symbolic of Green's growing acceptance of what has gone before and of the possibility of miracles, even in a Chicago hospital.]*

2-11: "Dead of Winter"

Shep and Raul bring in County's share of 22 hungry, ill-clothed black children who were found in an apartment without any adults. Shep is horrified by their condition and blames the parenting, which Benton and Malik pounce on as a racist comment, something that Shep urgently denies later. All of the children are malnourished, one of them has impetigo, and Trey, a young boy with cerebral palsy, has cigarette burns on his back and other injuries. Child Services explain that the court awarded custody of the children to the grandmother; the parents were crack dealers. They call for the grandmother.

Susan notices that one boy, Michael, has a non-reducable mass and calls Benton, who doesn't agree that the boy needs surgery. Susan demands that Michael be put on the surgical list for the following day. Jeanie takes Benton aside and, observing his harsh examination of the young boy, tells him not to take his problems out on other people and to get out of medicine if he can't find compassion within himself. Later, heeding Jeanie's words, he stays to comfort Michael who is scared of the operation. Meanwhile, the grandmother, Mrs Pool, arrives and explains that, believing the mother to have changed, she had given the children back to her. The grandmother defends the mother, but neither Haleh nor Susan seems sympathetic.

Benton/
Jeanie

Mark receives a summons at work: Jennifer is suing him for divorce. Doug is a little surprised: "If you can't make a marriage work, how the hell am I gonna?" he asks. Susan invites Mark round that evening, but he seems set to wallow in self-pity at home instead. Later, Mark sees Loretta - now no longer a prostitute, after finding a job with the help of Lydia *[episode 2-5]* - who has brought in her son with a fever. Jimmy is fine, but Loretta has had some vaginal bleeding recently. Before she leaves, Mark orders some tests and discovers that Loretta has cervical cancer; he asks Lydia to call her back. That evening, he changes his mind and decides to call on Susan.

Greene/
Lewis

Having already come into conflict with Benton over his examination of Michael, Jeanie has to work with him again when dealing with Mrs Saunders, an obese woman whose stomach cramps turn out to be twins! Later, Jeanie receives her first evaluation for her work in the ER. The comments are critical: Jeanie lacks assertiveness and needs to take control more, but ultimately may not be suited to work in the ER. Expecting the analysis to be the work of Benton, she is surprised to find that the verdict is that of Carol Hathaway. Later, Jeanie asks Carol if she has offended her somehow, but Carol insists it isn't personal. Meanwhile, Al attempts to give their relationship another go, but she is determined to make a clean break.

Jeanie

195

Benton/
Carter

Mrs Rubadoux is suffering from partial paraplegia, congestive heart failure, and renal insufficiency, though Vucelich denies it can be linked to the clamp and run technique. He and and Benton agree to try to arrange moving her to a long term care facility but her cardiac output is too low. Carter is put in charge of improving it. Carter becomes more friendly with Mr Rubadoux, 'Ruby', who deeply loves his wife and explains he's not ready to lose her. Benton approaches Vucelich, concerned that Mrs Rubadoux's problems are a result of his surgery, but he is told not to be so melodramatic. Vucelich argues that she was never a suitable candidate for the procedure and will be omitted from the study. Despite their difference of opinion (or because of it), Vucelich makes Benton a research associate, complete with office, parking space, and an increased salary. Carter's best efforts, however, are unsuccessful and eventually Vucelich tells him to give her dibutamine and ship her out. "She's dying, Mr Carter. Nothing you can do will save her." Carter speaks to Ruby but does not tell him how serious his wife's condition is, and gives him his beeper number. The man is delighted with Carter's sympathy, telling him: "You're the only person around here who gives a damn."

2-12: "True Lies"

Greene/
Lewis

Rachel has been staying with Mark for a couple of days and is clearly suffering from her parents' separation. To cheer her up, he and Susan take Rachel and little Suzie ice-skating, but Mark's daughter reacts coldly to Susan. Rachel comes to the ER with Mark and is cared for by E Ray, Malik and others while Mark is working. Later, he finds time to speak to her and explains that he and Jennifer are getting a divorce. Rachel is deeply upset and wants him to explain everything. Jenn arrives and tries to take Rachel with her, but she doesn't want to go. Jenn carries Rachel away, crying for her Dad and life as it was before.

Benton/
Jeanie

Vucelich invites Benton and guest to a dinner that evening. Eventually he asks Jeanie, who accepts. Later,

Peter deals with an emergency candidate for clamp and run. Although Vucelich won't be at the hospital for another half an hour, Benton manages to convince Hicks that he can perform the procedure and be finished by the time Vucelich arrives. However the surgery does not go well, and it is left to Vucelich to stabilize the patient. Hicks apologises for letting Benton's enthusiasm cloud her judgment and Peter, dismayed, cancels his acceptance for dinner - but has to change his mind again when he discovers he was filling in for a last minute cancellation anyway.

Carol eagerly announces that David Morgenstern has been brought in to the suture room wearing a Catholic school-girl's outfit. Sadly, it's only a kilt: Morgenstern has injured himself tossing the caber at a pre-Burns Night Highland Games. Fearing he would miss the celebration, and the coveted slicing of the haggis, he is overjoyed that his strapping nephews bring in their bag-pipes and a noble feast and continue the festivities in the ER.

Carol

At Vucelich's dinner, Jeanie and Peter share a joke, both being out of depth in the high-powered assembly. Later, Vucelich takes Benton ("Carl's new chosen one", as one doctor remarks) aside. It is clear that Benton's surgery was a disappointment to him, but he admires Peter's ambition. "I was beginning to fear that I see something in you that you don't see in yourself," he says. Benton insists that he wants to see it.

Benton/
Jeanie

Ross's father has been calling the ER all morning and Doug refuses to speak to him, asking Jerry to tell him that he has died. Later, he treats two boys who have been hit by a car; Carol recognizes one, Noah, as the son of a drunk she has treated before *[episode 2-1]*. Doug refuses to believe that Mr Crosset, the drunk, has changed his ways and angrily confronts him about not caring for his children. Carol, however, realizes otherwise and tells Doug that if he wants to beat up on a father, he should call his own. Later, he tries to do just that but hangs up. It's been a tough day: he and Susan share some of

Ross

Morgenstern's single malt.

Carter   Carter, having assuaged Ruby's fears about moving his wife, manages to see Mrs Rubadoux discharged and sent to a nursing home. His delight at finding Ruby and his wife are finally off his hands does not last long: Mrs Rubadoux suffers a relapse and is brought back to County, where Ruby insists on his wife being cared for by Carter. For the rest of the day, Carter tries to avoid Ruby and his questions. Dismayed that Carter hasn't told Ruby how serious his wife's condition is, Jeanie prompts him - but Carter continues to give Ruby false hope, arranging for Mrs Rubadoux to be admitted to neurology as part of a nerve stimulation study. However, Ruby is told by the neurologist that she will never leave the hospital, and he confronts Carter about his deception. In a heated moment, Mr Rubadoux demands the truth and Carter's temper flares: he tells Ruby outright that his wife is dying and won't leave the hospital. Ruby, with tears in his eyes, thanks him angrily for finally being truthful, and leaves.

2-13: "It's Not Easy Being Greene"

Greene   February 1st 1996. Mark unexpectedly arrives at work: it's his day off, but he has come in to ease the workload. His personal life is in turmoil: Jennifer is suing Mark for full custody of Rachel, and he needs to keep busy to avoid thinking about it. Mark takes responsibility for a 33-year-old who suffers from a mysterious seizure and dies on the table, despite Greene's best efforts. The wife accuses Mark of having screwed up, a point all too close to his heart with the O'Brien case which is nearing its end. Morgenstern and the hospital lawyer, Kathy Snyder, tell Mark of O'Brien's settlement offer which they favour but Greene storms out, refusing to let the case dog his career and pledging to fight it on his own if necessary. Greene asks Susan if she thinks he screwed up over the O'Brien case and, hesitantly, she says so. Having pondered the case records, Greene admits he missed the pre-eclampsia and now doubts his role in the heart case that morning. Ross insists that Mark sets himself impossible standards, and is backed up by the autopsy result which gives a verdict of no known cause of death. Later, Mark tells Susan that he did everything right that morning and the guy still died. The lesson? "You can't win."

Carol's shifts have been cut back which means less money just at the time that she has bought a house. She declines a take in Jerry's pyramid scam but another opportunity proposes itself: a specific type of worm dung, a rich fertilizer, which a woman patient tells Carol earns her up to six figures. Carol is asked to look after Mrs Henry's $5,000-tub of worms, but is later horrified when they are dumped outside in the freezing cold and soon encased under a thick film of solid ice. Despite warming blankets and a warm water lavage, most of Mrs Henry's worms don't make it and Carol has to break the sad news.

Carol

A teenage American football player, Ray, is brought to Ross with dizziness and headaches. A CAT scan rules out any physiological problems, so Ross talks to the young man about school and his personal life. Ross discovers that Ray has realized he is gay and is plagued by worries about telling his father and brothers. Instead of talking to the boy, however, Doug orders a psych consult and goes to lunch. Later, Haleh asks why Ross won't speak to the boy. Doug denies that he is homophobic, and insists that the boy's case falls outside his expertise. However, he clearly has second thoughts and seeks to talk to Ray in private - but with his father there to pick him up, Ray doesn't want to raise the issue again. Ross tells him to come back to talk to him if he wants.

Ross

Weaver tells Susan that Morgenstern believes Lewis is the best candidate for chief resident next year. Despite being concerned about balancing commitments, and having to work with Weaver, Susan proposes her candidacy. However, Kerry soons starts to irritate

Lewis/
Weaver

Susan, cancelling an ultrasound because of the expense and disagreeing with Susan's diagnosis in a trauma situation. Eventually, Susan tells Weaver point-blank that, if being chief requires having Weaver breathing down her neck all day, she doesn't want it: life's too short. "That's the first time I've seen you act like a chief resident," Weaver responds. "Maybe Morgenstern was right."

Benton/ Carter One patient away from publishing their study, Vucelich appoints Benton to construct a presentation and become his 'clamp and run ambassador to Europe'. Benton is thrilled and tells Carter to keep an eye out for clamp and run cases. Harper finds an aneurism case but Carter takes the credit, eventually having to apologize to Benton and Vucelich for misleading them when Harper discovers what he has done. However, the patient died on the table as a result of an unknown secondary condition, which Vucelich argues should exclude the patient from the study. Although Benton is concerned by the exclusion, the issue only occupies a moment of Vucelich's thoughts. Later, Benton examines the rules governing exclusion from a study, suspecting that today's case and Mrs Rubadoux may be omitted to improve Vucelich's results. He takes the case histories of several omitted patients for further scrutiny.

2-14: "The Right Thing"

Benton Having pored over the files relating to clamp and run patients, Benton confronts Vucelich about his grounds for excluding patients like Mrs Rubadoux. Vucelich answers Peter's queries but orders him to take the day to consider the magnitude of the study and its opportunities, effectively taking Benton off the surgical list for the day. With two of his scheduled operations cancelled by Vucelich, Benton has time to talk to Greene about his worries. Mark urges Benton to make certain of his claims: if he pursues this and is wrong, his career is effectively over. Later he discovers that Vucelich has expelled him from the study, telling everyone that he quit. Benton talks to Hicks but she merely encourages him to apologize: Peter will one day be a great surgeon, she says, but he hasn't the ability to be part of a team. Benton finds Vucelich and insists that, under the protocols, at least three cases should not have been excluded from the study. Vucelich snaps that he decides who is omitted and warns that if Benton questions his reputation he'll be taken off the surgical service for more than one day. Instead of heeding the warning, Benton goes to see the Dean - but after waiting for him for 20 minutes, he leaves. He confides in Walt that he has worked hard to make his career and now can't go any further: "I'm stupid enough to ruin my career but I don't even have the courage to do it the right way."

When Carter observes Greene and Lewis together on the train to work (actually in pursuit of tequila for Ross's birthday party) he draws his own conclusions and the ER is soon awash with rumour. Throughout the day, Mark and Susan are congratulated on getting together by most of the staff, much to their bemusement.

Greene/ Lewis

Susan Lewis and Carter treat Nathan Connolly, a drunk whose girlfriend, Angel, later arrives to care for him. Carter is curt with the pair who he regards as being a couple of losers, unwilling and incapable of changing their ways, which riles Susan. Susan speaks to Angel alone and discovers that she has AIDS: the girl is terrified that Susan will tell Nathan in case he leaves her but Lewis is legally bound not to tell him. Later, Carter finds Nathan and Angel drunk in an examination room and Susan has to pull him away before he punches the man. Susan speaks to Nathan alone and discovers that he doesn't know why Angel stays with him. Realizing Nathan cares so much for Angel, she tells him that she has AIDS and that he may too. Susan explains to Angel that Nathan wants to go through this with her, "if he has it," Angel adds pointedly. She doesn't think he will stay around if he doesn't.

Lewis

Despite his insistence that it's just an ugly rumour, today

Ross

is Doug Ross's birthday. He is unpleasantly surprised by the arrival of his father who insists that he has regrets about deserting Doug and his mother. Ross is dismissive and returns to work, not before receiving a card from his father which he later finds contains two tickets to the Bulls game. Ross goes for a long walk and decides to avoid the tequila festivities on his arrival back in the ER. He treats a number of cases, a few children suffering from bites after an incident at a zoo. Joseph, a young boy who shares Ross's birthday, is waiting for his father. Ross and Joseph share their birthday disasters.

Carter   With Benton removed from surgical service for the day, Carter is put back in the ER and spends most of the day bored and lethargic. Carter tries to keep his place on Vucelich's aneurism study, albeit without Benton, but is told there really is nothing for him to do. In the process, he neglects one of Susan's patients, much to her annoyance. Later, Jeanie takes Carter aside and explains that Mr Rubadoux has spoken to her: Mrs Rubadoux died yesterday and there is a memorial service for her at four o'clock that afternoon which Jeanie is to attend. The matter plays on Carter's mind and later he lashes out at Susan's patients again. Susan comments on his change of character: when he first arrived they worried he cared too much, now he hardly seems to show any compassion. "What happened to you, Carter?" she asks. Carter clearly considers her words and attends the final moments of the memorial service for Mrs Rubadoux. Finding Ruby, he commiserates and delivers an apologetic, well-rehearsed speech about his failings in the case, but Ruby's response is cutting: "This day isn't about you, Mr Carter," he says.

Greene   Greene breaks the news to Loretta that her biopsy proved positive for cervical cancer. They've managed to catch it relatively early but she will require surgery, a radical hysterectomy, and possible radiation therapy. The five-year survival rate is over 90 per cent but Loretta is still horrified: her two children will only be teenagers by then.

Jeanie treats T-Ball, an ER regular who complains of a hurt stomach. Carol takes Jeanie aside and tells her that T-Ball is in the Turkey file: he's trying to get drugs but if she leaves him for an hour, he'll moan but eventually give up and leave. Jeanie, however, checks his file and discovers he usually fakes a pain in his back and orders some blood tests just in case. Her suspicions prove correct: T-Ball is suffering from blood poisoning and is admitted to medicine. Carol nods approvingly, seeing Jeanie is acting on her own initiative now.

Jeanie

That evening, Ross having cancelled his party, Mark and Susan decide not to let the tequila go to waste and get slowly drunk. Mark is concerned that he has that "guy about to be divorced" look about him, especially since he bought a motorbike from a patient in a strange lifestyle choice. They talk about the affair they are meant to be having, and both agree, hesitantly, that if they were having one it would probably be torrid, as the staff had implied. For a moment, Mark and Susan share a lingering gaze, but Susan snaps out of it and gets some more drink.

Greene/
Lewis

[Again the Peter Benton veneer cracks, and what a hell of a way for it to happen! Breaking down Benton's defences gives the series some of its finest, most dramatic moments, and few come better than Peter's pathetic despair of his own cowardice at the end of the episode. Significantly, the more human side to Benton is played out before the culmination of Carter's descent into a callous disregard for his patients as the student takes as his own some of Benton's worst habits. Carter's relationship with 'Ruby' (veteran Hollywood star Red Buttons, who puts in the finest performance of any of the series' returning characters) moves from an initial purposeful compassion to deceitful, guilty avoidance in a matter of episodes, giving Noah Wyle a meaty plot to pursue. Carter's self-serving apology to Ruby at his wife's funeral is brilliantly exposed for what it is as Ruby remarks "This day isn't about you, Mr Carter." Also, The Right Thing sees a welcomed fleshing out of Jeanie and Carol, both of whom are limited in scope in the first half of the season, and there's that heart-stopping moment where Mark Greene and Susan Lewis almost kiss!]

2-15: "Baby Shower"

Greene   The ER is awash with pregnant women, many rapidly approaching delivery. Mark dives straight in to deliver a baby boy but has Dr Coburn constantly looking over his shoulder, clearly mindful of his mishandling of the Jodi O'Brien case *[episode 1-18]*. He surprises Coburn when he correctly deduces the woman, Mrs Wilson, is having a second set of contractions and delivers again, this time a breach birth. Weaver congratulates Mark on his skill. Things don't always go so smoothly: Jeanie helps to deliver a baby born with an addiction to crack cocaine, and Ross and Greene barely manage to resuscitate one child. Later, Mark and Doug are called to a more traumatic case: Dr Anna Castigliano has breast cancer, and withdrew from radiation therapy in the early stages of treatment so as not to harm the foetus. With only a few more months to live, Castigliano gives birth to a healthy baby girl: she didn't think it would be so hard to see her baby now when she knows she won't be around to see her grow up. At the end of the day, Coburn congratulates Mark on the deliveries: eight mothers to return to OB and nine healthy newborns. Mark insists the mothers did all the work.

Conni hasn't had her baby yet and complains that she feels like an elephant: if she doesn't have the baby by Monday, she will be induced. However, Conni hears from the other nurses, and later from one patient, that the beet soup over at Doc Magoo's has put many women into labour; apparently, according to Weaver, there's something in beets that makes the uterus contract. When it's time to clock off, Conni heads straight over to Doc Magoo's and asks for the soup. It's a set-up, and those are the key words - suddenly everyone jumps out with presents for Conni and the imminent newborn!

Carter   Today, Carter is being interviewed for a residency at County. His nervousness is not helped by Harper's revelation that she may be pregnant, although later her fears prove to be unfounded. Carter asks Benton if he has sent a final draft of his letter of recommendation to the interview panel; Benton says that he has already sent his one and only draft, a letter which Carter has seen and felt was only lukewarm in its praise. Meeting the competition makes Carter even more nervous. The interview itself, however, appears to go better than expected. Hicks, one of the panel, notes Vucelich's standard glowing report but all the interviewers are more impressed by Benton's recommendation which they regard as gushing: a 'solid' from Benton is high praise indeed! They tell Carter he's a good candidate, but note that they have many others up for the same position.

Benton arrives in the hospital in poor spirits, and is annoyed to discover that his morning surgery has been cancelled. Hicks explains that it has nothing to do with Vucelich: having been involved in the aneurism study, Benton has been away from regular surgery and it will take time for him to get back on the schedule. Seizing the opportunity to get back to work, Benton takes one of Greene's patients - a man who had a bad Valentine's Day and threw himself onto the train tracks - straight up to the OR. The man begins to haemorrage and Benton bets with another surgeon, against the odds, that he can save the man. Students line up to watch Peter Benton "raise the dead" and soon it's standing room only. Not content with the huge job still ahead of him, Benton decides to try to save the man's arm too, a longer than long shot. Later, Carter catches up with Benton and brings him a Chinese take-away dinner. He thanks him for setting high levels to achieve, being a good example, and asks if the man will live. Benton thinks so.

Benton/ Carter

Coming straight from a house visit with a woman from social services, Susan Lewis is directed to look after a pregnant 13-year-old called Tina. Tina's mother fails to arrive, but a couple with a vested interest soon show up: they are adopting Tina's child. As the wife rubs Tina's back to relieve the pain, the husband is concerned that, the mother having failed to arrive, Tina may be

Lewis

becoming too dependent on him and his wife - they can't adopt both the baby and Tina. However, when Tina delivers her mother arrives. The couple watch anxiously as Tina's mother is sympathetic to her daughter's desire to keep the baby, now she has held it in her arms.

Ross   Being around new fathers, and their promises always to be there for their children, makes its impression on Ross and he decides to visit his father at the Hotel Du Pre. On arrival, he is surprised to find that it isn't the dive he was expecting, and even more surprised to discover that his father, Ray, owns it. Finding Ray in the bar, he throws the two tickets to the Bulls game back at him. "You're not my father. A father is someone who was there, and you never were." Ray is apologetic and regretful, and manages to hold Doug there with drinks and old stories. Later, Ross's reserve having broken, they play table football. They play the best of three, with the tickets for the Bulls game, one for each of them, as Ray's chosen bet.

2-16: "The Healers"

Carol   Paramedics Shep and Raul are on their way back to the station when they are sent to a burning building. Explosions continue to rock the building as people escape from the flames. One mother, clutching a baby, says three of her children are still inside, at the back of the second floor. Shep refuses to wait for the fire services and races in for the children, reluctantly pursued by Raul. County is alerted to receive the burns cases and Carol discovers, much to her horror, that Unit 47 was first on the scene: both firemen went in, but only one has been found. As Greene, Ross and Carter work on the first survivors, Carol waits outside for the arrival of new ambulances. Eventually Shep is brought in to the ER, but Raul is still missing. Shep pleads desperately with Carol and the doctors to find his friend: he led him into that fire.

News hits County that Raul has been found, but Jerry
tactfully avoids mentioning how badly he is burnt. Shep
is overjoyed that his partner has been found, and asks
Carol to tell him he didn't leave him in there. Raul is
conscious, but very badly injured. Mark takes Carol aside
and tells her he has 85 to 90 per cent burns, mostly third
degree. Carol is horrified and later tells Shep, who cries
out in shock. Meanwhile, awaiting arrival of the burns
unit, Carter and Benton attempt to operate on Raul. As
soon as the wet dressings are pulled back, Carter reels
away. Horrified by the extent of Raul's injuries, Carter
struggles with one procedure but has to resign himself to
failure. Minutes later, he apologizes to Benton, who
reassures him: "It doesn't get worse than that." Just to stay
on his feet in that situation was something.

Carol/
Carter

Greene, Lewis, and Ross discuss the burns cases. It
seems the mother Shep and Raul met was responsible for
the fire; she has a baby who could possibly be ill and her
other children have been brought to the ER. The boy has
only first degree burns, the equivalent of a bad sun-burn;
his sister has been sent to another hospital but is okay.
Suddenly, the mother brings in baby Jamie with an
airway obstruction. Although the throat is swollen shut,
Ross is able to intubate Jamie. He sees the mother, crying
for her baby in the corner, and tells Mark "If it had been
her airway, I'd have let her suffocate."

Ross

Susan Lewis is paged while she talks to social services
about Suzie. It has been five months since Chloe
abandoned her baby, and Susan's plans for adoption are
running smoothly. Arriving late in the ER, Randi takes
Suzie up to day care while Lewis races to assist: she's too
late, and is chastized by Mark. Meanwhile, Chloe arrives
at County and heads for the nursery. Somewhat
belatedly, Randi tells Susan of her sister's arrival, causing
her to fear the worst and run to Suzie as fast as she can.
On arrival, she finds Chloe playing with Suzie as though
nothing had happened.

Lewis

His other duties at County being covered by Greene,

Ross

Ross sets off for the Bulls game where he will meet his father. Some time later, the game has already started and Ray still hasn't turned up. Doug goes to the hotel and throws the tickets back at Ray, who is flirting with a younger woman. Ray chases him outside and makes his apologies but Doug just says he was someplace else, not with him, exactly as it has always been. He's never been committed to anything, he tells Ray: "No messy details, that's what you taught me... Well here I am, dad. I'm you." Ray insists that although he's responsible for what he did when Doug was a child, anything his son does now is his own decision.

Carol   Carol is told that, although Raul is stable, he won't make it to morning. The family are on their way, but before they arrive, Raul speaks to Carol. She tells him the extent of his injuries and he knows he's going to die. He asks about the kids and is pleased to hear they'll be okay. "Because of you," Carol tells him, but Raul insists it is Shep who saved their lives. Later, Carol disovers that Shep blames himself for leading Raul into the fire. Carol tells him that they did what they had to do, and convinces him to see Raul. When he does, Shep can do little more than cry that he's sorry, as Raul reaches out a hand to him.

['The Healers' is an episode which drips with a sense of guilt, from Shep taking the call to the burning building because he needs the overtime, to Carol's relief at finding Shep only partially injured, but realizing Raul must be the paramedic who has been severely burned. Setting up the Shep plot for the rest of the season, the episode carefully advances Carol Hathaway's relationship with him through her delicate, honest handling of the situation. Despite characterization tending to take a back seat in the 'event' episodes, plenty of minor points about the rest of the cast are made, most notably Benton's compassionate support for Carter who fails to keep his head in trauma, and leaves ashamed. Benton's comment that "It doesn't get worse than that" establishes the horrific nature of Raul's injuries more effectively than any number of gory close-ups.]

2-17: "The Match Game"

The ER is understaffed, so Greene tells Lydia to get some nurses from a temp agency. The temp who arrives is none other than Carol Hathaway, who is sickened to discover that Jeanie Boulet's picture is plastered over reception as 'Employee of the Month'. Throughout the day, Carol and Jeanie swap responsibility for Hugo, an obese tramp who requires hosing down and later stitches. Hugo is brought back into the ER only minutes after leaving when Shep's new partner, Reilly, backs over him at the entrance. Shep is extremely hard on Reilly, and Carol has to tell him to go easy on his new partner. Shep thinks that he has been thrown a rookie by the department as a punishment for killing Raul. Though Carol reassures him that no-one blames him, Shep is unconvinced and leaves disconsolate.

Carol/
Jeanie

Benton assists Mr Bowman and his grandson, the surviving victims of a drunk driver who jumped a red light. Bowman is fine, but the boy has a damaged knee and a femur fracture. On checking the X-rays, and previous ones taken at County four months ago when the boy damaged the same knee playing basketball, Benton discovers that Bowman's grandson has a tumour, and that it was clearly visible on the first film - but Ross missed it. If it had been noticed, the cancer could have been treated much earlier. Greene tells Benton not to become further involved; he will take care of the situation.

Benton/
Ross

Meanwhile, Susan Lewis saves the life of the dangerous driver and is angry to find that he was high on cocaine. The mother insists that her son doesn't use drugs, but Susan fiercely continues to press her, and gets a slap in the face.

Lewis

Ross accepts that he missed the first diagnosis, and prepares to face his first malpractice suit - but hospital attorney Kathy Snyder insists that they are under no obligation to tell the Bowmans about the error. Ross accepts her decision but, feeling guilty, decides to take his own steps to a solution, personally paying for the

Ross/
Benton

chemotherapy. Benton, however, is furious and tells Mr Bowman the truth. Bowman angrily confronts Ross and tells him to stay away from his grandson. Ross, in turn, is confrontational with Benton for much of the rest of the day. Before Benton leaves, Greene confronts him about his actions: "This is about your guilty conscience," he tells him. "You didn't have the guts to speak up about Vucelich so you blow the whistle on Doug. The truth is a lot easy to tell when it's not your own career on the line."

Carter   Today Carter finds out if he made the match and will be staying at County as a resident. Harper tries to reassure him as he retches over the toilet, but he is preoccupied with his most recent failings - being wrapped up in the competition, using patients like guinea pigs. "Not any more," he tells her. "Patients come first." Whilst waiting for the results, Carter sees Mr Leadbetter, an extremely busy lawyer (soon to be a partner) who has suffered wheezing attacks. Carter is concerned and, after consulting preliminary tests, orders a haematological consult: Leadbetter is severely anaemic, and they need to know why. A little later, Carter finally receives his results: he is overjoyed to find that he has been accepted. Immediately whisking Harper off to enjoy champagne in a huge bubble-bath in a swanky hotel, he leaves Leadbetter to Susan Lewis. On his return to the ER, Susan is horrified to note that, not only has he neglected Leadbetter who, it is revealed, has leukaemia, but he has been drinking on duty. This is a serious offence and Hicks threatens expulsion, resulting in Carter returning to the bathroom for another round of retching.

Greene   Mark Greene is making sweeping changes to his lifestyle. Not only has he purchased a motorbike *[episode 2-14]*, but also he has grown a goatee beard, is wearing blue-tinted contact lenses (to Lewis's approval), and, with Doug, is off on the prowl to a jazz club that evening. Later, a female patient who directs 'infomercials' for a living invites him to dinner, and to star in a commercial - but Mark is a little put out to discover that the product to be advertised is a new hair restorer. Doug then tells him he has other plans for the evening, but, refusing to be put off, Mark goes to the jazz club alone. Dropping one of his tinted contacts, he gets into a conversation with Kathy Snyder, the hospital attorney. "What are you doing here?" he asks her. "Same as you, I suspect," she replies.

Meeting at Doc Magoo's, Chloe insists that she has got on a new program, is turning her life around, and is engaged to be married! Susan is unwilling to believe Chloe again, and tells her: "You abandoned your child and that's the best thing that ever happened to her." Chloe insists that Susan can't keep Suzie from her. Susan takes Suzy to day care and insists that if Chloe is seen near Suzie, she should be paged. Later, this happens and Susan races upstairs, only to find that there is no emergency: Suzie is taking her first tentative steps. That evening, Susan finds Chloe waiting outside her apartment: their conversation is brief and heated, during which Susan dogmatically insists that she is adopting Suzie. Chloe is enraged: "She's my baby, Susan, and I want her back."

Lewis

2-18: "A Shift In The Night"

Having spent all day travelling to Milwaukee and back, Mark Greene is called to cover the ER that night. He's been on three nights on a row, and refuses to come in until he hears Ross has whiplash from a minor car accident. On arrival, he is troubled to find that Susan and Kerry can't stay on and there are only a few residents, a psych intern, and Carter, working off his penance in the ER *[episode 2-17]*, to help him. With almost 80 patients in the ER between them at the start of the evening, Mark orders quick turnover, no unnecessary tests, and tries to get Morgenstern to close County to trauma for one night. Morgenstern disagrees: telling management that the ER can't cope might give them an excuse to close the ER down permanently.

Greene/
Carter

THE ER FILES

Greene   With patients and their troubled relatives pestering him,
          Greene has to tell Jerry to prevent anyone getting
          through without a chart. One of Mark's first patients is
          Omar, a young boy who has been drinking anti-freeze.
          With no ethanol in the ER, Greene has to order an IV of
          bourbon to prevent renal failure and sends him to
          another department. Next, an elderly woman is brought
          in by her daughter suffering from the warning signs of an
          impending stroke. Greene again passes her to another
          department, medicine, but Dr Randall discharges her
          early in the evening: she hasn't suffered enough of these
          premonitory attacks to require admittance. Greene calls
          Randall in at midnight to argue the case, but Randall
          refuses to change his decision and storms out.

Greene/   As Mark makes a quick getaway to grab a sandwich from
Benton   Doc Magoo's, he is witness to a car crash just in front of
          him. He tries desperately to free the children
          from the back seat but has to be pulled away by Shep
          who insists on leaving the firemen to do their work.
          When the first victims arrive, Greene and Carter work
          frantically and Greene reluctantly pages Benton, having
          tried to avoid it so far because of Benton's intervention in
          the Ross's missed tumour case *[episode 2-17]*. Benton is
          slow to arrive. Carter accidentally punctures his patient's
          heart and Greene manages to get the situation under
          control just as Benton arrives, having spent the last few
          minutes closing on one of his surgical patients. Greene
          fiercely shouts him down for failing to answer his page.
          Later, he finds Benton and tells him that they have to
          find a way to work together.

Greene   With the number of waiting patients rising, and the ER
          under more than considerable pressure, the tension
          mounts for Mark Greene. He finally manages to see a
          boy with a cut hand who has been waiting for hours, and
          the mother is angry to discover that, as the wound has
          been open and unseen for over six hours as they waited,
          he will have to come back in three days for delayed
          closure.

212

Reasoning that desperate times calls for desperate measures, Greene gets Carter and the nurses to help him treat those in the waiting room from a trolley. Minor injuries can be treated there, but no procedures are to be performed without a chart. Watching Greene weave between cases in the crammed waiting room, Jerry thinks he has lost his grip but Carol realizes he's having fun! Hours pass as he and Carter make snap diagnoses, give rapid treatments and move on. By dawn, and the arrival of the other doctors, the waiting room is virtually empty. Carter compliments Greene and says that the work in the waiting room was just how he thought medicine would be - helping people.

Greene/
Carter

[Another example of ER's *hallmark rapid-fire episodes, in the same spirit as the first season's* Blizzard *and the second season story* Baby Shower. *This time, it's Mark Greene at the centre of it all, battling against the ER's inability to cope and the consequences of his doomed marriage. There are some great reflective moments pitched into the middle of the chaos - Mark wallowing in a pleasant memory of the early years with Jenn before sadly dismissing it - and some welcome flashes of humour (vomit on Doug's shoes!). The episode also serves to reassure us about Mark Greene: not only does he cope against the odds, but he ends up having fun too, doing that which he is so suited to doing. The wonderfully enjoyable final minutes, where Carter and Greene ask each other what they are doing after the shift and neither has a clue, is casually bitter-sweet. Despite suffering a little from the proximity of* Baby Shower *and* The Healers *in transmission order, both of which have similar formats,* A Shift In The Night *is solid entertainment, throwing Mark Greene into the deep end, and watching him just about swim.]*

2-19: "Fire In The Belly"

Jeanie Boulet consults Benton on a possible candidate for an appendectomy but, looking at Mrs Mendoza's chart and not examining her, he tells Jeanie to discharge the woman. Later, however, Mrs Mendoza is brought back to the ER and this time the appendix is clearly the cause of her pain. Benton takes her to OR, but the appendix bursts before he can take it out, and it spreads infection. Later, he tells Mr Mendoza that a doctor misdiagnosed

Benton

appendicitis as food poisoning and that there's a chance his wife won't make it. But he fails to mention he was the doctor in question. He defends himself to Hicks by making a half-hearted attempt to blame Jeanie, but Hicks is clear that Benton is in the wrong. Having already told him that the general view among the surgeons is that he has betrayed Doug Ross, Hicks now tells Benton that he should not expect support from colleagues if news breaks of his own mistake. Benton takes note and tells Mr Mendoza the truth, though later it becomes clear that his wife will survive. He then finds Hicks and tells her that he has decided to go on record about Vucelich: "No more excuses."

Carol   The violence around Shep appears to be taking its toll. When a drunken man attacks Carol, Shep pounces on him, strangling him until they have to perform emergency CPR to keep him alive. Later, as Shep drives the ambulance, he and Carol witness a violent brawl. Shep calls for backup but, when one man throws a bricks at the ambulance window, Shep runs out and repeatedly punches the man. Carol has to pull him away but as she reaches out for him, he turns with his fist raised and nearly assaults her.

Carter   New surgical resident Dale Edson, a Harvard high-flyer, arrives and greets Harper, an old friend in more ways than one. Carter is immediately competitive and a little envious: he is allowed to handle one trauma, but is so wrapped up in organizing it that he fails to realize the woman is already dead. Carter is also concerned that, unlike Dale, he has not performed an appendectomy and makes this his new first priority. Carter hears of one appendectomy but it is Mrs Mendoza, and Benton, feeling angry and guilty, is already taking her to the OR. Later, he finds a candidate for an appendectomy and convinces Hicks to let him operate, but the pain turns out to be nothing more than a lodged toothpick. Carter is irritated at his first 'toothpick-ectomy' and a little concerned when Hicks explains that all interns will be ranked on their procedures: those in the bottom third will not be asked back. Later, Carter keeps Dale out of the ER so that he can handle the next trauma case, despite Ross having promised it to the newcomer but Harper realizes what he is doing. That evening, she explains that she is fed up of him "making suck points to become resident", and dumps him.

Kerry Weaver is fulfilling Morgenstern's desire to videotape trauma situations for teaching purposes and has asked Iris *[episode 2-17]* to set up video cameras in one of the trauma rooms. Meanwhile, Greene expresses his doubts about re-entering the dating game after Iris asks him to lunch. Later, as Kerry teaches from the recordings of traumas that day, she rewinds to find a tape of Greene privately explaining his concerns about his lack of sexual experience to Ross in one of the trauma rooms, much to everyone's amusement. However, Greene still goes on his date with Iris and they end up back at her place. After sex, she suggests they rewind the tape and review Mark's technique...

Greene

Ross is surprised to receive a gift of $25,000 from his estranged father. Having put in an unsuccessful loan application to cover the cost of the Bowman boy's cancer treatment *[episode 2-17]*, Ross needs the money, but suspects it may be dirty. When he arrives at his father's apartment, he finds Ray's girlfriend Karen staying there. She openly flirts with him.

Ross

Having spent much of her morning with the irritable and irritating Mrs Garvey, Susan is not in the best mood to attend court where Chloe is appealing for visitation rights. On arrival, she discovers that her father will no longer support her, deciding that he doesn't want to choose between his two daughters. He insists that Chloe has changed, that Joe, her fiancé (a police officer) is a good man, and that Susan has not given Chloe the chance to prove she has turned her life around. In the hearing, Susan sticks to her case, refusing to accept any settlement. However, the judge decides that Chloe is responsible and presents no danger to Suzie, and

Lewis

privately advises Susan that if she tries to keep custody of Suzie, she will lose. That evening, Susan drops Suzie off with Chloe. She explains that she has been so angry with Chloe for so long that she cannot bring herself to be happy about her apparent change of character. Chloe, though, is adamant that she can be a good mother to Suzie: that is what she wants to be, more than anything.

2-20: "Fevers of Unknown Origin"

Carter   Since Raul's death, Shep's outlook on life and those around him has changed. Saving a girl from the rubble of a crumbling building, Shep angrily dismisses the mother's concerns and tells Carol that "stupid people shouldn't breed". He snaps at Reilly, his new partner, throughout the day and is curt with him when they go to a gun-shot wound case, where the concerned friends of the victim hamper their attempts to treat the 14-year-old. While Reilly and Carol are otherwise occupied, Shep firmly pushes one insistent, troubled boy away from his injured friend, causing him to fall against a table which knocks him unconscious. Reilly is angry when Shep insists that the boy just fell, and he files an incident report.

Carter   Carter's sub-internship is coming to a close with a last-minute rotation in plastic surgery, or "the beautiful people's specialty" as Benton disparagingly calls it. Hicks, however, informs Carter that to graduate with his class he still has to see a certain number of paediatric patients; Doug Ross has agreed to take him on for four weeks to make up the shortcoming. Typically laid back, Ross tells Carter just to show up, hang out, and get an 'A'. Later, Carter says goodbye to Harper, who is taking an OB rotation at Parkland in Dallas. Despite their changeable relationship, they part on good terms and Carter says that he will miss her.

Weaver/   Today, the name of the 'Resident of the Year' is
Benton   announced, and Kerry Weaver is on edge. Meanwhile, Benton speaks to Dr Bradley about a letter he wrote to

the ethics committee concerning Vucelich's study. It seems that Dr Vucelich published an addendum to his article which included the omitted cases, thus avoiding confrontation with Benton over the issue. Later, Carter alerts Benton to trauma two and on arrival he finds cake, wine, and plenty of congratulations. Benton seems pleasantly overwhelmed to be 'Resident of the Year'. He later discovers from Hicks that he was nominated by Carl Vucelich.

Ross has slept with his father's 'boss' and girlfriend **Ross** Karen, which he recognizes is "really perverse" - but as Greene notes, it has put him in a good mood. She meets Doug after work, and tells him that Ray has gone abroad with a substantial amount of her money, and now cannot be contacted. Ross reassures her that "he'll turn up, he always does," but adds that it could be years.

Greene treats Loretta Sweet, who virtually collapses as **Greene** she enters the ER. He is horrified to discover that Loretta, now receiving treatment for cervical cancer, has suffered radiation burns and seems unaware of what to expect as a consequence of the treatment. Mark confronts Loretta's oncologist, Dr Howard, but he simply states that he gives his patients as much information about side-effects as they need. When Mark becomes more persistent, he asks: "Is this a relative of yours?" Later that evening, Mark meets Jennifer who has decided to negotiate terms of settlement with her husband without using lawyers. The discussion is friendlier than either expected, and they end up sleeping together - although they both agree after the event that it was a bad idea.

Having been paged, Susan Lewis arrives at the ER on **Lewis** her day off and throws herself into her work. One of her first patients is a pregnant woman of 21 weeks who has high blood pressure, a problem which caused her to lose a baby at this time in her previous pregnancy. Despite Weaver's frustration, Susan insists on performing an ultrasound and discovers that the woman has a tumour on her adrenal gland: it's serious, but the baby will be fine. Later, Susan realizes that a man who has accidentally taken an overdose did so because he couldn't read the prescription: he is illiterate. Weaver and Mark, pondering the candidates for the next chief resident, are both impressed although Kerry is hesitant, fearing that Susan allows her personal life to interfere with her duties. Indeed, throughout the day Susan is plagued by flashbacks to an incident where she was searching through her apartment, crying, as baby Suzie bawled somewhere in the distance. In fact she was searching for 'Mr B', Suzie's favourite toy, to quieten her during the car journey to Chloe's new home in Phoenix. Distracted by the loss of the baby, Susan hardly hears Mark and Kerry advising her about her chances of making chief resident. She completes her day in the same distracted state, before returning to her empty, quiet apartment...

2-21: "Take These Broken Wings"

Lewis Susan Lewis is visiting a therapist to cope with losing Suzie to Chloe. Her life consists of working, sticking to a routine: things are getting back to normal - that is, how they were before the baby. But, thoughout the day, events have succeeded in breaking through her reserve, beginning when she listens to the beautiful singing of a church choir, rehearsing for a christening. Afterwards, she settles a bill at the day care centre and finds Suzie's paint handprint picture on a wall, which she carefully folds away and pockets. Later, Susan and Weaver deal with a six-month old baby girl who has the hallmark symptoms of 'shaken baby syndrome'. Susan is angry and upset, but Weaver manages to calm her down to avoid a confrontation with the mother, while they organize family services and the police to deal with the case. "The healers are always taught to move on," Susan explains to her therapist. "I can't seem to do that now." She fell in love with baby Suzie, she says. "For the first time in a long time, I didn't feel alone."

Continuing his work with Doug Ross, Carter treats T C   Carter
Lucas, a jaundiced ten-year-old girl with a passion for
basketball. With T C on her own, and her coach having
to deal with all the other members of her team, Ross asks
Carter to stick close to her. Later, as she and Carter
argue the finer points of basketball, Benton examines T
C and decides that she needs a liver transplant urgently.
He orders that she be moved up to status two and kept in
the hospital. Carter breaks the news to T C that she
won't be able to play in her tournament. He offers to
watch the playoffs with her in an attempt to lift her
spirits, but she remains depressed.

Al Boulet arrives in the ER suffering from a long bout of   Jeanie/
flu. Weaver observes that he is losing weight and has a   Weaver
fever, so orders a chest X-ray and some blood tests.
Jeanie discovers her estranged husband is in one of the
wards, and checks his chart. Disturbed by his symptoms
and the tests ordered, she rings the lab and asks them to
speed up the results. Later, Jeanie pre-empts Weaver by
guessing correctly that Al has AIDS. Jeanie decides to
break the news. Weaver asks if Jeanie has had an HIV
test, but Jeanie hasn't. "How many married people get
tested?" she asks tearfully.

Karen has heard from Ray Ross: he's in Mexico, but she   Ross
doesn't know if he is coming back or if he will return her
money. When Doug says that he is disappointed that his
father will not come back, she asks if their relationship is
just Doug's way of getting back at him, and attacks him
for not being sympathetic about her lost money. Later,
Ross tells Greene that he is concerned by her accusations
but accepts that he was unsympathetic: Ray gave him
$25,000 of Karen's money, $15,000 of which he has
already used to pay for the Bowman boy's chemotherapy.
Ross visits his mother to explain the situation, and asks
for money to bail himself out. This she does, and later
Ross returns the money to Karen: Ray never gave him a
dime during med-school, and he was taken aback by the
gesture. Karen starts to laugh and kisses him: "Ray stole
over two hundred and fifty grand," she tells him - but she

is grateful for the gesture.

Greene Loretta and her children, Annie and Jimmy, arrive in the ER. Greene discovers that Loretta is now suffering from abdominal pain as a result of her cancer treatment. The pressures of the treatment are taking their toll on her ability to look after Annie and Jimmy, who roam the ER with Iris's video camera when the infomercial director is brought in suffering from an allergic reaction to cats. Loretta begins to cry, explaining to Mark that her children have no idea where she will be from day to day. She may need surgery and has no idea what to tell them any more. She is pleased to see them when they reappear: Al Grabarsky and Lydia, now engaged, have been looking after them and Mark Greene will look after them that evening.

Carol Reilly and Shep have been interviewed independently of each other by an investigator, David Haskall, about the injuries sustained by the Vietnamese boy Shep pushed on to a table *[episode 2-20]*. Carol agrees in advance to support Shep's side of the story but Haskall picks holes in her account, forcing her to change her version of events slightly. Nevertheless, Reilly later tells Carol that the investigation has been dropped, but warns her that she isn't doing Shep any favours: right now he is dangerous and should not be on the paramedics staff. Shep arrives overjoyed and tries to persuade Carol to celebrate with him, but she brushes him off, still considering the implications of Reilly's words.

['Take These Broken Wings' *is that rare creature, a poor* ER *episode. Most of its problems stem from the episode's format and direction (by Anthony Edwards, whose debut is less than glowing). Susan's therapy sessions have a gimmicky staged quality which state, rather than illustrate or explore, that her inability to let go of baby Suzie is the product of more deep-rooted emotional insecurities. The flashbacks become a little jaded and the story switches carelessly to Carter's treatment of T C Lucas and to Carol's interview about Shep, with jarring shifts of perspective. This is all the more unfortunate as Carol's growing understanding of her mistake in excusing Shep, and more importantly Jeanie's tragic discovery about Al, are pretty distressing.]*

2-22: "John Carter, M.D."

Mark Greene agrees to support Kerry Weaver's bid for an attending physician post in the ER, on the understanding that Weaver supports Susan Lewis for chief resident. "I think I just sold my soul to the Devil," he tells the nurses. Greene is true to his promise and Weaver is made attending, but he is angry to discover that Linda Martins is the new chief resident. He storms off to find Weaver who explains that they offered the post to Susan Lewis, but she turned it down. Susan tells Mark that her encounter today with a 46-year-old cancer patient has reminded her that they don't know how much time they have. She had something, baby Suzie, but now all she has is work, and that's not enough.

Lewis/ Weaver

Carol confronts Shep who insists he only needs a little time to sort himself out, and refuses to see a psychiatrist. When she presses the subject and voices her concerns, he gets into his car and leaves. At work, Carol discovers that County sent a baby home before a serious heart problem could be diagnosed and finds Weaver and Lewis defending the hospital's case in general terms. Later, she and Susan treat a 46-year-old man who they discover has lung cancer, but who leaves fearing the cost of the tests as he has no insurance. When an insurance company orders that a girl with a painful leg fracture is moved to another hospital for treatment, Carol is enraged and suddenly announces she's quitting her job. She returns home to find Shep and confronts him again about his change of character since Raul's death. "I can't do this, Shep. I have finally gotten my life together; it's taken me a long time... I love you, but you need help. And if you can't get it together to get that help, I can't be with you."

Carol

Loretta arrives in the ER, scared about her forthcoming surgery and a little overwhelmed. Mark tries to reassure her and discover that her chief concern, as ever, is for her two children. She asks him if he will agree to be their

Greene

guardian should something go wrong. Mark hesitantly declines, but reassures her that she's going to make it. "Damn right I am," she agrees.

Ross/
Greene

The hospital pharmacy contacts Ross, concerned that he has prescribed 100 percodans for Karen. Ross is worried - he prescribed ten, not 100 - and finds Karen to ask her about the discrepancy. She denies changing the prescription at first, but then bitterly throws the pills back at him, telling him he can count them if he wants. Later, Greene tells Ross that Jenn is getting remarried. Ross says he never liked her anyway - she's scheming, manipulative, and has skinny legs. "What you doing looking at my wife's legs?" asks Mark. "I'm your buddy, I'm not dead," Doug replies. Doug explains about Karen and the percodan. Greene tells him to get out of the relationship but Doug is resistant: after all, she is cute. Mark says she has great legs...

Jeanie/
Benton

Jeanie Boulet sends a sample of her blood to be tested for HIV, and meets Al before she gets her results. He is baffled by the information that he has been given, and has been told to make a list of all his past sexual partners in the last ten years. "It's not much to be proud of now," he says. "It wasn't much to be proud of then," Jeanie angrily retorts. Jeanie, in turn, finds Peter Benton and explains the situation with Al. "Get tested, I'm sorry," is all she quickly says. Later, her test results come back positive.

Carter/
Benton

It's the day of Carter's graduation, and for choosing his surgical team for next year, but Benton is cold and refuses to attend Carter's celebrations: "You were my assigned med-student, I was your assigned resident. You don't owe me anything, okay?" Throughout the day, Carter calls on T C Lucas *[episode 2-21]*, who still urgently needs a liver transplant. She is scared and, with her parents away, Carter stays to comfort her, at the cost of missing his graduation. Later, he finds Benton sitting alone and pensive in a room after his conversation with Jeanie. He tells Carter he missed his graduation too, though he was in surgery. For the first time that day, possibly much longer, Benton appears friendly and taps his student affectionately: "You take care of yourself, Carter," he says. Carter finds Morgenstern and changes his choice of surgical team from Dr Nancy Langdon's 'red' team to the "real meat and potato stuff" of Benton's 'blue' team. As Carter is about to leave, E Ray passes him a parcel from Benton: a lab coat, with 'John Carter, M D' proudly written on the chest. Suddenly, more patients are rushed in through the doors, and Susan calls on 'Dr Carter' to assist...

Series Three (1996/7)

3-1: "Dr. Carter, I Presume"

July 4th, 5.45 am. It's Carter's first day as a surgical intern [or first-year resident], and he joins the 'blue team', taught by Benton, which also includes Drs Leung and Dixon, Harvard-educated Dale Edson, Harper Tracy's friend *[episode 2-19]*, and Dennis Gant. Departing surgical intern Dr Melvoyne takes a perverse delight in giving the new batch their gruelling schedules, and warning them about Benton, who he refers to as "an intern's worst nightmare".

Carter

As Benton arrives for work just before 7 am, he's met outside by Jeanie. She has received the result of her HIV test, and tells Peter it's positive. Awkwardly, he tells her he's sorry, and asks if she is going to tell Greene: Jeanie plans to tell him this afternoon. Benton is still waiting for his result, which he should get sometime today. Later however, Jeanie goes to a clinic at County General for the first time, and in the waiting room a man who was previously a surgical technician at Southside advises her not to tell her co-workers. Although he couldn't be sacked, he was constantly re-assigned and given impossible shifts until he felt forced to resign. He tells Jeanie to go to a clinic at another hospital, and she decides to take his advice. When Weaver asks her later how Al is and whether she has had her result yet, Jeanie

Benton/
Jeanie

tells her the test came back negative.

Carter   Benton subjects his interns to a merciless test over breakfast. He reserves his greatest disdain for Carter, telling him to take the first night shift, and to cover the ER during the day. Throughout the morning Carter finds himself constantly second-guessed by Benton and the nurses, and he becomes very irritable. The nurses decide that he needs a little "potty training", and Haleh volunteers to do it. Meanwhile, the admits area is buzzing with rumours that County General may be closed, as reported in the *Tribune* and the *Chicago Sun-Times:* the mayor has set up a commission to see how $200 million can be cut from the health-care budget, and closing County is "one of the options" they're considering. On a happier note, the staff are looking forward to the 4th July barbecue and softball game (ER staff versus paramedics) this afternoon at Grand Park.

Weaver/   Weaver manages to frustrate virtually everyone
Greene   throughout the day by introducing a scheme for protecting confidentiality on the admissions board. She hands everyone a huge booklet containing "a few hundred easy to remember two-letter combinations of our most common patient complaints", and dictates that social security numbers should be used instead of names. Only Benton bothers to acquaint himself with the new system, memorizing the acronyms over lunch. Greene is also less than pleased with her plan to introduce regular twice-weekly meetings for attendings, and shows no enthusiasm for the lecture she plans to attend on Saturday, regarding 'modern architecture for emergency medicine management'. Eventually he snaps, and re-introduces patients' names, "and complaints, in English", to the board - to loud cheers from his co-workers.

Benton/   Jerry absent-mindedly tells Benton that the test results he
Jeanie   wanted from an outside lab were ready "a couple of hours ago", and with curt thanks, Benton finds an empty room and makes a telephone call to the lab, claiming that the results are for a patient. He is relieved to hear that the

test has come back negative. Later, he tells Jeanie and she tells him about her decision not to tell her colleagues that she is HIV positive. He frowns. "Are you asking me to lie for you?" he says. Taken aback, she says that she just doesn't want her private life spread all over the hospital, but Benton says he doesn't know whether he would be right to keep quiet about it.

Randi complains to Doug that she's been taking messages for him all day from a woman named Gretchen. She arrives in person later and they arrange dinner, but as soon as she has left the hospital he calls her answer-phone and leaves a message calling the date off, saying he is swamped with work.

Ross

The time comes for most of the staff to leave for the 4th July picnic, but there is a problem for Carol Hathaway: as head nurse she is expected to cover for a colleague who is off sick. "Tough being boss, eh?" says Malik. "You could always quit again," Haleh teases her. But Lily agrees to cover for her until 10 pm, and Carol joins Greene, Lewis, Ross and others for the picnic. During the softball game (which the paramedics are winning easily), she sees Shep arrive late with a new girlfriend, and they exchange a few words. The game stops for everyone to see a firework display, which especially delights Susan who is, after all, in need of some light relief.

Carol

At another barbecue, Benton meets his sister Jackie and brother-in-law Walt, who suspects he's only come to see Carla, a woman with whom Peter obviously shares a close relationship. Carla asks him why he doesn't come round to her restaurant any more. "No time for old friends?" she teases. He's got an hour here and there, he says. "It only takes an hour, Peter. Don't you remember?"

Benton

Meanwhile, Carter is not only covering the ER but also surgical wards, SICU, OR prep, the trauma team, pre-op and all the surgical admits. In the midst of it he manages to find a little time to get some sleep, but Haleh wakes

Carter

him persistently with tedious questions. Weaver tells him whatever he did to upset the nurses, he should apologize immediately! Later he is called away to deal with a drunken man who put his fist through a window. There are also multiple burns victims on their way. Soon he is called upstairs to decide treatment for a man with an abdominal aneurism and then called back down to deal with a boy whose fireworks caught fire in his apartment. Feeling out of his depth he asks for someone to call a doctor, and has to be reminded that he is the doctor. Thankfully, Gant arrives early for his shift and helps him out, before they go for another breakfast with Benton. Some of the pressure is relieved when Carter makes his peace with the nurses by buying them some doughnuts. Greene later finds him standing outside the ER entrance, obviously worn out, with two hours more of his shift to go. He gives him a sparkler, which cheers him up a little, and reassures him: "You're gonna make it."

3-2: "Let The Games Begin"

Jeanie/ Benton
At her first appointment with her doctor at the HIV clinic, Jeanie is prescribed a cocktail of drugs: 14 pills a day. She is determined to pay for treatment herself, not from her insurance. The doctor supports her decision not to tell her co-workers at the ER, and says that if she uses universal precautions and is careful with sharp objects, there should be no risk of passing on the virus to patients. On the train to work Jeanie opens a letter which turns out to be a $3,200 bill for Al's HIV medication. When they meet later he tells her that his new job doesn't give benefits, but she is clearly angry and he accepts that his bills shouldn't be her responsibility. Later, Jeanie is livid when Benton dismisses her from an operation he is conducting, telling her he doesn't want his patient to contract HIV. He would have quit his job at once, he says. "But you didn't test positive, did you?" Jeanie snaps back at him.

Carter/ Benton
A loud, talkative woman named Betty knocks on the door of Carter's apartment in the morning. She lives in the

same block, and noticed that he was a doctor from his name on the mailbox. Talking with a cigarette in her mouth, she tells Carter she's a little short of breath. Suddenly Carter realizes he's overslept and rushes out, giving some hurried advice to Betty as he leaves. He arrives late for surgery with Benton and Morgenstern, who are discussing Benton's plans to undertake a cardiothurasic fellowship with Wayne Lentloff. Morgenstern is dismissive of Lentloff, and suggests a paediatric fellowship instead.

As Carol helps to bring in a patient, Ross tells her that her car is being repossessed. Carol is in financial trouble, and has decided to sell her house. Later she borrows Greene's motorbike and drives home for an appointment with Elizabeth, her estate agent, but Carol's mother has told Elizabeth that the house isn't to be sold after all. Before Carol can persuade her that her mother has made a mistake, Elizabeth says she's glad: the house is in such a poor state she would have had endless difficulty in selling it. "Frankly," she says, "I'm impressed someone managed to sell it to you."

Carol

Greene and Weaver are called away for coffee with Morgenstern, who tells them that there's a meeting scheduled for 5 pm today to announce a hospital closure: either Southside, Central, or County. He has spoken recently to Donald Anspaugh, chief at Southside, who is worried he will lose his job. He tells them Anspaugh's reputation as harsh and a crackpot is justified: "The guy's completely lumpy," he says. At the meeting, the representative of County Health Services announces the closure of Southside, and reveals some staff consolidation measures - among them, to Morgenstern's dismay, the appointment of Donald Anspaugh as chief of staff at County General. In the ER later, the staff hold an impromptu party to celebrate the non-closure of the hospital, and Anspaugh introduces himself to Greene. In the staff room, Weaver tells Morgenstern that Anspaugh might not be so bad. "Look how everyone thought it was going to be when I came aboard," she points out. "That's

Greene/
Weaver

true," Morgenstern says, and promptly asks her out to dinner, and perhaps a movie. Weaver agrees: "Maybe a midnight show at the Village. Have you seen *Caligula?*" Meanwhile, Ross arranges dinner with Heather, a young doctor, who complains that he never arranges anything more than a few hours in advance.

Greene/
Lewis

Having earlier discussed their recent disastrous blind dates, Mark and Susan are surprised to see each other at the fun-fair later, each with another blind date! Neither's evening is going particularly well so far, but when they join up as a foursome it seems that their dates get on far better with each other than they did with Mark and Susan. While the new happy couple are fetching drinks, Mark and Susan sneak off, and enjoy the rest of the evening in each other's company.

3-3: "Don't Ask, Don't Tell"

Greene/
Lewis

Mark Greene and Susan Lewis walk to the hospital together; Mark is envious of the fact that Susan is going on holiday to Hawaii later today - while he looks after her cat! Anspaugh does nothing to relieve his gloom by calling a meeting to discuss the forthcoming increase in patient load following Southside's closure. The new chief announces some 'efficiency measures': the doctor who has seen the least patients during the day will have to wax Anspaugh's car. Mark is now even more envious of Susan's holiday, until suddenly she suggests that he could come with her. Mark doesn't know what to say and leaves hurriedly, promising that they can talk later. While he asks Ross whether he could have misunderstood the romantic overtones of her invitation, Susan tells Carol she thinks she's made a mistake. "He was appalled; he couldn't wait to get away," she says. "I'm such a fool."

Carter/
Benton

After having been woken up again by Betty this morning *[episode 3-2]*, Carter is distressed to see from the surgical schedule that every surgical intern except him and Gant are in the OR today. He also notices the name of Abby Keaton on the schedule, a very highly respected

228

paediatric surgeon from Southside, and correctly guesses that Benton will try to get an elective fellowship with her. He later finds Benton waiting anxiously to talk to Anspaugh, and Benton agrees to let him book an OR for a woman with a fat tumour just to get rid of him. Anspaugh tells Benton to talk to Keaton, but he will only hold Benton's cardiothurasic elective for him until 6 pm today: if he hasn't seen Keaton or reported back to Anspaugh by then, neither fellowship will be his.

Benton spends the day trying to get a message to Keaton, but she is constantly in surgery. Meanwhile, Carter claims the fat tumour removal is a more exotic operation so that he can use the OR sooner, and is embarassed when Anspaugh arrives during the surgery, his interest piqued. In the next room, Gant is assisting on an appendectomy with a Dr Simon, which angers Benton: Gant is his intern, and is only permitted to work with him. He assigns him to mundane duties for the rest of the day. Gant tells Carter he doesn't know if he can take abuse like this for a whole year. Later, Carter is shocked to see Betty in the ER suffering from smoke inhalation after her whole apartment block - including Carter's apartment - burned down in a fire. Benton, meanwhile, arrives late at Anspaugh's office to find a young woman at his computer, eating pizza. He snaps at her for not knowing where Anspaugh is, but then she introduces herself as Abby Keaton, and invites him to talk about the fellowship.

Benton/ Carter

Maggie Doyle, an intern from Southside, arrives today and immediately gets on Carol's bad side by parking her BMW in Carol's empty parking space. Together they treat a man, Mr Sadowski, who is suffering from kidney stone pain - and who also happens to be an ex-teacher from St Monica's, where it seems both Carol and Maggie went to school. He tells Carol he's glad she made the grade and became a doctor, and Carol seems uncomfortable to have to correct him. Her attempts to make conversation with Doyle then fall flat when she gives her very brief answers, but Doyle does reveal that

Carol

her father is a policeman and her mother is a nurse. She tells Carol she was kicked out of nursing school: "I was never very good at following orders." Meanwhile, an elderly male patient's claim to have been attacked by a kangaroo is confirmed by television and radio reports that animal control officers are tracking an escaped marsupial in Ukrainian Village. Later, two of the officers arrive at the hospital, one having been accidentally shot by the other! Jerry works out that the animal is probably in his neighbourhood, and calls the Australian Embassy for advice on how to feed the kangaroo if he should find it. Later, on her way home, Carol sees the escaped creature, rummaging around in some dustbins...

Greene/
Lewis

Having spent the whole day with one patient, Mr Johnson, who constantly appeared to be on the verge of death, Greene is handed the waxing polish to use on Anspaugh's car. He tells Ross that "I've given it a lot of thought, and I've decided to be spontaneous", and is on the verge of accepting Susan's invitation when she gives him an awkward apology, saying that she hadn't meant it as a serious suggestion. With neither of them very sure of the other's feelings, Susan tells Mark she'll see him in ten days, and leaves to start her holiday.

Jeanie/
Weaver

Benton, Weaver and Jeanie treat a man who has been impaled in the chest by several large shards of glass. When Weaver asks Jeanie to remove some of the glass, Jeanie makes her apologies and leaves the room, fearing that she might cut herself. Kerry later finds her outside, and asks for an explanation, but Jeanie merely says she didn't feel well. Kerry asks after Al, saying that it must be difficult to be sick all alone. She tells her about a lawyer friend of hers who is HIV positive and hasn't told his co-workers. "It's got to be hard to carry that around all day," she says. "It is," Jeanie finally replies. Kerry tells her she's glad Jeanie decided to carry on working. "It'd be a real loss to the patients if you quit," she tells her.

3-4: "Last Call"

6.02 am. In Doug Ross's apartment, a woman gets out of   Ross
his bed and struggles to open the door. She is in a daze,
the combined effect of cocaine and tequila from the
previous night. Doug insists that she can't drive home,
and takes charge of her car. On their way to her flat, she
has a seizure of some kind, flailing her arms about wildly
and foaming at the mouth. Doug drives her to the ER,
where Greene and Weaver take charge of her. Carol asks
Doug what her name is, but he doesn't know and goes
out to her car to search for a registration or some kind of
ID. He identifies her as Nadine Wilks, but by the time he
returns to the trauma room she is dead.

Carter tells Gant about his problems living with his   Carter/
parents again, after his apartment block burned down   Benton
[episode 3-3], and Gant offers him a room at his place
instead. But another problem remains: a set of slides
Benton was planning to use in a lecture today were in
Carter's apartment when it was destroyed, and Benton
starts the lecture before Carter can explain. He trails off
awkwardly, and the lecture is rescheduled for tomorrow
morning. Later Abby Keaton meets Benton and Carter
in the cafeteria and asks for their help with a young
patient, Laura Armitage, who is reluctant to have another
in a long series of operations. Carter persuades her to
consent, and Keaton tells him to scrub in for the surgery,
in which Benton's performance is impressive. Later he is
less successful at giving advice and reassurance to
Laura's mother, and Keaton tells him that he has to
improve his manner with patients and relatives. "You've
got great hands. Now you've got to show some heart,"
she tells him. After work, Benton pays a visit to the
restaurant owned by Carla Rees *[episode 3-1]*. She is
delighted, but surprised, to see him. "You must have a
taste in your mouth for something, to come all the way
out here," she says, seductively...

Jeanie is feeling nauseous, perhaps as a result of her   Jeanie
cocktail of HIV pills. With Wendy, she puts a splint on a

man's ankle, helped by the attractive man who brought the patient in. He is a dance instructor, and the nurses take delight in having him teach them a few steps - but he is clearly more interested in Jeanie. For the first time in ages, Jeanie looks just a little happy as he encourages her to dance in the waiting room. When she has finished dealing with his friend's ankle, he asks her out to dinner. Reluctantly, she tells him that she can't, and he leaves feeling rather rejected.

| Greene/ | Greene is surprised when Ross says he is staying in the |
| Ross | ER for the start of his shift, having arrived much earlier |

with Nadine Wilks. He tells him Nadine tested positive for cocaine, and Ross angrily says he'll provide a specimen. As a 12-year-old boy is brought in with a gun-shot wound to the chest, Weaver tells Greene she's also concerned about Doug's alcohol levels. She joins him in trauma, watching over his shoulder, which annoys Doug even further. Later, he is curt with the police officers who question him about Nadine, asking him if he prescribed or gave any drugs to her. Greene is present for the interview. Later, a woman arrives at the ER looking for Doug and he meets her outside: it's Claire Wilks, Nadine's sister. She tells him Nadine died like she had lived: drunk, high and alone. Doug tells her that actually a friend brought her in, but she replies: "I know what kind of friends she had at 4 am." She adds that Nadine was epileptic, but often didn't wear the bracelet that would warn people of her condition.

Carol   Carol has arranged to have dinner with her mother this evening, and is not looking forward to it. E Ray suggests she should attend his yoga classes at Malcolm X Community College, which Doyle adds was where she studied her first year: it has a very prestigious pre-med night-school, she tells her. Carol then talks to a 15-year-old girl who needs a pelvic exam, but does not want it done by a male doctor. She tells Greene she can do it herself but Greene insists it needs a doctor, and assigns Doyle. Maggie hasn't done a pelvic exam in six months, though, and Carol has to guide her through it. Later,

Carol's mother arrives early, and they go for dinner at Doc Magoo's. Carol admits she's sick of teaching interns how to earn quadruple her salary, but her mother says there's nothing she can do about it. Maybe not, Carol says. Regarding her financial worries, Carol's mother suggests that she might give her some money as "a kind of rent", so that she could stay over at Carol's house on Saturday nights.

After her mother has left, Carol bemoans the fact that her mother will be staying with her for one night a week from now on, but thinks about Carter's suggestion that she could always work Saturday nights. As she leaves, Carol looks at the course-book from the community college which E Ray has brought in, tears out the page about pre-med courses, and puts it into her pocket. At the station, she finds Doug Ross waiting for her. "I think I really did it this time," he says, and tells her about his conversation with Claire Wilks. He never told her that he was anything but Nadine's doctor. But Carol says she won't let Doug cry on her shoulder, and she won't reassure him that he's a great guy after all. "I'm just not playing," she says. "You're on your own." She leaves him to make his way back to his flat, where he finds Nadine's bracelet lying discarded in his bathroom. His answerphone plays back several messages from different women, all wanting him to call them back - he erases them all.

Carol/
Ross

3-5: "Ghosts"

It's Hallowe'en, and the effect of thunder and lightning outside is heightened by the faulty lighting inside the ER. Weaver and Gant deal with a suitably weird patient, who is dressed and made-up as Frankenstein's Monster. Gant performs well and is encouraged by Weaver, but when Benton arrives he is harsh on the young doctor and has Carter take over from him. Afterwards, Gant tells Carter he's worried about Benton's lukewarm evaluation of his work, but Carter says he had exactly the same from him last year. Later, both help Keaton and Benton treat an

Benton/
Carter

eight-year-old girl injured in a hit-and-run incident, while Greene and Carol try unsuccessfully to save her father. Carter holds her hand as she goes to surgery, and tells her her father is okay, although he knows he has died: a decision Benton criticizes, but Keaton agrees with. Benton is then sent to fill in for Keaton trick-or-treating with a group of children from the wards, which he does fairly badly. Later, Carter himself goes to the girl after her surgery and tells her that her father is dead.

Greene/ Weaver   As various members of staff discuss the supposed 'ghost' on the fifth floor of the hospital, experienced as a rush of cold air, Greene is more concerned about Susan's imminent return from Hawaii. Anspaugh calls him to his office and advises him that Weaver is moving ahead on the track to tenure, having had her interesting research topic approved. He suggests that Greene could do a study on one of the subjects Weaver considered and rejected: namely, pus.

Benton   After spending some time trawling through obscure journal articles for Benton, Gant finds his teacher and demands to know why he has been given a mediocre evaluation. Benton agrees his work isn't mediocre, but says he has to do better than the other interns: because he is black, people will assume that he has been employed to fill a quota. "If you want to prove them wrong you have to work twice as hard, stay twice as late, to be twice as good." Gant asks if Benton himself ticked the 'African-American' box on the equal opportunities form, and Benton says he didn't. "Maybe you should just tell people," says Gant, "so you don't have to keep proving it all the time."

Jeanie   Jeanie and Doyle are assigned to treat an elderly woman in the end stage of a fatal disease, who appears to have taken an overdose of medication and is the subject of a DNR [do not resuscitate] order. As Jeanie tries to resuscitate her, Doyle questions whether they should even try. Together they talk to the woman's husband, Mr Jennings, who reveals that it was he who gave her the overdose, on her request - but then became afraid and called the ambulance. Later, Mrs Jennings dies, and her husband tells Jeanie he doesn't know if he did the right thing. "You stayed with her," Jeanie says. "You helped her when she needed you." When she meets Al later at Doc Magoo's, she tells him about the couple, her voice cracking. "We didn't have that kind of marriage, did we Al? We didn't love, we didn't cherish, we didn't respect. And now you've killed me." She walks out, leaving Al stunned and silent.

Carol is 15 minutes late for her first pre-med physics lecture, where her young lab partner William compliments her nurse's outfit, assuming it's a Hallowe'en costume! Later she accompanies Doug Ross on the 'health-mobile', a roving healthcare bus which tours the poorer (and more dangerous) parts of the community - a scheme pioneered by Anspaugh at Southside. Their involvement in the scheme has an off-putting start when a girl, Charlie, stumbles in pretending to have a knife-wound as a Hallowe'en prank. Her real request is for condoms, which Ross reluctantly gives her when she implies that she is a prostitute, although he doesn't believe she's even 15 years old. He and Carol then deal with a real stabbing, having to perform some impromptu surgery in the pouring rain before taking the victim back to the ER in the bus. On their way back, Carol tells Ross about her course and he offers her a few words of encouragement.

Carol//
Ross

Susan arrives back in the ER, but she reveals to Mark that she never made it to Hawaii: her fear of flying overcame her in Phoenix when she was meant to change planes. Instead she stayed with Chloe and baby Suzie. She accompanies Mark to the 'haunted' fifth floor, where Mark is supposed to pronounce death on a patient. At first he goes to the wrong man and both doctors jump when he wakes up, saying: "Next bed, doctor." Reaching the correct patient, both feel a rush of cold air go right through them. Later they go to a Hallowe'en party at the Jazz Note club, where most of the staff are in attendance

Lewis/
Greene

and Haleh is a singer! Mark tells Susan his worries about Weaver and tenure, but her advice is not to get too caught up in his job: there is more to life. Hesitantly, he asks her to dance...

3-6: "Fear of Flying"

Greene/ Lewis
Lewis has to overcome her fear of flying when she and Greene fly in a helicopter to the scene of a horrific car accident involving a family of four. The nearest hospital is Boon County, but it doesn't have a trauma centre, and Greene and Lewis find they are the first on the scene. The driver of the other vehicle is dead at the scene. While Greene puts the family's father (David Herlihy, a paediatrician) into the chopper, Lewis finds the mother, Gail, trapped in the car with her children - seven-year-old Zach, and Megan, who is only ten days old. Zach has facial fractures, and Lewis is concerned that his airway is obstructed. Greene helps her bag him and move him into the chopper. Mother and daughter are left to be taken to Boon County once they've been retrieved from the car, while father and son are taken to Cook County General.

Carol
Carol soon becomes impatient with the incompetence of Rhonda Sterling, a 'float' nurse from medical surgery replacing Haleh while she is on vacation. She keeps a patient waiting for potassium while she spends ages trying to find it, then insists the patient must continue waiting while she takes her break. Carol orders Sterling to assist with Ross and Carter's treatment of young Zach Herlihy, but when asked for saline she almost stops his heart by administering the potassium instead. Once his breathing is stabilized, Zach is taken up to the OR for surgery to deal with a pancreatic injury. Carol tells Rhonda she shouldn't be working in the ER. "You think I don't know that?" Rhonda says.

Greene/ Lewis
Greene and Lewis manage to revive David Herlihy, Zach's father, but are concerned when he seems not to remember the accident or be able to understand where he is. Greene demands a rush on the head CT he has

ordered, as Lewis prepares to go back and retrieve Gail Herlihy and the baby Megan from the crash-site.

Jeanie and Doyle take charge of the body of an elderly man who has died of prostate cancer, and asked to respect his wish to be cryogenically frozen, alongside his wife who died eight years ago. Jeanie dutifully calls the cryogenics company in California, who tell her to keep the man on ice until they arrive - she and Doyle then go to Doc Magoo's to request all the ice they can spare. When the cryogenics company rep arrives Jeanie doubts his medical qualifications, but they administer the medicine he asks for. After all, it can't do the patient any harm...

Jeanie

As Greene treats the relatively uninjured Gail Herlihy, Ross, Gant and Benton examine baby Megan. Her pulse and colour are fine, but her abdomen is distended and she cries constantly. Benton decides she needs an exploratory lacorotomy, and pages Keaton. He finds Gail in trauma room one and gets her to sign the consent form, although she is used to having her husband David make decisions like this. Keaton asks Benton and Gant to join her for Megan's surgery. They locate and repair her perforated intestine, but as they prepare to close Keaton is called away to deal with Zach, who Carter thinks may be bleeding again. Keaton tells Benton to close on his own: "Nothing fancy," she tells him. Shortly after she leaves, however, Benton sees what he thinks is fibre debris on the surface of Megan's liver. He attempts to clean it up before closing, but causes it to bleed instead, and after a long period of trying to correct his mistake, he surrenders his pride and lets Gant fetch Keaton.

Benton

Greene tries to explain to David Herlihy how his wife and children are progressing, but David seems to forget information from one moment to the next, constantly asking why he is in a hospital bed. Greene decides to re-unite him with Gail Herlihy, and Lewis brings her into the room. It's a risky strategy, but on seeing his wife David does seem to recover his memory of the accident.

Greene

Greene tells the couple that Zach has recovered and that Gail can see him, but he has not been informed about Megan's progress for some time.

Benton   Keaton is furious at Benton's mistake with Megan: the baby has lost 100 cc of blood, roughly one-third of her volume. Benton has inadvertantly ripped away the liver capsule, and Keaton has difficulty stopping the bleeding. Once stabilized she is taken to the neo-natal intensive care unit, but there her lung collapses and she stops breathing for 22 minutes. She is revived and stabilized again, but her condition looks poor. Keaton takes Benton aside and tells him he ought to have called for her as soon as he knew he was out of his depth. He ignored her specific instructions, assuming that what he knew about surgery in adults could be used to perform surgery on an infant. "You arrogantly and blindly think you have all the answers," she tells him, and adds: "If that baby dies, it'll be my responsibility - but it'll be your fault." As Benton walks away from the NICU, Gant arrives needing him to sign a code sheet, and tries to offer some comfort, telling Benton that everyone makes mistakes. "Any other words of wisdom, Dr Gant?" is Benton's sarcastic reply. As the lift doors close on him, Gant tells him: "You're a real prick, you know that?" Later, Benton returns to NICU and stands over Megan and her bypass machine, trying to recite the Lord's Prayer - but to his horror he finds he can't remember the words.

[Another episode driven by one particular event, although it's more subtle than usual, splitting up the members of the Herlihy family for the various doctors to deal with. Each plot is interesting in its own way, with the added dimension of Greene and Lewis hinting at their their attraction to each other: on one occasion Susan catches Mark watching her for no reason at all, and later Mark catches her doing the same thing, which leads us to believe that something is, at last, about to develop between them. But the most dramatic storyline is Benton's treatment of baby Megan, in which his usual overconfidence is shown to have devastating consequences. Abby Keaton's merciless criticism is brilliant and well overdue, but it's rather more satisfying to hear Gant call Benton "a real prick", which must have had millions of viewers cheering him on.]

3-7: "No Brain, No Gain"

As Carter arrives for work, Gant continues on a torturously long shift - and he still has 18 hours to go. The two of them agree to keep a look out for one of Dale Edson's patients who has gone missing - a Mr Percy, who has a tumour in his throat. Benton, meanwhile, is where he's been for most of the last six days - with baby Megan Herlihy *[episode 3-6]*. She is haemhorraging, but Keaton tells him they have only recently given her a blood transfusion: the best thing they can do for her is to do nothing. She adds that, for now, Benton should be more of an observer than a participant, in all cases: he has to learn patience to grow as a surgeon. But when Benton takes charge of one of Ross's patients, a 13-year-old gun-shot victim who has had no pulse for twenty minutes (Ross has already called time of death), Keaton doesn't object. Benton manages to get the boy's heart beating again, but Ross and others are sure that he is brain-dead.

Carter/
Benton

Greene meets Carol on the way to work, and when he accidentally calls her Susan she realizes what's on his mind. Carol tells him to put all the staff out of their misery and ask Susan out! Carol is preoccupied with Rhonda Sterling again throughout the day: unfortunately Jerry called for a 'float' before Carol could veto Rhonda. Greene, meanwhile, takes up Carol's suggestion and asks Susan to dinner tonight. She says she is busy, and seems hesitant about committing herself to another night, adding that they need to talk. Later, Greene treats a comparative anthropologist who is studying the mating habits of humans and birds. He seems convinced by her assessment of staff and patients' romantic intentions, including her view that Wendy is coming on to Jerry, and that Susan is romantically involved with Morgenstern! He tells Carol but she doesn't believe a word of it. Susan certainly hasn't mentioned anything, but then Carol agrees that if she was seeing Morgenstern, she wouldn't tell either.

Greene/
Carol

Ross/
Greene

Greene and Ross clash again, this time over the case of a young boy with an infected human bite on his finger: Ross wants to call the police because the father won't allow his son to have IV antibiotics, but Greene says oral antibiotics could be used instead. Ross accuses Greene of being incapable of respecting his decisions. At first Greene claims that it's nothing personal, but Ross says he's been "on a moral high-horse ever since I came in with that OD" *[episode 3-4]*. Later, Greene admits that he let his personal feelings cloud his judgement, and there is a kind of reconciliation. "You don't need to beat me up about making a mess out of my life," Ross says. "I like to do that myself." Ross tells Greene he's seeing a psychiatrist.

Carter

Carter finds Mr Percy, who is trying to eat some sweets Wendy has brought in - despite the fact that he cannot swallow anything because of the tumour. Carter is invited to join Anspaugh, Edson and a visiting Japanese surgeon for the operation, but when he talks to Mr Percy it becomes obvious that he doesn't understand what is happening. Carter tells Edson they should call a psych consult, but is afraid to force the issue with Anspaugh and the surgery goes ahead. It seems successful, and Carter's performance impresses Anspaugh. Afterwards, he accompanies Anspaugh and the Japanese surgeon to dinner and karaoke.

Carol

Rhonda Sterling's incompetence reaches its peak when she mixes up the bag containing the patient's belongings, which she puts on ice and gives to the surgeons, and the bag containing the patient's amputated foot - which she hands over to his understandably shocked wife! Carol tells her that the mistake is the most incompetent, horrifying thing she's ever seen. But before she can be referred to a review board, Rhonda resigns, claiming that the hospital has deliberately moved her to a department she's unfamiliar with so that she can be forced out before she can gain her maximum pension. Carol and Chuni don't believe her story, but then Lydia (whose pension will reach its maximum after another year of work) receives a letter telling her she's to be transferred to neurology three times a week starting tomorrow...

Benton comes to the end of his surgery as Keaton watches from outside, commenting that it's a lot of work to save an organ donor. As the boy's mother arrives, Benton takes him off the ventilator: unless he breathes by himself within ten seconds, the boy is brain-dead. After an agonizing wait, Benton finally pronounces death. Keaton asks him if he really thought the boy would live. "I guess I did exactly what you said," Benton says. "Rushed ahead, didn't think...I took that vent off, and I actually thought that kid would breathe." Keaton tells him he should check on Megan Herlihy before he leaves tonight: unexpectedly, the baby is showing signs of recovery. Her mother, Gail, calls it a miracle; Benton simply stares in disbelief.

Benton

Carter returns to the ER and Edson tells him Mr Percy stroked out after surgery. "Pity you backed out on the psych consult," Edson remarks. "Could have saved his life, such as it was." Furious at Edson's smug attitude, Carter shoves him against a locker and Edson punches him back, but the fight stops abruptly when Abby Keaton arrives. Later, as she stitches up Carter's injured nose, Keaton tells Carter to call her Abby - and then leaps on him with a passionate kiss!

Carter

After work, Mark Greene pays a visit to Susan's apartment. He asks her how long she and Morgenstern have been going out, but of course she doesn't know what he's talking about. She tells him that Morgenstern has been helping her get her transcripts together: she's transferring her residency to Phoenix. Her stay with Chloe and baby Suzie convinced her that she needed to be with them. She's happy now, for the first time in a long while, and she's finally moving on. He doesn't know what to say. "I know," she says. "I'm going to miss you." They hug, and he tells her he'll miss her too...

Greene/
Lewis

3-8: "Union Station"

Ross and Chuni organize a session of free immunizations

Ross

241

as part of the community healthcare project. Charlie *[episode 3-5]* arrives with her friend Gloria's baby son Ahmed, although she claims Ahmed is hers so that she can sign for the immunization. Later, the results of some routine lab tests on Ahmed give Ross cause for concern and he tries to contact Charlie, but fails to find her at the emergency shelter she has given as her address.

Greene/ Lewis — It is Susan Lewis's last day in the ER, and Mark Greene is behaving oddly - asking for Susan's help where it isn't really needed, while displaying a short temper around almost everyone else. Ross, Chuni and others have bought a number of leaving presents for her and a large cactus-shaped cake, but Carol thinks Susan would rather slip away quietly - especially as she doesn't have much time to spare between the end of her shift at 2 pm and the departure of her train from Chicago's Union Station at 4.20. Meanwhile, Lydia has called off her wedding plans with police officer Al Grabarsky, because he kept putting off the big day. Later, when Al brings in a patient, Carol tells him to be more bold: "If you want to be with her, be with her." She reminds him that there's a chaplain in the hospital...

Benton/ Carter — The Herlihys arrive to take home baby Megan, who has now recovered. Benton is awkward when they give him and Keaton their grateful thanks, but Keaton tells him never to begrudge a good outcome. As she goes back into her office Benton is surprised to see Carter there, but Keaton explains he is helping her write an article. Later, the three of them operate on a small baby with a partial small bowel obstruction, and both Carter and Keaton are surprised when Benton backs out, admitting he's out of his depth.

Greene/ Lewis — Mark discusses his feelings for Susan with Doug Ross, who tells him he has to say something before she goes, but Mark feels that there's no point now. Susan, meanwhile, has been chastised by Weaver for her involvement in one of Mark's cases, and she takes Mark aside to tell him he can't put her in the way of his conflicts with Weaver any more. She tells him she's anxious about losing the 'shorthand' of their professional relationship, but he clearly has other concerns, and the conversation ends awkwardly.

Carter and Keaton continue their 'article' in her office, which seems to include more kissing than actual research. They both agree that what happened last Thursday - and Saturday afternoon, and evening, and Tuesday before rounds - is strictly personal, and nothing to do with work. Later, Benton is surprised to see Carla pay a visit to the hospital, purely to see him. He introduces her briefly to Carter and gives her a tour of the ER - but when Carter is called away to the OR, she takes the opportunity for a passionate embrace in the suture room...

Carter/
Benton

In a break between traumas, the hospital chaplain conducts the wedding of Lydia and Al, who have decided not to wait any longer. The service is beautiful, despite various distractions like Al's police radio going off, and Chuni walking past yelling something about a stool sample! Mark and Susan watch the ceremony from opposite sides of the room, and find themselves looking at each other. After the throwing of the bouquet (which Susan catches), Mark apologizes for his earlier behaviour. "I guess I've proved I'm no good at goodbyes," Susan says. "I just don't want to go unless I know we'll always be friends."

Greene/
Lewis

On her way to work, Jeanie is met by Al, who presents her with a large batch of divorce papers. He tells her he's willing to give her the house, the car, everything: his medical fees will be paid for by the state if the value of his assets falls below a certain level. She won't have to worry about him any more, he says.

Jeanie

Annoyed at another attempt to 'float' the ER nurses - this time, Haleh is moved to neurology for the day - Carol has an angry meeting with Mary Cain, who is responsible for nurse management. She tells Mary that the 'floats'

Carol

should at least make more sense: ER nurses could be 'floated' to ICU, where their skills might be more appropriate. Mary takes up the suggestion, but on condition that Carol joins the hospital-wide 're-engineering' committee, which meets once a month, and Carol reluctantly agrees. But the nurses are less than happy with the compromise, and as Carol explains its virtues Haleh warns her: "You're beginning to sound an awful lot like management..."

Greene
Lewis
Just as Susan's shift ends, the paramedics start to rush in with as many as eight victims of a large motor vehicle accident, spoiling the plans for a farewell party. Susan does a short tour of the trauma rooms, and says goodbye to Ross and Carol, but not to Greene, who is busy with a patient and doesn't notice her in the doorway - although she looks at him for a long time before finally leaving. When Mark realizes she's gone he is upset and becomes even more irritable. Eventually Ross takes him aside and tells him he has to catch up with her before she leaves, and tell her how he feels - or he'll make himself and everyone around him miserable for the rest of his life, like he has today. Mark thanks him, and begins to run - first catching a taxi to Susan's flat, but she has already picked up her luggage and left. He runs at a break-neck pace across town to reach Union Station, but it looks like the train has gone - until a porter tells him it's leaving from another platform.

Greene/
Lewis
Mark finally catches up with Susan literally as she's getting on to the train and it's ready to leave - and she is delighted to see him. "You came to say goodbye!" she says. "No," Mark says, breathlessly. "Stay. I want you to stay." Finally, he tells her he loves her, and admits he's stupid for not saying it before. "No, it's okay," she says. "I knew. In a way, I knew." He tries to persuade her to stay: they belong together, he says. "Tell me you don't feel the same." She just says she's sorry. "Mark, you are my best friend," she says. "I don't know how I'm going to make it without you." But she has a new life, and it's going in a different direction. "I don't want to lose you," Mark says,

his eyes wet with tears, and they share their first - and only - kiss, before the station porter reminds Susan that the train has to leave. "I'll never forget you," she tells Mark as she closes the carriage door. As the train pulls away she tells Mark that she does love him, but he either doesn't hear or can't believe she's said it. "I love you!" she yells again. "'Bye!" The train slowly disappears out of view, leaving Mark exhausted, confused and alone on the platform.

[Aagh! It had to happen this way, from the moment Sherry Stringfield decided to leave the show - but the inevitability can't make it any less painful. Anthony Edwards brilliantly shows us the emotional side of Mark Greene that so often remains hidden, breaking into tears as he finally tells Susan he loves her. Susan's brush-off and disappearance to Phoenix, with nothing more than a brief kiss and cheery wave, may have seemed a little harsh - but the truth is that Mark really did leave it too late to make his move. There was certainly a time in the second series when Susan was making all the moves, and in series three even inviting him to Hawaii wasn't enough to prompt Mark to take the plunge. Still, you've got to feel for him, and we can only hope that if and when Anthony decides to leave the series, the writers will send Mark Greene off to Phoenix, where we can at least imagine him and Susan living happily ever after.]

3-9: "Ask Me No Questions, I'll Tell You No Lies"

Greene calls a staff meeting to organize the extra workload caused by Susan's absence, putting each doctor's duties into a colour-coded display on the chart - green is, of course, taken. Ross tells him he thinks Mark is over-reacting to a broken heart, but Greene insists he's just doing his job.

Greene/ Ross

The doctors rally round to cope with the large amount of work they are faced with, but it is Gant who has to deal with the lion's share. Benton, meanwhile, is becoming nervous about his abilities in paediatrics, and starts to notice that Keaton is getting on well with Carter. Abby, though, has recently arranged to spend several months working in Pakistan and when Carter seems distressed by

Carter/ Benton

the news, she tells him she assumed neither of them had long term plans for their relationship. He hesitantly agrees, and they discuss plans for the evening

Jeanie/
Greene

As Jeanie treats a woman with sickle cell anaemia, Greene attends to Al Boulet, who has come in to the ER for treatment of an AIDS-related illness. He tells Greene that he and Jeanie are divorced. Greene then talks to Jeanie about her husband's condition, obviously concerned that she might have contracted the virus, but she tells him she tested negative. Later, Jeanie confronts Al, saying he should never have come to County General, and they argue fiercely. Al tells her she has a right to be angry and that he feels desperately guilty that he gave her the virus, but hating him won't change anything.

Carter/
Benton

Gant's workload has increased to 20 patients, but he refuses help from Carter. "Benton wants me to pull my weight, I'm damn well going to pull it," he insists. But Carol gives Carter the next surgical patient to come in, assuming Gant is jammed already. Hearing this, Benton disagrees, saying Gant is just slow. Gant catches up with Carter later and tells him he did him no favours by taking the patient: the best way to help him would be to leave him alone, he says. Meanwhile, Benton assists Keaton with surgery and he asks her how she thinks Carter's doing, but Keaton throws the question back at him. He admits he's doing fine, has learned fast and is very good with children. Keaton says he ought to tell him that, saying it's important for the teacher to keep his intern informed about his progress: "It's very easy to get discouraged in a vacuum."

Greene/
Jeanie

Greene decides to look at Jeanie's medical records - giving the spurious reason that he is worried Al never informed his wife - and discovers she is HIV positive. He confronts Kerry, having seen her and Jeanie talking earlier, demanding to know why he wasn't told. Kerry is furious that Greene has looked at Jeanie's records, committing a serious breach of confidentiality. But

Greene is undeterred and goes to see Anspaugh, telling
him that there is a rumour about an HIV-positive staff
member in the ER. Anspaugh tells him the hospital will
deal with the situation, but has to be cautious to avoid a
discrimination suit. When Greene presses him, he
reminds him that at this stage it's only Mark's suspicion -
"and please, don't correct me if I'm wrong."

Carol attends a meeting of the 're-engineering' committee
for the first time, and is alarmed when Mary Cain
announces that the system of 'floating' ER nurses to ICU
will continue indefinitely. Mary stresses that money has
to be saved somewhere, but she seems to accept Carol's
argument that emergency patients and nurses should get
preferential treatment: later, Haleh reads out a memo
from management saying that ER nurses will be exempt
from 'floating' from now on. When she tries to give
Greene the good news, though, he snaps at her before
she's even started, assuming she's about to complain
about her job and saying that he's sick of hearing it. Carol
tells Doug he should talk to Mark, and try to get him out
of his current mood: if he carries on this way, he'll soon
have no friends left.

Carol/ Greene

Jeanie asks Greene for an evaluation on her sickle cell
patient, and he says he'll do it - and tells Jeanie to cover
the waiting room for now. Checking up with the records
department, Jeanie discovers that someone inspected her
medical records at noon today. To add insult to injury,
Greene fails to attend to the patient Jeanie referred to
him. "You get to make the rules," Jeanie says to Greene,
"and then you get to break them by going into my file."
Greene tells him she should have told him much earlier,
but Jeanie says it's better this way: "You know about me,
and I know a hell of a lot more about you." Later, she
returns to Al and apologizes for blaming him for her HIV
status: she wants it to be somebody's fault. He admits he
hasn't told anyone at his workplace either, fearing they
would treat him differently.

Jeanie/ Greene

As they leave the hospital, Greene and Ross talk. Mark

Greene/ Ross

247

apologizes for his behaviour: "I was a..." He falters, and Doug fills in: "a vicious, humourless, pain-in-the-ass." Mark tells him work just isn't fun for him any more, and Doug thinks he understands what he means. "It's okay to miss her," he tells him.

Benton/
Carter

After work, Benton finds Carter in the car park, ready to drive away (although really he's waiting for Keaton). Carter is shocked to hear Benton finally admit he's doing good work. Abby waits until Benton has left, and then gets into the car. They drive off to a small snow-covered forest, where Abby helps Carter with one of the Carter family's Christmas traditions - felling a Douglas fir tree for the family home. Abby asks whether they're allowed to cut down the tree - aren't they trespassing somewhere? - but Carter tells her his family owns the land. He finds a suitable tree, but instead of felling it the couple, happy and wrapped up warm like kids, indulge in a snowball fight.

Ross/
Carol

Doug meets Carol outside her college as she comes out of her exam, and he suggests they go for a drink - just as Carol's lab partner William arrives, and suggests going for ice-cream instead. With a shrug and a smile, Doug agrees...

3-10: "Homeless for the Holidays"

Jeanie

Christmas Eve. The Chicago streets are white with snow as Jeanie Boulet rushes to a meeting with Kerry Weaver. Her test results have just revealed no viral nodes - it appears that the drug cocktail is working. Jeanie rashly hopes that the hospital won't have to make a policy decision but Weaver insists that Jeanie is too important to be relegated to administrative duties.

Carter

Dennis Gant, who has been on duty since the previous morning, is on bad terms with his girlfriend, Monique; an old row has erupted again. Gant tells Carter that Monique won't be joining him in Chicago this Christmas and she won't be able to attend the Carter family's

Christmas party. Later, Carter discovers that Keaton has had surgery cancelled and can now make his party so he tries to rearrange with Gant. Dennis, continuing a 34-hour shift, is a little crestfallen but insists that he'll be all right. But when Carter tries to arrange for them to meet the following night he discovers Gant is on duty then also.

County's legal department have advised that a policy decision regarding HIV-positive health-care workers should be made by each section. At a secret meeting, Dr Anspaugh informs Mark Greene and Kerry Weaver that they have to decide where the ER stands. Meanwhile,the reception desk is buzzing with rumours: Jeanie Boulet is told in confidence that someone in the ER may be HIV positive. Greene and Weaver discuss their positions but their confrontation is heated. Greene insists that his medical concerns do not run to bigotry, but Weaver fears that they could run to depriving Jeanie of her job. Weaver explains that she would rather break the law than open Jeanie's tragedy to public scrutiny, and thereby bring on frivolous law suits and mass hysteria. Later, both doctors reprimand the nurses for gossiping about their current deliberations. Jeanie walks past as Weaver explains that she and Mark are deliberating over hospital policy, and that 'Employee X' could be any member of staff. However, Jeanie is tired of the insinuations and rumours: she asks that she stop being referred to as Employee X and announces that she is HIVpositive.

Greene/ Jeanie/ Weaver

Charlie *[episode 3-5]* returns to the ER with her friend Gloria's baby. Ross finds blood in the infant's nappy and wants the mother to come to the hospital but Charlie appears nervous and later tells him that Gloria can't come. Ross finds a tumour in the boy's abdomen and schedules an operation but is angry that the problem was not noticed earlier. Charlie is concerned that she will be thrown out of Gloria's house where she has been staying. Later, Gloria arrives to see her son but Ross refuses to let her, threatening the intervention of social services. Gloria

Ross

leaves with Charlie in pursuit, accusing Ross of being just the same as all the others.

Jeanie/ Weaver

Greene and Weaver continue to debate the policy decision, now with Jeanie present. Mark wants Jeanie to continue work within boundaries, not working on deep penetrating poorly visualized cavities, and Jeanie says that she wouldn't feel happy working on injuries of that nature anyway. To counteract the view that dementia may set in, Jeanie suggests a physician monitor and Weaver volunteers. With progress made, Jeanie leaves the meeting but notes a change in attitude among her colleagues. Hathaway says she wishes she had known but Jeanie curtly asks if that would have made them friends. Later Carol explains about her attempted suicide and the response of her friends on her return to work - if they're not friends, perhaps they should be.

Ross/ Carol

Ross returns home to find Charlie outside his house: she stole his wallet and took his address from it. She and Gloria have argued and she hopes to crash at Doug's place. Instead, Ross calls on Carol Hathaway and asks her to take Charlie for the night. Carol is reluctant: it's already 'Christmas in the Ukraine' in her house, complete with eight drunken sword-dancers re-enacting the Purges in her front room. Nevertheless, Charlie gets on well with Helen Hathaway and Doug is able to convince Carol to let Charlie stay.

Maggie

Maggie Doyle treats Mrs Lang, a survivor of long-term domestic abuse who insists that her broken jaw is the result of an accident. After some time, Doyle manages to convince Mrs Lang to admit that she is being abused. Mr Lang arrives, apologetic for failing to fix the top step of the ladder earlier; Doyle asks him to leave the exam room. Later, as they wheel a covered body through the corridor, she and Malik tell Mr Lang that his wife is being kept in over night for observation. When they are outside, however, they uncover Mrs Lang and Doyle gives her a bus ticket to a women's aid refuge, paid for from the staff's football betting-pool.

Carter and Keaton are exchanging Christmas gifts when Benton arrives at Abby's office. Carter dives behind her desk and overhears Keaton deny Benton a place on the next paediatric surgery rotation. Keaton explains to Benton that he doesn't live and breathe for children; he has taken the rotation desiring a challenge, not from love. Benton leaves, downhearted.

Carter/
Benton

Having bought a sled for Rachel, Mark Greene plans to visit his daughter later that day to give her this Christmas present. Later, however, Greene is lumbered with a shabby dog called Nicky after his owner, a homeless burns victim, dies in the ER. Inspired, Greene cleans up the mangy animal as the perfect Christmas gift for Rachel but on arrival at Jenn's house discovers that Craig, Jenn's new husband, has already bought her two labrador puppies. Mark quickly says the dog is his own and he just wanted Rachel to meet him. He quietly thanks Nicky when he takes a bite out of Craig's hand!

Greene

Al arrives in the ER with a Christmas card addressed to both him and Jeanie. They talk amicably and much of the tension between them appears to be fading. He also gives her the star from the top of their Christmas tree, which later she uses to put the finishing touches to the ER's tree decorations. Doyle notes that the star is an heirloom and should go on Jeanie's family tree. "It just has," says Jeanie.

Jeanie

3-11: "Night Shift"

It's about 20 degrees below in Chicago as Mark and Chuni, now seemingly closer, arrive at the ER to begin the night shift. It's tenure review week and, as if it weren't enough that he's in direct competition with Weaver, Greene is being criticized by the legal department for failing to co-sign cases. Weaver is aiming for the prize tenure with a last-minute study of the effect of exercise on the circadian rhythms of night shift workers, in the course of which she subjects both Jeanie and Wendy to a series of tiring tests. Meanwhile, Greene treats a deranged woman who is suffering from meningitis. He

Greene/
Weaver

decides to perform a spinal tap without her consent, bypassing legal who have said all such decisions should go through them. Greene explains to Chuni that he believes his chances of making tenure are almost zero "but, hey, I did my job and I can do my job somewhere, tenure or no tenure". Mark asks Chuni if she wants to grab some breakfast, which ultimately leads to her staying over...

Benton   Benton still wants a second paediatric rotation, despite Keaton's failure to recommend him. Anspaugh suggests that Benton speak to Dr Kenner, but the paediatric surgeon can do nothing without Keaton's approval. Benton attempts to speak to Keaton but, on his arrival at her office, he finds her and Carter entwined on the sofa sharing their final moments before she leaves for Pakistan. Later, Benton and Abby speak alone. Abby cautiously approaches the subject of blackmail, but Benton doesn't want a recommendation based on anything other than his skills as a surgeon. Keaton regretfully tells him that she still can't propose a second rotation. "You've got the makings of an excellent surgeon," she tells him. "But not a paediatric surgeon."

Carol   The hospital budget has been released and there's a crisis conference first thing tomorrow which Carol has to attend. ER nursing is $94,000 over budget, and two nurses have to go. Despite Carol's protests, Mary leaves the decision to her. Carol decides to consult the budget and schedule, and is given advice by Randi: cutting overtime and reducing shifts to eight hours will save $100,000. Carol is enthusiastic and tells the nurses, who react badly. Lydia mentions the forthcoming contract negotiations and says that if management tries to force this upon them, the nurses will strike.

Ross   Despite his new year's resolution "to resist charitable impulses", Doug assists Carol on the routine maintenance survey of the ER. Their work is interrupted when Charlie arrives and asks Ross for $100 to pay off a pimp, who she says is going to kill her. Doug refuses and

252

Charlie flies into a fit of rage, calling Doug a child
molester.

Dennis Gant is angry that Benton has refused him two
days' leave to sort things out with Monique. Carter has
heard Gant's girlfriend troubles for two weeks, and tries
to avoid Dennis throughout the day. Even a little
competitiveness with Doyle cannot excuse Carter
indefinitely, and Gant manages to catch up with him. As
the two talk over dinner, Benton bursts in and accuses
Dennis of failing to monitor a critically ill patient, almost
resulting in the man's death: "If you can't do the job, or
you don't want to do the job, then you don't need to be
here." Carter, taken aback by Benton's abruptness, sees
Gant is dismayed and starts to reassure him when he is
beeped and has to run. Dennis goes to Anspaugh and
Carter is called to comment on the severity of Benton's
reprimand but, caught between two colleagues, he
indicates that Benton's words were harsh but perhaps not
inappropriate.

Carter/
Benton

The maintenance survey takes Carol and Doug to a
storage room which holds romantic memories for them
both. Carol reassures him that he was right to refuse
Charlie's demands. Later, Charlie staggers into the ER,
her face badly bruised and her jaw and right arm broken.
Carol suggests that she was raped: later, Charlie confirms
this to Ross, but makes him swear that he won't call
social services. Once she is asleep, however, he does just
that.

Ross/
Carol

As Carter and Doyle continue competing with each
other, the paramedics bring in a young black man who
has been hit by a train. No-one is sure whether the man
fell or jumped. Benton rushes into the ER and asks for
someone to page Gant. The man's face is badly messed
up, he's lost an eye, and there's brain matter in the hair.
His pulse is failing. Suddenly a pager starts beeping and
Benton realises it's coming from the patient. The pager
gives their room number - Doyle realises the patient is
Gant. Carter and Benton pause, horrified, then

Carter/
Benton

frantically try to save him as he flatlines...

[Night Shift *would be little more than an average episode without the final few moments, and in a way that's the point. As the story of the night shift at County unfolds, our attention is drawn to the higher profile concerns of Mark Greene's conflict with the legal department, Ross's relationship with Charlie, and Benton's failure as a paediatric surgeon - and not to the character who has fallen between the cracks, Dennis Gant. Gant's problems are deliberately underplayed - even the instance which launches Benton's torrent of criticism is enacted off-screen - cleverly mirroring the precise circumstances which lead inevitably to the episode's final scene. Carter's spineless failure to support Gant is all the more harrowing in retrospect, and Benton's hard line on Gant is loaded with guilt. The last sequence of the episode is a flash of realization, as the doctors frantically try to save a colleague they had all but forgotten...]*

3-12: "Post Mortem"

Carter   "What happened? I guess that's the question. How could this awful senseless thing happen? I mean, I've seen traumas from plenty of accidents since I started my training, but this was someone I knew..."

Carter/   It is the day of Gant's memorial service, and the police
Benton   are still uncertain whether to adopt a verdict of accidental death or suicide. Anspaugh has called in Dennis's colleagues to try to discover if a hospital policy or harsh teaching methods were in any way responsible. Carter asks Benton if he could say a few words at the afternoon service but Benton simply says that he's no public speaker. He's a little preoccupied with Anspaugh's investigation but Carter reassures him that no one is blaming Benton. Benton quickly replies "Why would they?" Later, Carter finds Benton's evaluation of Gant, unread, and is angry to find that it is very positive. He confronts Benton with it in the OR, when they assist Dr Hicks: "All he ever got from you was harping and criticism, and now he's dead and you're going to have to face it."

Carol   Angered by the hospital management's renegotiation of contracts, Carol's entire afternoon shift has called in 'sick'. Management organizes some temporary nurses and call in staff from other departments. Carol, Mark and Kerry insist that the ER is closed to trauma, but a homeless man who has been crushed by a dumpster is rushed in by his friend. Carol assists, rushing between the supply nurses, none of whom have up-to-date experience in an ER, but they are unable to save the man's life. Later, Kerry and Carol are horrified to find that the cause of death was incorrect blood type given to the man by Carol in the confusion. Mark and Kerry argue that it was an understandable mistake in the circumstances, but Carol insists on reporting the incident. Though Drummond concurs with Mark and Kerry, Carol isn't so willing to accept the error: she has to face herself in the mirror, knowing what has happened.

Although he has heard from Morgenstern that the police have ruled Gant's death accidental, Carter's guilt is welling up and he tries to arrange a meeting with the hospital counsellor, Dr Pomerantz. She had helped Gant when he was settling in, and recognizes his name as one of Gant's friends. She urges him to come to talk to her about survivor's guilt but he insists that maybe he feels that way because he is guilty. All Carter knows for sure is that he wasn't much of a friend. Carter/Benton

A patient, who has flown in from Gabon, via Paris, is placed in isolation on suspicion of being infected with the ebola virus. Greene introduces Jeanie to Greg Fischer from infectious diseases, who quickly rules out anything exotic, and they later discover it to be a case of malaria. Later, Weaver suggests Greg as Jeanie's personal doctor for her HIV treatment - he joined County after his business partner died the previous year from AIDS. Jeanie and Greg get talking about a shared interest in astronomy and Greg invites her for a pre-dawn comet watch. Jeanie

Ross discovers that Charlie now hates him for calling Ross

social services. She thinks that, having admitted she was raped, Doug is trying to lock her up. Ross promises he won't put her in a home and that no one will hurt her. He tries to get some details from Charlie about her living relatives in the hope that she can be placed with them, but Charlie is more interested in being adopted by Doug. He says he's not ready, but if he was she'd be the first on his list. Meanwhile, social services find Charlie's mother ten blocks away - not in Cleveland as Charlie had said - but the woman has admitted to fights at home, and social services are concerned about Charlie going back there. Later, Ross is asked to return: Charlie has claimed Doug will adopt her, and the mother is only too willing to be rid of her daughter. Doug denies this and explains they talked about the precise opposite. Charlie starts screaming and he leaves.

Jeanie   After an unsuccessful comet watch at four in the morning, Greg and Jeanie go to Doc Magoo's. He kisses her, but she pulls away. She explains she is HIV positive and apologizes for not saying anything earlier but she was having fun. The conversation descends into an awkward silence.

Carter/   Anspaugh and Hicks leave Gant's memorial service, and
Benton   thank Carter for making the arrangements and expressing everyone's sentiments. Benton arrives late, and Carter deliberately introduces him to Dennis's father to make Benton feel uncomfortable. Dennis Gant senior says that his son greatly respected Benton, and Benton finally admits to having been hard on him. Later, Carter meets Benton on the train platform and they talk more. He knew he was hard on Gant - he thought it was the best way for him to learn - but he doesn't need Carter to tell him how he feels. Carter says if he wants to go through this alone, he can. "We'll both keep our distance... do our work, pretend like nothing happened - we're good at that. Look what that did for Dennis Gant."

3-13: "Fortune's Fools"

Jeanie takes a look at Mike Patterson, a young husband who is suffering from migraines and dizziness. Greg Fischer is called to assist and apologizes to Jeanie for not having contacted her: she sharply retorts that she didn't expect him to. Greg diagnoses neuro-syphyllis. It's a sensitive issue and he would like Mike told privately, but Jeanie insists Cindy Patterson be told too: Jeanie knows full well how failure to communicate can ruin a marriage. In the end the Pattersons insist on hearing the news to-gether but the doctors are surprised to find Cindy was the culprit, not Mike. In the course of events, Jeanie and Greg's relationship becomes more tense and eventually Greg snaps at her. He tries to apologize for that, and for his initial shock at Jeanie's condition. She angrily replies that if he doesn't want to date an HIV-positive woman, then that's fine.

Jeanie

Benton sees Carla Rees in the waiting room and speaks to her. She reveals that she is pregnant with Peter's child and that she is waiting for an obstetrics appointment with Dr Coburn. Later he finds that everything is fine with the baby, although both of Carla's sisters had miscarriages in the first three months of their pregnancies. Carla has decided to keep the baby - but she doesn't expect any help from Peter. Meanwhile Peter has forgotten about a surgical presentation he is supposed to make with Carter, and Carter is pushed by Anspaugh to begin without Benton. Having finished his own part of the presentation he tries to cover for Benton's absence, but faces tough criticism. Eventually, he tries to placate the audience with a terrible joke he heard from Morgenstern...

Benton

It's prospective intern day and Anspaugh has called in Greene and Weaver to take three of the brightest applicants on a tour of the ER, independently of each other. Weaver has produced a huge introductory manual, which Greene casually throws in the bin. While Weaver's tour is thoroughly dull (including the progress of a urine sample through the ER, and Morgenstern's life story!) Mark's is livened up by being interactive and revealing,

Greene/ Weaver

257

especially when one patient, Heather Morgan, chats him up and offers to buy him a drink. The offer is left open-ended, but a time and place is set. In fact Mark's relationship with Chuni ended earlier in the day: Mark had planned to break it off, although in the end Chuni beat him to it. At the end of the day, Anspaugh announces that none of Weaver's group signed up, but all of Greene's allocated County as their first choice. Much to Weaver's dismay, Anspaugh directs Mark to consider an academic appointment as a tenure is soon to become available. That evening Mark meets Heather at Finch's Bar, only to find his group of applicants have come along to see if he took up the offer, and to buy him a drink!

Carter/ Benton

Carter confronts Benton, furious that he has let him down, allowing Carter's reputation to be trashed in front of every surgeon in the hospital. Benton gives a fleeting apology which is barely sincere. Later, Hicks asks Carter if she should be worried about Benton. Carter insists that Benton's skills aren't impaired but Hicks seems more concerned that Benton is wasting Carter's talents, and offers him a place on her surgical team. He accepts, and asks Benton to sign him off the blue team in favour of the red. Benton cares little what Carter does, and Carter is worried that Benton barely cares about himself or his reputation any more.

Carol

A newspaper has printed the story that an ER patient died when a nurse gave him the wrong blood during the sick-out. Haleh realizes this puts paid to management's zeal in placating the nurses, and removes public support for their efforts. Carol puts the nurses straight: it wasn't the fault of a temp; she did it. Carol accuses Mary Cain of selling her out to benefit management in the contract negotiations. "This isn't labour politics," she tells her, "a man died." Meanwhile, Haleh is unconvinced that Carol didn't know about the leak, and tells her that the revised contract has been withdrawn from negotiations. Carol is isolated from both camps, and resolves to go to the newspaper and explain that the accident had nothing to do with the sick-out. Mary is astounded at Carol's actions and tells her to see Drummond, a senior manager, who is on the warpath. Carol returns from Drummond's office, telling Haleh to take over negotiation of the contract: Hathaway has been suspended.

3-14: "Whose Appy Now?"

Doug Ross attends to a man named Jad Houston, who has cystic fibrosis, and whose girlfriend Katy has brought him to the ER suffering from an attack. Katy says that Jad is 19 and has signed a DNR [do not resuscitate] order, but Doug insists on helping him until the order is confirmed. Jad's doctor, a paediatrician, reveals that Jad is actually seventeen although his birthday is three weeks away. As such he's too young to have a DNR order and needs parental consent. Jad doesn't want to die on a respirator. His mother, however, orders Ross to aid her son if he suffers another attack. Ross tries to persuade Jad's mother to respect his wishes but, at first, she ignores his attempts. Eventually, after much thought, she agrees to Jad's request and signs the order.

Ross

Mark Greene has double-booked a date, but rather than cancel one he has decided to see both women. He intends to have dinner with Polly MacKenzie, whom he has been dating for some time, and go to a ball game with Heather Morgan, the schoolteacher he treated recently. He consults Doug who tells Mark that he's playing with fire and that women can smell deceit: he knows from past experience! Mark blows off his date with Polly by pretending to have a cold, but then has another date to contend with - Nina Pomerantz, the hospital psych, who asks him to dinner. They arrange drinks at six. The balancing act collapses, however, when all three women arrive in the ER that afternoon: Polly recognizes Nina as an old friend and together, with Heather listening, they discover Mark's activities. They all dump him, with only Nina saying she may have lunch with him some time. Stuck for a date, he asks Chuni, who declines, and Mark later settles for dinner with Doug!

Greene

Carter competes with Maggie Doyle over procedures. Their rivalry ends when Maggie's knowledge of firearms saves Carter: she warns him about extracting a bullet from an AIDS patient, which Maggie realizes could be razor sharp. They are both annoyed when their patient is given to another surgeon and they are allocated an appendectomy instead. Carter, however, scrubs in eagerly when he sees the patient is Benton: Weaver caught Benton performing an ultrasound on himself and diagnosed appendicitis. In the OR, Shirley takes plenty of photographs to commemorate the occasion and Carter gets into the swing of things, playing 'Ride of the Valkyries' and 'Mack the Knife' over the OR loudspeakers!

Jeanie   An outbreak of staphlyococcus among ER patients forces Jeanie and Greg to takes swabs from every member of staff - but as the disease is spread by someone not washing their hands after using the toilet, they have to be discreet. After much confusion and searching, they identify Jerry as the culprit, who to Jeanie's horror, is surprised to learn you should wash your hands after *every* visit. Having given Jerry a quick lesson in bathroom hygiene, Greg asks Jeanie out on a date but she makes excuses, saying they should keep their relationship professional. However, treating an AIDS patient who she had cared for when he previously had pneumonia, Jeanie is moved by the man's love for life and rethinks Greg's proposition. They meet for dinner and afterwards Greg kisses her. She pulls away, and asks if he isn't afraid. He answers with another kiss.

Ross   Jad is in respiratory failure, with his mother and Katy at his bedside. As his mother watches him fade away, she suddenly demands Doug intubate him - and Katy agrees. Ross reminds her that she signed the order, but she tells him to rip it up. After some hesitation, Ross intubates him. He apologizes to the boy, but the only response he gets is a feebly raised third finger.

Carter   Doyle goes to a shooting range and Carter tags along, having hesitantly asked her out. Suddenly she tells him to hide her: a woman in a red sweater has arrived at the range. She's Doyle's ex-girlfriend, Amy Elliot, a cop - they broke up two months ago and she's "jealous as hell". Carter is so shocked, he shoots out one of the range's lights in panic.

3-15: "The Long Way Around"

It's Valentine's Day, and Carol pays a visit to her local convenience store. In the next few minutes, she finds herself in the middle of a hold-up as two men, a short man with a Scottish accent and a taller American, threaten store-owner Mrs Novotny with a gun. As she hands over the money, her elderly husband arrives with a shotgun. One shopper runs for the door, and in the confusion, the shopkeeper shoots the taller man but is himself shot twice in the chest by the Scot. As the shopkeeper falls to the floor, Carol watches from behind a freezer cabinet. The Scot sees the escaping customer talking to a policeman in a car outside and he and his friend try to escape through the back door, but it's locked. The elderly woman is weeping and refuses to give them the key. They're all trapped inside the shop as the police arrive outside.

Carol

With Mrs Novotny's crying beginning to annoy the American robber, Carol comes forward and announces she's a nurse. The Scot, Duncan, refuses to let her help the more injured Mr Novotny and instead tells her to assist his American cousin, James. James keeps his gun trained on the other hostages: Angie, a school teacher; Lockhart, the bakery delivery man; Mr Duzak; the Novotnys; and Robert Potter, a ten-year-old. Carol tells James that his gun-shot wound is serious, but he refuses to let a doctor in. She dresses James's wound with items from the store, and is given permission to see to Mr Novotny who is critically ill. With the help of Mrs Novotny and Angie, Carol performs CPR on Mr Novotny and manages to get a pulse but he dies, and his body is dragged to the back of the store.

Carol

Carol   Duncan leaves Carol alone in the store room for a while
         and she finds another boy behind the shelves who has
         gone unnoticed. He tells Carol that there's a door behind
         him, but it's locked. She urges him to stay where he is,
         though he is armed with a baseball bat, and says she'll try
         to get the keys. At the front of the store, James and
         Duncan argue. Carol takes the opportunity to see to the
         other injured customers - Mr Duzak has a fractured wrist
         and Angie has a burnt hand - and to ask Mrs Novotny
         for the keys, but they are behind James. Carol also tries
         to reassure Robert, the young boy, but he is still
         frightened by Duncan. Duncan gets Robert to play on
         the pin-ball machine but warns that if he doesn't hear
         him playing it, he's liable to turn around and shoot.
         While Duncan answers the phone and speaks to the
         police, Robert clambers up on the machine and onto the
         roof. Duncan chases after him but falls on the glass
         surface of the pin-ball machine, cutting his face.

Carol   Carol treats Duncan but tells him that James's condition
         is now critical and that they need to get him to a hospital.
         She needs some glue to seal Duncan's wounds; Mrs
         Novotny directs her to some - and to the keys. Suddenly
         the boy from the store-room tries to attack Duncan, but
         Duncan is warned and turns to shoot him. Carol stands
         in his way but, to placate Duncan, tells him about the
         door and gives him the key.

Carol   Duncan leaves James in the store, and takes Carol with
         him. They escape through the back door, up the fire
         escape, on to the apartment block behind and down into
         a back street. Duncan is pleased that they finally made it
         and agrees to let her go at the end of the alley, but before
         they get that far a police car pulls into the alley and
         Duncan is ordered to drop the gun. Instead he turns and
         runs. Carol yells at him not to run but he ignores her,
         and is stopped by three shots to his back.

Carol   Duncan is rushed into County ER, with his cousin
         wheeled in behind, as Carol barks out the details of their
         injuries. She insists on calling procedures and

determining treatment, but has to be called away by Ross and Weaver. Carol tries to comfort Duncan, but they lose his pulse. Meanwhile, Weaver finds that James's bullet probably hit his spleen and he's sent up to the OR, but he'll probably be alright. The race is on to save Duncan as both Weaver and Ross work on him, but it's clearly a losing battle. Duncan dies on the table, and Carol calls time of death. Carol checks on the other hostages, who are fine, and Angie thanks Carol: "You really saved our lives in there; none of us could have done that." Carol apologizes to Doug for her conduct in trauma but he tells her to ignore it; he's just happy she's okay. Weaver catches up with Carol and says that they've missed her around the hospital. She's missed it too. "I love my job, Kerry," she says, and leaves for home.

[Though perhaps not to everyone's tastes, The Long Way Around *stands out among* ER *episodes for its very different feel. With only the last few minutes set in County, the emphasis is firmly on the talents of Julianna Margulies and Ewan MacGregor, who carry the episode forcefully. MacGregor's character is given the freedom to develop and is treated intelligently. But the story is really that of Carol Hathaway, superbly developing the problems of her suspension from the hospital and her desire to become a doctor. The highlight of the episode, however, is shared with Doug Ross, as he dismisses her apologies for her behaviour and asks if she is okay. Doug's questions are delivered with an understated, but compassionate, sincerity which underlines his feelings for Carol.]*

3-16: "Faith"

Today is a big day for Carol: not only does she find out about her future in the ER, but also it is the day of the medical school admissions test. She discovers that the safety committee has ruled her mistake was the result of systems problems and not of negligence. Carol can start back today, but that still leaves the question of whether to take the exam: Doug urges her to think about it. Later, Doug interrupts the nurses' celebration of their victory in the contract negotiations to find that Carol has taken the afternoon off. He arrives at her house that evening and she tells him she took

Carol/
Ross

the test and now has to wait to find out if she's good enough. "You are," Doug tells her.

Greene   Greene and Doyle treat Louise Cupertino, a 35-year old Down's syndrome patient suffering from respiratory failure. Louise will need a heart transplant, but her mother tells Greene that Louise has been refused a place on the transplant list. Maggie is horrified, and she and Greene decide to take it up with the transplant committee. Mark discovers that it was Nina Pomerantz who turned down Louise's application. Nina feels Louise wouldn't get the post-operative care required. Greene accepts all the perfectly logical, bureaucratic reasons for refusing Louise's case but argues an emotional line. Louise can make people laugh and smile, she can reach out to people. He asks Nina not to let her die. Later, he returns to Louise and finds her playing with a Down's syndrome man, who turns out to be Maggie's brother, Jimmy. Meanwhile, Nina has taken note of Mark's plea and approved Louise's application.

Jeanie   Greg tries to get out of a date with Jeanie, and she accuses him of being unromantic and lacking spontaneity. In response, he organizes a picnic outside in the freezing cold! He tells Jeanie he thinks that they should start sleeping together. Jeanie doesn't answer, but later asks him if they could slow down their relationship. Greg is a little taken aback, but respectfully agrees.

Carter   Carter examines a woman with abdominal pains who has survived on a lifetime of cooked breakfasts. He believes she has appendicitis, but is unsure, and requests Hicks's opinion. Instead, Anspaugh and a team of students arrive. Anspaugh humiliates Carter by dismissing his opinion, instead diagnosing congestive heart failure. Later, the patient suffers more severe abdominal pain and this time Hicks is requested in person. Carter explains that he believes Anspaugh has misdiagnosed what is in fact a case of atriol-fibrillation, which puts the patient at risk of heart clots. Anspaugh is called and is shocked at Carter's accusation, but agrees and orders immediate surgery, which he tells Carter to perform: he's the only one around there who seems to know what he's doing today!

It is Jad Houston's eighteenth birthday *[episode 3-14]*, and he has signed the DNR order. He has requested that Doug Ross be the doctor to take him off the respirator, and Doug agrees. Katy and Mrs Houston are told that Jad will probably not survive longer than a few minutes without the respirator, but they have already said their goodbyes. Ross removes the tube and looks on stunned as Jad, after a moment's struggle, begins to breathe for himself. Refusing any further hospital assistance Jad and Katy leave, but Katy pockets Ross's card behind Jad's back and they leave the hospital without telling Mrs Houston where they are going.

Ross

Greene is called back to Louise. Mrs Cupertino won't sign the surgical release needed to give Louise the transplant, and no amount of persuading by Doyle or Kayson can help. Greene discovers that Mrs Cupertino feels that she won't be alive for much longer, and that in two years or so Louise will have to be placed in a home without her. She and Louise can live together in Heaven.

Greene

Benton meets up with Carla, who complains that he hasn't spoken to her since he heard she was pregnant. Benton says he needed time to think about it, but is ready to support her. She will have none of it: even his financial support is unwanted. Later, in the ER, Benton is on the receiving end of Carter's jokes about his appendectomy: Carter shows around his photographs of the operation, notably one of Benton's appendix in a jar on his mantelpiece! Benton still seems dazed and confused. Later Hicks catches up with him, standing alone in the OR. He admits that he hasn't been well since Gant died, and his mistake with the baby and Keaton's failure to recommend him. "Six months ago I thought I was invincible and now... I don't even know. I guess life isn't working out the way I thought it would." He tells Hicks about his guilt over Gant's death, and she replies: "We all

Benton

have to find our own way, Peter. You're not invincible, you're a young doctor, learning, making mistakes, saving lives. It takes a lifetime - you just have to have faith."

3-17: "Tribes"

Greene   Two gun-shot wound victims are rushed into the ER after a shooting at a burger bar. Greene works on the more critically injured white man and orders that the black teenager, Kenny Law, be searched for needles and weapons. Kenny's brother Chris insists that Greene help Kenny, but Greene says he is seeing to the most seriously ill patient first, and calls security. Kenny then crashes, and Greene has to fit a chest tube. Chris is frustrated and angry with Greene and grabs Benton, demanding he help as well. Benton orders the OR to be ready for Kenny.

Weaver   Weaver sees to a disabled man who was hit by a car while 'jay-wheeling'. The man, Brown, is high and Kerry orders a blood alcohol test. She and Greene discuss getting him into a clinic for addiction, but Greene sees all manner of problems ahead. Despite this, Weaver manages to get Brown a place, but the man is unwilling to attend and demands painkillers. She bribes him into checking in to detox for two days in return for some strong painkillers, but the man later discharges himself. "We made a deal," she appeals angrily. "Yeah, well," he says, having got what he wanted, "never trust a junkie."

Benton   Hicks and Benton operate on Kenny Law. Hicks asks Benton if he thinks she has poached Carter from him. Benton, stirring trouble, wryly comments that she would only have done so if it was for Carter's benefit. Later, Hicks offers Benton a place on her team, suitable for his talents as a good general surgeon. At first he's a little hesitant, but Hicks comments: "It's not about ambition, Peter. It's about healing people." Benton accepts - and he'll be working with Carter again.

Greene   Chris Law confronts Greene over his preferential treatment for the white patient. Greene defends himself from charges of racism, but Chris Law retorts: "Just another shot nigger's what you saw." Meanwhile, Greene is asked to look after Rachel for a few days while Jennifer sees her mother, who has had a heart attack. Jenn is concerned that Mark can't handle it but he insists that he can, although later he has to ask Maggie Doyle to look after Rachel for a while. Back in the ER, the shooting incident has brought friends and well-wishers to the side of the Law brothers. Kenny Law is a bright basketball hope, and the waiting room is soon crowded with many of his team mates. Greene asks Malik to move on some of Kenny's friends, but Malik is clearly concerned that Greene doesn't want to do it himself. A little later, Ross calls Greene away from Rachel to another gun-shot victim, this time a white basketball player from a rival team, and suggests that this could be payback for Kenny Law. Greene and Chris stare hard at each other as the white player is brought in.

Carla Rees is brought into the ER, having been involved in a rear-end shunt from a truck. Jeanie examines Carla and finds that the baby is fine, but Carla has a broken ankle and will need stitches in her arm. Unfortunately, Carla is scared of needles. Jeanie and Dr Coburn need to perform a test on her to rule out any compatibility problems for the baby, but the needle scares Carla and she asks if there's another way. Jeanie says they need to know the father's blood type, so Carla tells her that the absentee father is Peter Benton; Jeanie is taken aback, but tries not to show it. She pulls Benton out of surgery on Kenny Law to obtain a blood sample, and he is concerned about Carla. He asks if Carla asked for him or wanted him to stay away, but Jeanie tells him she said neither. Carla begins contractions but Jeanie halts them, helping Carla over her fear of needles to get an IV working. Later, when she is sleeping, Benton calls round to see her. He finds the tape of her ultrasound and gives a faint half-smile as he sees the baby boy wriggling on the screen.

Benton/
Jeanie

Mark Greene talks to Chris Law, having discovered from

Greene

THE ER FILES

the white man's parents that their son, Billy, was a drug dealer and that it was only a matter of time before something like this happened to him. Kenny was an innocent bystander in the drug-related shooting, but Greene still tells Chris to convey to his friends that there's no need for retaliation. Chris is angered by the implication that he had something to do with the recent shooting, and Greene tries to get out of it. Their conversation becomes heated: Greene says he sees gunshot victims every day, but Chris says that's not Mark's brother on the table.

Greene   The white basketball player is saved by Carter in the OR, but Kenny Law dies on the table. Greene asks Malik if he will join him when he breaks the news to the Law family but Malik simply says that if he's scared, he should call security. Greene tells Chris the news, but the moment is horribly tense. Chris Law breaks down and is comforted by his friends. Later, Greene, having talked to Haleh, tells Doug Ross that he made racist assumptions but tried not to act on them. He also breaks the tension with Malik by accepting that he was right to question his actions.

3-18: "You Bet Your Life"

Jeanie   It's nine years to the day since Al and Jeanie married, and Jeanie has heard that her viral node count is up. Greg says that it's nothing to worry about, and proposes to rechristen the date by taking her away for the weekend. Al arrives with a bouquet of roses for Jeanie, but she refuses to accept them and throws them in the bin. Jeanie and Weaver are called to a woman, Suzanne Alner, found bleeding and unconscious in her car at the side of the road. They discover that she overdosed on her AIDS pills and more. Jeanie brushes the woman's hair back: "Why would you want to hurt yourself like this?"

Greene/   Greene is told by Anspaugh that he and Weaver are up
Weaver   for the same teaching position and that, although Anspaugh has personally backed Greene, Mark needs to

find a case and write it up to show he isn't illiterate! At that moment, Iva Blender is brought into the ER with acute abdominal pains. Greene thinks it's a rare case of porphyria, and the perfect case to write up. But in fact she just enjoys having surgery done on her: in Nina's words, she's "a total fruitcake". Nina and Mark discuss his relationship with Rachel, but suddenly they realize Iva is alone. On X-raying her, they discover Iva has eaten an entire tray of instruments, and she now demands surgery. Greene suggests an endoscopy to Iva, and sells it as being an extremely painful and invasive procedure! He's called away, however, to pick up Rachel. Rachel's teacher explains how Rachel has been having social problems at school, getting into fights, and even claiming to have leukaemia as a way of getting attention. On his return to the ER, Greene finds Weaver has already performed the procedure and now proposes to co-author the article. She even has a title - 'The Woman Who Ate The ER'.

Weaver intercepts a call from Cryogen Labs to a fictitious Dr Markovic. Jerry has been pretending to be a doctor to sell his sperm to pay for an expensive new sports car! He insists that he has an IQ of 150 but Kerry is horrified - she has an IQ of 145 - and demands he retakes the examination. Having failed to get Doug's assistance, Jerry gets fifteen per cent on the test - less than the rate expected for just guessing at random! - and Kerry blows the whistle on his scheme. But that doesn't stop Malik from having a go...

Weaver

Jeanie's patient wakes. She shows her a picture of the woman's daughter and asks where she is: the woman says she killed her. Later, Jeanie discovers that the little girl died the previous month from an AIDS-related illness, having contracted HIV from her mother. Suzanne, now blind from the methanol she ingested, wants to tell her husband, Roger, that she's sorry and Jeanie encourages her. On meeting Roger, Jeanie is shocked to find that he is pleased that his wife is dying and in pain: she cheated on him, infected him with HIV, and then passed the

Jeanie

virus on to their daughter. He insists he has been waiting
for this for a long time.

Ross/
Carol

Doug finds Carol poring over a medical textbook,
checking her answers from the medical entrance exams
and convinced that she has failed. Doug tells her that
nurses do things doctors wouldn't think about doing -
just as Doyle calls her away to clean up a 'major code
brown' (a very dirty and smelly task!). Later in the
trauma room, Maggie and Carol virtually come to blows
over the best way to treat an elderly man rushed in with
congestive heart failure. Carol disagrees with Doyle's
assessment but finds Doug agrees with Maggie, who
later confronts her about second-guessing the doctor's
actions. "We grew up in the same neighbourhood and
now she's a doctor," Carol tells Doug later. "I'm a nurse
and I gotta take orders from her all day long and I hate
it."

Jeanie

Suzanne Alner is delirious, blind, and very near death.
Hearing Greg's voice, she mistakes him for her husband,
and begs his forgiveness. Jeanie tells him to say that he
forgives her but he can't bring himself to say anything,
and watches as the woman slips away. Later Greg tries
to apologize to Jeanie. They agree not to go out that
night - Jeanie is uncertain whether or not it has anything
to do with the Alner case - and part company on muted
terms.

Carter

John Carter treats Mr Bartok, an overweight inveterate
gambler. Carter decides on preventive surgery but
Anspaugh refuses to operate: Bartok is septic, and liable
to die on the table. Carter convinces Hicks that, although
the man is a high-risk patient, they have nothing to lose.
Together they operate, but find rampant gangrene in
Bartok's stomach; Carter urges them to press on with the
surgery anyway. Anspaugh bursts in, demanding to
know why an operation is being carried out on a
candidate already turned down for surgery. Carter is
called to Anspaugh's office and makes a formal apology,
but learns that Mr Bartok survived the surgery. Later,

Carter hears from Hicks that he is on probation but still in the surgical programme. He thanks her but discovers Hicks wanted him kicked out but Anspaugh let him stay. "John Carter is not a law unto himself, " she says, "I hope you learnt that. You won't get another chance."

Benton tries to find Carla, but learns that she was discharged the previous night. He tries to look at her confidential file but is caught by Dr Coburn, who refuses to answer his fears about gestational diabetes. Later Benton returns to OB and, having failed to speak to Carla and making sure Dr Coburn is not there to catch him again, gets her ultrasound video by pretending she is a surgical patient. He takes it to another doctor who says the baby is fine, but becomes suspicious of Benton's reasons for asking and asks him to leave. Later, Benton calls on Carla but she refuses to see him. He tells her over the intercom that he wants to do the right thing, to support their child and be a father to it. She comes to the door and tells him to come back on Saturday morning: she'll need some help around the house.

Benton

That evening, Jeanie visits Al and apologizes for rejecting his gesture. "I don't hate you," she says. "I don't want to be angry anymore; I don't want to be that kind of person." He says he never meant to hurt her and she starts to cry. She's missed him, and he has missed her. They hold hands, then hold each other close.

Jeanie

3-19: "Calling Dr Hathaway"

Carol has received her medical school examination results, but is so sure of bad news that she has carried the unopened letter to work. On arriving, Weaver congratulates her: she already knows Carol passed with flying colours. While the news gets around the reception that Carol's off to med school, Carol and Doug spend much of the day assisting a baby boy, Joel Thompson, found unconscious in his crib. Joel's mother Andrea gets in the way of Doug's work, but Carol lets her stay until they have to insert a chest tube to re-inflate the boy's

Carol/
Weaver

271

lung. Carol promises to bring Mrs Thompson to her son if his condition deteriorates. While Carol is being taught by Weaver how to appreciate a pseudocyst, Joel wakes up but Andrea is not alerted. A little later, Carol breaks from her lesson with Weaver when she hears Chuni call for more blood for Joel. She races to get Andrea but when they arrive Joel has died: he crashed ten minutes earlier. Chuni announces the time of death.

Greene   Rachel is annoyed that Mark has forgotten about giving a talk to her Brownie troop. What's more, he has to take on another shift because he has double-booked two doctors' holidays. Later, he treats Mr and Mrs Smythe, a strange couple who complain of a button up the nose and a bucket vacuum-welded to Mrs. Smythe's butt! He consults Nina Pomerantz about the two deranged individuals, who insists they are really investigators working on innovative problem-solving in emergency medicine. Mr Smythe suggests that Greene's name could be mentioned in the highest levels of government, even to Hilary Clinton. Nina adds: "Well, if she ever gets her ass stuck in a bucket, she'll know who to call." Mark manages to get around his Brownie commitments by organizing a tour of the ER for the troop, which seems to placate Rachel. Nina congratulates him on another piece of innovative problem-solving and they arrange to go out bowling that evening (with Emma, Nina's daughter, and Rachel), although they agree that next time they'll go out without their kids, and exchange a brief kiss.

Carter   Carter is not only late but also unprepared for rounds with Anspaugh. Anspaugh asks Carter increasingly difficult questions until he can't answer them, just to put the young doctor in his place. He explains to Maggie that he was just humiliated by Anspaugh. She tags along to trauma two where a gun-shot wound victim being treated by Benton is saved by Carter with a novel method he read about in *People* magazine! But when it comes to scrubbing in for surgery in the OR, Anspaugh refuses to let Carter help. When Benton has to rush off to see Carla, Carter is given Benton's cases. He has to save the recovering gun-shot wound victim, Gunderson, when he suffers respiratory arrest as an allergic reaction to a post-operative antibiotic administered by Dr Dale Edson. Edson failed to take a full case history: Carter calls Anspaugh and tells Edson to prepare an excuse. Instead, Dale falsifies the history. Carter tells Maggie, who urges him to tell Anspaugh the truth and later unsuccessfully tries prompting Carter and Edson in front of Anspaugh. Maggie is furious with Carter, who she says doesn't want to break the rules of the surgeons' club. Carter speaks to Dale privately, who admits he screwed up and promises he'll do anything for Carter but Carter wants nothing from him and says that if anything like this happens again, he'll bury him.

In the morning, Benton hurriedly shows Carla how to test her blood. She's upset when he has to leave, though she is expecting the nurse at ten o'clock to give her a shot of insulin, and is dismayed to find that little seems to have changed with Benton. Later that day, Benton returns to Carla and gives her the injection she needs: the nurse didn't arrive, and Carla had to call Peter. Again he has to rush off, but when Carla gets up to go to the store for food, he offers to go for her and takes a personal day on grounds of family emergency. That evening, Peter cooks for Carla but again has to leave to prepare for tomorrow. She accuses him of never wanting the baby, but he protests that he never said that.

Greene

Carol is unhappy about breaking her promise to Andrea. She finds the heart-broken mother and urges her to spend some time with her son, to say goodbye. She leaves them together in a quiet room while she is shown how to intubate a patient by Weaver: Chuni remarks that Weaver has a new pet student! But the new relationship is challenged when Kerry wants to use the room set aside for Andrea to treat a patient. Carol insists Andrea and Joel be left alone. Weaver admires Carol for her compassion but tells her that she has to stop thinking as a nurse to be a med-student: in reply, Carol reminds her that she isn't a med student. Later, Carol returns to

Carol/
Weaver

273

Andrea as the mother says a final prayer for her baby boy. That evening, she joins the other nurses for beer and pool. They wonder why she's given up the idea of med-school. She responds: "Let's just say, I really like what I do... "

3-20: "Random Acts"

Greene   Greene is confronted by Chris Law, the brother of Kenny Law, the young basketball hopeful who died in Mark's care a few weeks previously *[episode 3-17]*. Chris is angry that the hospital billed his mother for $19,000; he believes Greene's actions were racist and contributed to his brother's death, and is angry that the morgue lost Kenny's body for two days. If his mother receives another bill, he says, "maybe I'm gonna kick some ass. Maybe I'll start with yours." Later Mark speaks to Doug, having verified that the mortuary did lose Kenny's body between the hospital and the funeral parlour. Doug says he should inform security, but Mark insists that Chris was just blowing off steam.

Benton/   Hicks offers Benton the chance to assist at a kidney
Carter   transplant being carried out by two of the country's most prestigious surgeons. Benton jumps at the chance, and manages to get Carter a place on the donor team. Carter begins to thank Benton, but Benton cuts him short as he races off to meet Carla for their appointment with Dr Coburn. Carla tells Benton that she doesn't want any more help from him because he barks orders at her and, discovering Coburn is going to be further delayed, tells him to get back to work. Meanwhile, Carter meets the transplant patients: Carl Twomey is giving his kidney (in return for a stereo and jet-ski) to his older sister Jean. Carter promises Jean that he'll stay with her kid brother. Jeanie has been spending more time with Al, and stayed on his couch the previous night. "I didn't want to be alone but I didn't feel right calling anyone else," she admits. Jeanie is concerned to find that Al has proven resistant to some medication, and tries to get him on a new trial headed by the Infectious Diseases clinic at

County General. She manages to convince Greg to get him an interview. When the time comes, Greg interviews Al himself. He discovers from Al that Jeanie is back in her husband's life, and that she's been staying over a lot recently. Greg assures Al a place on the trial but confronts Jeanie over their relationship, suggesting that Al is using her to get new medicines. Greg asks Jeanie if she still loves Al. She hesitates, but says that she doesn't know.

In the OR, Carter brings Carl's kidney through to Benton and the recipient team, and is asked if he would like to scrub in for the second act. Carter jumps at the chance, but is horrified later when Carl begins to haemorrhage. He watches from the other room as the surgeons have to open Carl again but can't join him, though he promised Jean he would, until the transplant is completed. Thankfully the bleeding is soon under control, and after the operation Carter asks Shirley to beep him as soon as Jean is awake. Carter and Benton join the post-operative diagnosis to hear some of the best minds on the subject, but Benton is clearly concerned when Carter leaves to visit Jean. Carter explains to Benton that he left the meeting because he promised Jean, and asks if that's a problem. Benton says he doesn't know if it is. He leaves to visit Carla, who has been admitted after Coburn managed to prevent her from going in to premature labour.

Benton/ Carter

Chuni, Carol and Jerry are laughing at the manuscript of a lurid romantic novel, set in an ER and found behind the desk. With character names like Nurse Hallidan and Martin Bean, they agree to be careful with it - and proceed to make plenty of photocopies! Weaver discovers the novel, and the thinly disguised version of herself as an ultra-bitch attending physician with a shrivelled limb, and Carol tries to reassure her that the book is only a bit of fun - and that the seduction scene is really hot. Kerry seems pleased with the response and Carol thinks Weaver is the author, though she denies it. Virtually everyone is implicated in the writing but Kerry

Carol/ Weaver

275

manages to make Carol the chief suspect: after all, she has recently had time away from work to write it...

Greene/ Anna
Mark Greene is washing his face in the rest-room, as a gloved hand grabs the back of his head and bangs it on the sink. He is wheeled round and smashed into the mirror before being repeatedly punched and kicked into one of the cubicles. Without his glasses, he is unable to see his attacker who appears to have left, but as he staggers to the exit the beating begins again, ending with the attacker stamping on Mark's hand. Greene manages to stagger to the door, but fails to alert anyone. After what seems like hours, Doug stumbles on Mark and calls for help. Anna Del Amico assists and they manage to get Mark to trauma. With some frantic work, Doug, Kerry and Anna manage to stabilize him as the rest of the ER staff look on. Mark wakes up and Doug tells him he's okay, and jokes that he's signed him up for shifts that weekend. But Mark can't remember a thing...

[If there's a message to this episode it's that nothing goes right for Mark Greene! The brutal attack is appallingly savage and unrelenting: the viewer is lulled into a false sense of relief as the beating pauses, only to discover that the unseen perpetrator is still present and launches into another, more violent assault. The continuation of other storylines, including the introduction of Anna Del Amico, is painful to watch as Greene struggles to alert his colleagues. Meanwhile, Jeanie's romance with Greg Fischer comes to a close, and it seems she will go back to Al. Carter too is alarming Benton with his compassionate regard for patients above surgeons! Random Acts *establishes many of the themes to be explored in the fourth season, with Greene's assault lending an oppressive tone to the proceedings. On a lighter note, the lurid romantic novel provides an amusing sub-plot: can it be mere coincidence that the otherwise out-of-context pause beneath the end credits is a picture of Weaver with one eyebrow raised?]*

3-21: "Make A Wish"

Carla's contractions have begun and this time there's no way to stop the birth, which is two months premature. Dr Coburn tells Benton to gown up and join them if he wants to be present. In the delivery room, Benton harangues the doctors about the procedures and constantly asks questions. Coburn takes him aside and tells him his only job is to get Carla to breathe and focus. Dr Del Amico is called to assist when complications arise, and they order a vacuum extraction. The baby is finally delivered, but it's silent. The boy has a discoloration of the skin, and has to be intubated and resuscitated. He is sent to the intensive care unit, where Dr Tabash orders virtually all possible tests to be carried out. Their son is stable but critically ill: he may have a blood infection, and the doctors aren't sure if his lungs can sustain him. Tabash asks what the baby's name is, but Benton replies: "He doesn't have one."

Benton/
Anna

Jeanie and Al are closer still. They exchange gifts over the course of the day - Jeanie getting a microwave oven and a cafetiere for Al, and Al buying Jeanie the remote-control garage-door opener she always wanted. They share a drink by candlelight on Al's drive.

Jeanie

It is Greene's first day back to work since the attack, a week ago. Although he insists he's fine, the staff notice him wincing and clearly in pain at various moments throughout the day. Meanwhile, Weaver discusses the installation of security cameras and bulletproof glass in the ER. Maggie offers a selection of defensive weapons, including a 'staser' and a mace spray, and even suggests a gun but Greene rejects her offer. Later, Greene meets a police detective following Mark's leads. All the leads he gave the police have proved clear, but Greene seems dissatisfied with the result: he cannot accept that he was the victim of a random act of violence. Later, Nina asks Mark if he's all right, but his tone says it all. At the end of the day he is still extremely unsettled, reacting to one stranger as though he is about to attack him.

Greene

Doug makes it widely known that it is Carol's birthday and even threatens a surprise party, but later tells her that her colleagues have already prepared one. He reassures her that he's got her out of it by saying they were going out for dinner together, but Carol is suspicious. At the

Carol/
Ross

end of their shift, Carol and Doug return to Carol's house so she can change for dinner. As she enters, she finds herself amid her surprise party. "Oh God, I hate you for this," says Carol, but Doug replies smugly: "Worked out well, don't you think?" He explains that he felt some of her previous birthdays ("You mean the ones I spent with you") have been rotten, and he just wanted to make sure she had a good one for a change. When it's time to blow out the candles, her friends place their rings on the cake so that she gets her wish. She holds Doug's gaze before blowing them all out.

Carter   Carter is having second thoughts about surgery and has the feeling that he might be in the wrong place. He looks after Mr Lensky, a middle-aged man with a perforated ulcer who needs immediate surgery. Despite the urgency of his case, Lensky refuses surgery and Carter discovers that the man's father died on the operating table during gall bladder surgery, a supposedly straightforward procedure. Weaver directs Carter to a non-operative treatment, which he finds and takes to Anspaugh. He tells Anspaugh that Lensky doesn't want surgery, but is asked in return if he really thinks this is about Lensky's desires. "I don't believe I should cut somebody open just because I can," Carter retorts. Anspaugh is dismayed: he is worried that Lensky doesn't want the surgery, but more worried that Carter is willing to help the man risk his life by refusing it. Later, at Carol's birthday party, Carter takes Weaver aside and asks what it would take to transfer from his surgical specialty to emergency medicine.

Benton/   Jeanie discovers that Carla has given birth and finds
Jeanie   Peter upstairs, standing in the hallway outside Carla's room. He tells Jeanie the problems his son is having and she reminds him that he has friends, and urges him to go in to speak to Carla. An hour later, Benton hears from Tabash that the baby's condition hasn't improved. Benton is concerned for the boy's sight, but Tabash insists that there are more immediate problems. He proposes a new experimental treatment that runs the risk

of mental retardation, as opposed to continued lung problems if his condition persists. Benton apologizes to Dr Coburn for his behaviour, revealing that today is the first day that he has ever felt afraid. He sits down to explain Tabash's procedure to Carla, and says that they have a decision to make...

3-22: "One More For The Road"

Carter speaks to Anspaugh about his concerns: he is contemplating changing his specialty, leaving the surgical programme. Anspaugh is furious and reminds Carter of the contract he made with the hospital. Carter is on the surgical programme, irrespective of what he thinks. Carter assists Jeanie and Weaver with Burt Kromkey, a very elderly man suffering from paralysis in part of his digestive tract. His wife is clearly unable to take care of him and Carter and Jeanie try to convince her to put her husband in a home, but she ignores them. Carter consults a social worker, a dietician and a physical exercise therapist about the man, and calls a number of nursing homes trying to find a couple's room for the Kromkeys, but comes under attack from Anspaugh for neglecting his job. He is late for rounds, and Anspaugh demands that he comes now or never again; Carter shouts that he'll be there if and when he can.

Carter

Greene is plagued by memories of the attack, and is not getting much sleep. He tells Maggie that he's considering carrying a gun. Greene speaks to Chicago PD who have photographs of suspects, but Mark can't remember the incident clearly and eventually picks one very hesitantly. The detectives are concerned about Greene, and offer a list of help groups. Mark insists that he's fine but once the men have left, he flies into a fit of rage and begins to smash the lounge. Later, Doug finds Mark smoking outside: Doug tells Mark he needs help, and that his door is always open, but Mark is dismissive.

Greene

Weaver observes Al's presence in the ER and notes that he and Jeanie are back together. Jeanie values Kerry's

Jeanie/ Weaver

279

opinion but Kerry refuses to pass judgement. She asks why this has happened. Jeanie admits that she doesn't know but says that she's happy now, happier than before. "And that's because of Al?" asks Kerry. "No," Jeanie replies, "it's because of me. I'm not afraid any more."

Ross/ Anna

On Doug's recommendation, Anna Del Amico talks to Carol, while they treat a young man with a hip pain, about getting an apartment on the west side. Anna orders a large number of expensive tests, but is angry when Ross cancels them and dismisses her patient without her knowledge. Ross, meanwhile, seems preoccupied with Hathaway, who is going on a date that evening. When a young girl is brought in, wearing tattered mud-covered clothes and suffering from an overdose, Anna resents Ross being called but Carol explains that Doug knows the girl: it's Charlie. Doug angrily calls for Charlie's mother but is told by Charlie's pimp, Tommy, that she is in prison for possessing drugs. Charlie has graduated to smack and when told she has to see a social worker, she runs.

Benton

Having slept that night in the intensive care unit, Benton begins his day unprepared and unfocused. Hicks notes that he is preoccupied and is surprised when he leaves the OR when beeped. Tabash discusses the case of Carla and Peter's son: although there is no brain damage, oxygen starvation may have resulted in mental retardation. Jackie finds Peter in the Chapel. He admits that he didn't know it was going to be this hard, and is worried that he can't handle it. He tells her he misses his Dad, and Jackie is taken aback for a moment. That evening he returns to the ICU and finally holds his son in his arms. He gently begins rocking in the chair, as Carla watches him from the corridor.

Carter

Later that day, Carter tries to explain his feelings to Anspaugh. As much as he finds surgery a challenge, he can be a better doctor - looking after the total care of his patient - than a surgeon. Carter feels he can make a difference in people's lives and asks Anspaugh not to make him give that up. Anspaugh's facade cracks for a moment: "I've often wondered, over the years, if I made the right decision, in becoming a surgeon," he says, "but you seem so certain." He asks about Carter's patient and is told that he got the Kromkeys into a nursing home together. Anspaugh tells Carter to find him in the morning and they'll sort something out.

Leaving work that evening, Greene is harassed by several youths on the train who demand money. He decides to get off early but they follow him. Halfway down the platform, Greene wheels round and pulls a gun on the men who step back on the train before it leaves. Greene breathes heavily, still terrified, and later runs along a bridge, throwing the gun into the water. He stands, panting and frightened by his actions.

Greene

Anna and Doug search the streets for Charlie, and Anna reveals that the girl reminds her of herself. Seeing Doug is preoccupied, she correctly guesses that he and Carol were once together. Doug leaves and catches up with Carol outside her home. At first Carol is bemused by Doug's lingering gaze but they soon fall into a long, passionate kiss.

Ross/ Carol

Series Four (1997/8)

4-1: "Ambush"

Doctors Anspaugh and Morgenstern have given a PBS team access to the ER to make a documentary, which will highlight the problems facing the hospital. Cameras are set up in main reception and trauma one and also in the staff lounge, much to the surprise of Doug and Mark who bad-mouth the camera crew while unknowingly being filmed. The cameras are not welcomed by all members of staff, notably Anna, who refuses to sign a consent form to allow the crew to film her. Dr Morgenstern also looks flustered and uncomfortable before the cameras.

Carol/ Ross	The documentary team asks Carol about nurse-doctor relationships, which she insists are an exaggeration. However, when she later helps Doug Ross she leaves her microphone running and accidentally reveals that they are now seeing each other again. When they realise the camera crew know, they quickly separate. Clearly this is a relationship no one is supposed to know about.
Benton/ Corday	In between dealing with a gangland double-trauma and being unpleasant to Carter, Benton is introduced to Elizabeth Corday, a visiting surgical lecturer from Great Britain, who relieves him of part of his busy schedule.
Carter	Carter is finding adjustment to his new specialty difficult. Benton has not spoken to his former student since he left surgery: he is short with him in trauma and later when Carter finds a spleenectomy for him. Carter also discovers that he is once again an intern, forced to resit his first year as a result of changing specialty. And he is embarrassed when his lecturing to camera is cut short when he is covered in vomit. Worse still, he fails to alert an attending physician when one of his patients goes into arrest and dies as a result.
Weaver	Weaver comes to the aid of Morgenstern whose earlier flushed appearance has developed into radiating chest-pain: he is on the verge of a heart attack. Malik quickly commandeers Jeanie's heart monitor for Morgenstern, prompting the cameraman to ask if the ER operates a double standard, one service for doctors and one for everyone else. Weaver bluntly puts down the question as she rushes Morgenstern to the cath-lab.
Greene	Doug Ross thinks that Mark's agreement to do the documentary is a sign that Greene is back on his game but events indicate the contrary. Mark disagrees with one of Jeanie's calls only to be proven wrong in front of the cameras when test results confirm her diagnosis. He is also upset to discover that the documentary team have heard about his assault [*episode 3-20*] and persist to question him about it. Greene has no intention of letting

282

the documentary team present him as the poor pathetic victim but he eventually concedes to a full and frank interview on the condition that the team does not use footage of Carter's error in their film. Before the camera, he admits that he was attacked in the hospital. The worst thing was not the injury to him but that some of the world's violence has leaked into the ER - and that's hard to accept. Mark is scared of losing control of what's outside, but also of what's in him.

['Ambush' was a real gamble, but one which paid off brilliantly. Filmed live, the cast and crew were required to record the episode twice, once for east and once for west coast transmission. The sheer audacity of it (and the enormous publicity it generated) made it one of the highest rated programmes of all time in the States with an enormous audience share. Of course, it can't be denied that a lot of people tuned in just to see if it would be a huge cock-up, but they were to be disappointed. *'Ambush' is* riveting television, and stands up to repeat viewing. All the characters are reintroduced extremely effectively, and Edwards gets to put in one of his finest performances in the last scene. There are also some very nice technical touches, in particular the drummer in reception who provides an approximation of the familiar instrumental music as a trauma case is rushed in. With plenty of hints of events to come, notably Greene's suggestions that his assailant was found but not charged, *'Ambush'* transcends the novelty of its format to lay strong foundations for the fourth season.]*

4-2: "Something New"

Weaver informs Mark that she has been made acting chief of emergency medicine in place of Morgenstern who is drugged up on morphine and hallucinating. Meanwhile, Greene's post-traumatic stress continues. He chastizes Carter for ordering expensive tests on a drunken woman only to discover that Carter correctly suspected that the woman has multiple sclerosis. When Heather, an ex-girlfriend turns up suggesting dinner, he blows her off. For much of the day, Mark and Carol interview candidates for the new desk clerk's position. Mark seems ready to settle for a congenital liar so Carol tells Weaver that she would rather re-advertise the post.

Greene/
Weaver

Greene is sharp with Carol for going behind his back and later offers the job to Cynthia Hooper, a rather dippy candidate, without consulting anyone. Greene's condition has been exacerbated by a note from a solicitor: the Law family is suing the hospital.

Jeanie   Al is unwilling to tell his boss that he is HIV positive and is trying to think up a new excuse to get away from work and attend the clinic to receive his medication.

Benton/   Dr Tabash successfully takes Peter and Carla's baby off
Corday   the ventilator without complications, despite Benton's prior hesitation. Carla is delighted and determined to get on with life, starting by giving their son a name. Both fight for their surnames, which merely indicates how little either can see the three of them as a family. Eventually, they settle on a compromise, Rees Benton.

Meanwhile, Benton is asked to show Elizabeth Corday around the hospital. Together, they operate on a gunshot victim and later a second, during which it becomes clear that Benton has underestimated the new surgeon. Benton is also taken back by Corday's refreshing effrontery when she tells the elderly Dr Reedlove that he is remarkably short!

Carter   Carter arrives in a good mood, looking forward to receiving his first student, but soon finds that, as an intern, he now has to run all procedures by Maggie Doyle whom he instructed last year. In fact, Carter's power relations with other members of staff are in a state of flux. His student, George Henry, turns out to be a researcher with no interest or experience of practical medicine and Carter is quickly able to humiliate him with a variety of unpleasant procedures. But such power is short-lived as Henry identifies a rare brain illness associated with his research that Anna and Carter both missed. Trying to locate Henry amid the hospital labs also leads to Carter exposing his expensive shoes to radiation and having them confiscated. To cap it all, Carter discovers that the ER has taken him up on his offer to work for free and that his pay cheque is an administrative error!

By contrast, Anna's student, Chastity Lee, is enthusiastic and well trained. However, Anna has problems of her own. Doug Ross wants her to see more adult patients while on her rotation. Doug takes one of her child cases but misses whooping cough, which Anna suspected and failed to tell him about. Although the boy is seriously ill, and starts to vomit blood, he is stabilized. Doug confronts Anna but she stands her ground, insisting that the boy was her patient.

Anna/
Ross

Carol's increasing impatience with Mark Greene is highlighted by the case of an eighteen-year old girl who is dehydrated and does not want her parents informed of her condition. A pregnancy test proves negative but Carol realizes that the erosion of the girl's tooth enamel indicates bulimia. Greene's order to 'treat and street' the young woman makes Carol uncomfortable. Meanwhile, Doug and Carol's relationship appears to becoming more serious, crowned by the gift of a drawer to Doug so that he can keep a change of clothes at Carol's house.

Carol/
Greene/
Ross

4-3: "Friendly Fire"

The ER is $1.7 million over last year's budget so far this year and Kerry has approached Anspaugh with a plan to put them back on budget within six months. Anspaugh contrasts Weaver's proficient management with that of Morgenstern and indicates that some would not like to see the latter continue in his post. Kerry is officially made acting ER chief and is promised a full evaluation of her position when Morgenstern returns. Determined to solve the department's financial problems, Weaver's first target is Ross whose paediatrics fellowship is underwritten by the ER. Doug is told to apply for independent funding or lose his job. Next she prevents overtime payments for the nursing staff despite Carol's objections. Unsurprisingly, Weaver's friendly approaches to staff like Maggie Doyle are received coolly.

Weaver

In fact, the ER budget seems dangerously threatened by Jerry's incompetence. While speaking to the wife of a Texan who shot himself in the foot, Jerry examines the couple's personal grenade launcher - and blows up the ambulance bay in the process! Jerry soon finds himself put on the night-shift...

Carol   Carol assists Casey, a 'hero' who grabbed a loose cable to prevent two men being killed but badly cut his hands in the process. Although she defends him against his employer, who threatens Casey's chances of claiming benefit by twisting an insurance claim, Carol discovers that her patient was smoking dope on duty and caused the accident. Meanwhile, Carol gets a little frustrated when she suspects Corday of chatting up Doug. In fact, Doug tells Corday he is not interested and Carol later has to apologize to him but clearly she still has problems trusting him.

Carter   Carter and Greene look after a twenty-seven year old woman who will die due to swelling at the brain-stem. They decide to approach the husband about organ donation but just as they do the woman starts to talk and move again. However, x-rays show that she needs emergency surgery. The confusion earlier makes the husband unwilling but after pressure from Greene and Carter the husband relents and signs the consent form.

Benton/   Benton and Carla argue about circumcising Rees. Carla
Corday   is in favour and approaches Anna to perform the procedure, which she does, not realizing that Peter did not share Carla's feelings. Peter confronts Carla who explains that she was mad with him but he stands his ground. Meanwhile, Benton's respect for Corday appears to be growing (especially when she calls Anspaugh an 'old tosser.')

Carter   Carter is annoyed when Maggie Doyle pulls him off a trauma case to perform sutures and gives the case to Anna instead. Although Greene explains that Anna's student is more capable than Carter's, allowing her to run procedures, Carter suspects that Maggie has a thing for Anna. In fact, Carter is the one who is pursuing Del Amico and she and Carter arrange to do their laundry together that evening. The date proves to be a comic disaster, with Carter putting their hoagies in the dryer with his clothes.

Al and his fellow construction worker, Billy Nelson, arrive in the ER. Both have been involved in an accident and Al has bled on his friend but so far has said nothing about his HIV status. Jeanie manages to convince Al to tell Bill, who will need to go on a drug cocktail pending the results of a blood test, but Bill reacts badly and refuses to let Jeanie take his blood sample. — Jeanie

Heather asks Mark out again but he once more tells her that he's busy. Meanwhile, the bulimic girl [episode 4-2] returns to the ER suffering from internal bleeding due to repeated vomiting. Doyle is angry to find that the girl was inadequately treated by Greene, who has to admit his mistake. Carol, however, defends Mark. It should not be left to doctors to go the extra mile for all their patients: there needs to be a safety net. After a frustrating day, Greene calls Heather and they meet for dinner but the date unsuccessful. Mark is impotent and, embarrassed, makes his excuses and leaves. — Greene/ Carol

4-4: "When the Bough Breaks"

Peter brings Carla some emergency medical equipment for the baby: Rees is being released today. Later, at the hospital, Corday bumps into Peter as Rees is being taken away by Carla and her sister. Benton is obviously uncomfortable that she has found out the truth. Having a son is making a difference: during the day, he desperately tries to save a crack baby but Greene calls off his efforts. Amid the chaos of the ER, he walks to a telephone and calls Carla to ask if Rees is okay. Later, Corday offers to cover for Benton so that he can go home - she says she will explain to Hicks. At Carla's he watches mother and son sleep next to each other. — Benton

Greene   Jenn tells Mark that his recent moods have been affecting
          Rachel. She has decided to keep her away from Greene:
          "Call me when you have your life back together." At
          work, he is more than usually cranky although he won't
          admit it. Amid run-ins with Hathaway, Mark treats a
          man who thinks he is an angel. The angel tells Mark that
          he is 'lost in negative energy' but also that Cynthia is
          attracted to him. That night, Greene offers Cynthia a
          ride home.

Carter/   Carter is trying to approach his internship with a change
Benton   of perspective and to enjoy it. He and Anna meet their
           new med-students, James and Ivan. A motorcyclist who
           was involved in a high-speed chase with police is brought
           in. Carter orders an abdominal CT before alerting
           Benton, in response to Benton's insistence on one for an
           earlier candidate, but now finds his patient crashing in
           the ER. Benton arrives and rushes the motorcyclist to the
           OR while chastizing Carter for not calling him sooner.
           Carter talks over the incident with Anna and decides to
           confront Benton about his attitude to him. Benton is
           angry that Carter wasted three years with him and didn't
           give Benton the chance to talk him out of his change of
           specialty.

Ross   Weaver's cost-cutting measures continue to irritate
           members of staff. She finds Doug's research proposal
           and suggests that, although his thesis has been proven by
           another hospital, he could perform a sample study in the
           ER. Weaver insists that Doug finds private funding for
           his project or he will have to look for work elsewhere.

Jeanie   Al comes in to have his stitches removed earlier than
           expected. He has been sacked from his job on the
           construction site for a rather lame reason and does not
           believe that he will get another such job in Chicago now
           that people know his HIV status. Meanwhile, Jeanie has
           to attend to an old man who has a collapsed lung. In her
           desperate attempts to put in a chest tube, she decides to
           break her agreement and put her finger into the man's
           side, exposing him to the risk of infection. Weaver arrives

and angrily dismisses Jeanie. Jeanie removes her gloves and finds, to her relief, that they did not split and that she is not bleeding.

A high-speed chase has ended in a collision between a police car and a school bus, injuring several children. Amid the confusion of the multiple traumas, Carol notices a trail of blood leading to the women's toilet. Doris, a heroin addict who had previously attended the ER, *[episode 4-1]* is pregnant and crowning. Just before Carol can get to her to help, Doris delivers the baby but it is unresponsive. Greene and Benton, who is momentarily stunned, fight to save the child but the baby dies. Doris demands a lawyer saying Carol dropped the baby and Carol has to fill in a report form but finds that Greene is cold and won't defend her. She complains that Mark failed to treat Doris correctly on previous occasions, but he says that the ER can't help people who can't help themselves. Carol disagrees - they are precisely the people they should help.

Carol

Anna continues to have her authority as a paediatrician challenged when a woman brings her asthmatic grandson into the ER but will only see Ross. Ross orders a stool sample but discovers that Anna had already ordered one and not told him. He angrily confronts her but has to break off when the bereaved mother of one of the school bus victims arrives.

Anna/
Ross

4-5: "Good Touch, Bad Touch"

Carol has come up with the idea of a clinic, a voluntary service housed in the ER to catch those patients who would normally fall through the cracks in the system. The women and children's day clinic would use an exam room in the ER two or three days each week and be staffed by volunteers. Weaver is lukewarm, fearing expense or disruption to nursing care, but later gives Carol a number of books on grant applications and fund-raising. Although she hadn't envisaged herself at the head of the clinic, Weaver says that for a good idea to come to

Carol

life one person has to sit down and make it happen. Later, Carter suggests private foundations and mentions that his grandmother is in charge of one. Carol decides to approach her.

Benton   Caring for Rees has taken its toll on Benton who is inadequately prepared for surgery. When he answers a question incorrectly, Anspaugh tells him to leave and address his backlog of paperwork, leaving the patient in the capable hands of Dr Corday, Benton's new rival. Later, Corday finds Benton and offers to get him a place on Romano's team: Benton declines as he has too many commitments. Anspaugh, however, is concerned: the hospital was willing to help when Rees was in NICU but now Corday has raised the bar for surgical residents. She risks making them all look bad. Later, Corday introduces Benton to Romano who takes an instant *liking* to Peter.

Greene   Greene's mood continues to worsen. He cuts Benton short on a question about parenting, refuses to finish his medical examination of an excitable 65 year old woman, and grabs a violent patient's wound until the man begins to cry and settle down. The cause soon becomes clear when Cynthia discovers that Mark is due to give a deposition in the Kenny Law malpractice suit that afternoon. She comforts him but the deposition does not go well: Greene is flustered by the questioning, becomes increasingly angry and accuses Chris Law of assaulting him.

Anna/   Anna sees a 20 year old college athlete who is suffering
Ross   from shortness of breath. An x-ray reveals probable testicular cancer, which has spread to the lungs. Anna refuses Doug's offer to perform the examination and carries on regardless, causing much embarrassment for Anna and the young man who gets an erection. Anna leaves him and is later dismayed to discover that the athlete has gone missing. However, eventually, the man returns. Anna offers Doug's services but the athlete wants Anna to stay.

Dale Edson, today's surgical consult to the ER, cannot resist making remarks at Carter's expense. He also tries to make Carter jealous by saying that Dr Robert 'Rocket' Romano is back in the hospital and letting him scrub in later that day. When he makes an excellent save and finds an urgent surgical case, he can only watch as Edson and Romano take his patient up to surgery. Although Weaver congratulates him on a good call, Carter nevertheless begins to wonder if he has made the right decision in transferring to the ER. He checks on his former patient in surgery and finds Edson telling the man's wife that the operation was successful. Edson introduces Carter but the wife is more concerned to thank Dale. Carter talks to Benton who says that Carter is twice the surgeon Dale will ever be.

Carter

Jeanie and Al enjoy a drink in a bar until Billy Nelson arrives *[episode 4-3]*. Billy starts to shout, demanding to know if Al got HIV from drugs or sex. Although Jeanie tries to convince Al to leave, he gets into a fight with Billy. Jeanie stands by helpless, calling to Al as he beats his old friend unconscious...

Jeanie

4-6: "Ground Zero"

Carol spends the day preparing her presentation to Millicent Carter, head of the Carter Family Foundation and John Carter's grandmother. Carter tells Carol that his Gran loves stats and figures and to avoid politics, religion and baseball - his Gran is still pissed off about that inter-league play! Meanwhile, Carter is getting closer to Anna by empathizing with her lack of money. Naturally, Anna is annoyed when she hears from Carol that Carter is 'real blue blood' and decides to tag along with Carol to see Millicent Carter. Suddenly confronted by the family mansion, Anna accuses Carter of being patronizing. He is apologetic but Anna is still fuming. Meanwhile, Carol and Millicent get on well: Millicent approves of Carol's proposal and more especially of Carol and gives her a cheque for $75,000 - seed-money for the clinic.

Carol/ Carter/ Anna

291

Benton/
Corday

Benton discovers that Dr Hicks' schedule has moved forward and that Corday took his gastroplasty that morning instead of calling him in from home. Later, he discovers that the surgery he was given in lieu by Corday was in place of ground-breaking surgery with Romano, which is being covered by Channel 5 news. He again confronts Corday but he soon gets his own back by suggesting that Corday begin an appendectomy without Anspaugh, thereby landing her in trouble. Corday insists that she is not being manipulative but Benton decides to err on the side of caution and tries to muscle in on Romano's team himself. Romano decides to consider Peter's request.

Weaver/
Jeanie

Anspaugh tells Weaver that Synergix Physicians Group (SPG), an ER management consultancy, is being hired to balance the ER's budget. Weaver insists that she has made headway but Anspaugh says that she should welcome SPG or risk finding herself made a scapegoat. Weaver attends the SPG presentation, given by Dr Ellis West, and asks some perceptive questions that put West off guard. Afterwards, he sweet-talks Weaver to dinner. Weaver confides in West that she will have to sack eight physician's assistants, including Jeanie, to balance the budget. West gives Weaver some advice on breaking the news but Jeanie takes it badly. When Jeanie returns home, she finds the house full of candles. Al has found looking for work in Chicago impossible since his HIV status went public but has found a job in Atlanta with an old friend. He asks Jeanie to come with him to Atlanta.

Greene/
Ross

Mark is relieved to find that the Kenny Law malpractice suit has been settled by the hospital out of court but this respite is cut short when he is served with a civil suit from Chris Law for violating his brother's human rights. Doug tries to help by putting Mark in touch with a lawyer he knows but Greene is short with him. Doug complains that being Greene's friend has become increasingly hard while Carol suggests that she look at the statute of limitation on post-traumatic stress - they've cut Mark Greene more than enough slack. Greene's temper increases as the day goes on and his failure to treat an eccentric woman almost leads to her death. When he insensitively shouts at an old woman who is hard of hearing that her husband will die, the whole ER stops. Ross pulls Greene away but Mark shuns him and runs for the door. Cynthia follows. Mark explains to her that he's losing control and in the heat of the confession they kiss. That evening, Doug arrives at Greene's apartment and is greeted at the door by Cynthia in a dressing gown. He is about to make his excuses but Greene sees that he is upset. Ross has heard that his father has died in a car wreck and is leaving to arrange the funeral. Mark agrees to take his holidays and go with him.

4-7: "Fathers and Sons"

It's a sweltering hot November day as Mark and Doug drive through the desert en route to Barstow. The highway patrol inform Doug that his father ran a stop sign at 120mph killing himself, a woman in his car called Sheri Fox and Pedro Lopez, a father of six, who was driving a pick-up truck with which Doug's father collided. Ray Ross was four times over the legal limit for alcohol. Doug is bitter about his father's stupidity, especially as it resulted in other deaths. He and Mark head to the motel where Ray was staying.

Ross/
Greene

The landlady recognizes Doug as Ray's son, the doctor, whom Ray always talked proudly about. Doug discovers a collection of photographs and movie reels of him as a child among his father's possessions. He is more surprised to find his father's Cadillac in the garage: it must have been Sheri's car that Ray wrecked that night. They take it for a spin and Doug reminisces upon how he learnt to drive in that car, how his father would turn up in it unexpectedly and they would disappear for days together in it. Suddenly, they run out of petrol. He and Mark look in the trunk for an emergency supply but the petrol canister is empty and the boot filled with hundreds of child's toys belonging to Sheri's child.

Ross

Ross   Doug and Mark sleep in the Cadillac on the highway but
            are rescued in the morning by a truck driver. The car
            refilled, Doug wants to find the Lopez family and speak
            to them. He discovers that today is the day of the funeral
            and together he and Mark attend the service. Doug is
            clearly upset by the sight of one of Pedro's youngest
            sons, innocent of all around him. They don't stay; Doug
            can't think of anything to say to the family. Instead, they
            recover Ray's property from a pawnbrokers: an old
            movie projector, diamond rings, Rolex but no wedding
            rings - he wouldn't pawn them, they are told. Mark buys
            a tacky necklace engraved 'Cynthia,' which Doug objects
            to, before they head back to the motel.

Ross   Mark later finds Doug trying to ring his latest sweetheart
            - Greene notes that it sounds serious and wants to know
            who it is. After much pestering, Mark finds out that
            Doug is back with Carol and is astonished. That night
            they watch the movies. Doug finds it easy to hate his
            father for controlling his life, and that of his mother. He
            is angry that he never got to tell his father so but the old
            movies show a tender side to his father he had perhaps
            forgotten. Doug tells Mark that he's in love with Carol.
            It's the first time that's happened.

Greene   Greene confesses to Doug that he and his father barely
            speak but when Doug discovers that Mark's parents live
            in San Diego, only a short drive away, he insists of taking
            Mark to see them. Mark's mother is pleased to see him;
            Doug quickly makes his excuses and leaves them alone.
            Mark's relationship with his father, however, is stilted
            and they say little though they haven't seen each other in
            a long time. Mark discovers that his father has emphy-
            sema and needs oxygen: at dinner, his father refuses his
            help when an uncontrollable coughing begins. His
            mother also has high blood pressure. That evening,
            waiting for Doug, Mark speaks to his mother. He thinks
            that his father doesn't care about him or Rachel. His
            mother insists that's not true and that Mark always
            assumes he knows more about people than he actually
            does.

Doug returns: he has informed Sheri's family. Her son is in Arizona, living with Sheri's ex-husband. Doug tells Mark he should spend more time with his family but Mark insists that there is no point and tells Doug that he didn't miss much not having a father around. Doug is angry: Mark's father was always there for him. He tells Mark to get his head out of his ass.

Ross/ Greene

Overnight, Doug and Mark return to the motel. Greene admits that he's been acting like a victim, been self-pitying. He has always wanted to control but has lived his life waiting for something bad to happen - and last spring it did. Now he doesn't know what will replace the old Mark. They arrive back at the motel to find Carol waiting for Doug. Later that day, Doug scatters his father's ashes in the desert. He loved him and hated him - never simple is it, he says. Carol, Doug and Mark drink tequila shots to Ray's memory.

Ross/ Greene/ Carol

4-8: "Freak Show"

Greene hands Carol a note addressed to 'CH' which Doug wrote before he left Barstow. She is about to open it but finds the ER packed with people expecting the opening of the free clinic: Cynthia has advertised the clinic one week early. Mark gives Cynthia the tacky necklace he bought for her in Barstow and she is ecstatic but she is more pleased by his apparent change of attitude. Later, Cynthia kisses him and tells him that what he wrote was really sexy - she has read the note to 'CH', which Carol left behind the reception desk! And her answer is yes! Later, Carol finds the note and reads it - it's the rip your pants off kind not the sentimental type - but that evening it's Mark Greene and Cynthia who get the benefit of Doug's hot note!

Carol/ Greene

Anna insists that she is no longer annoyed with Carter but she still seems a little curt with him and he asks for a truce. Meanwhile, George Henry returns to the ER to resit his rotation: Carter was unable to evaluate many of the skills tested because Henry barely turned up!

Carter/ Anna

Throughout the day, Henry complains about his allergies but later collapses and starts wheezing in the trauma room. Anna and Carter quickly discover Henry's hands have turned red beneath his gloves - he is allergic to latex. Together they save Henry who claims to have had an out of body experience: Anna and Carter were his angels, together they saved his life. He joins their hands.

Greene   Greene treats Herb Speevak, a solicitor who has been bitten by a python. 'Flora' the snake ate the neighbour's jack russell terrier and Herb was defending the snake's owner. Herb is treated and discharged but continues to loiter around the ER. Later, Greene finds that his lawyer thinks Herb has taken over the case. Greene complains that he can't pay Herb's fee but Herb suggests an alternative: if Mark allows him to perform some minor procedures, he'll make the law suit disappear.

Jeanie   Maggie Doyle tries to convince Jeanie that she should fight her dismissal on the grounds of unfair dis-crimination. Doyle believes that it may have something to do with Jeanie's HIV status but Jeanie is not so sure. At work, Weaver tells Jeanie that she has put in an excellent reference for her for a physician's assistant post at Atlanta Memorial Hospital but Jeanie is still short with her. Later, she hears that Al's job in Atlanta has fallen through. During the day, Jeanie finds that a new nurse has been hired despite the hiring freeze and overhears that Kerry has awarded herself a $25,000 pay rise as a result of becoming acting ER chief. She confronts Weaver but her explanations do not satisfy her. Jeanie tells Anspaugh that she believes her dismissal was due to her HIV status. Despite Weaver's protestations, Anspaugh appears to back down and will reconsider Jeanie's redundancy.

Benton/   Romano has heard that Benton and Corday have issues
Corday   and therefore has reservations about letting Benton join his team. He asks Benton if he has the time to put in his best efforts; Peter hesitates but says yes. Later, Benton finds a one-in-a-million surgical case: a 12 year old hit-

and-run victim, Rodney Price, has a rare genetic defect which has reversed the positions of his abdominal organs. Benton pages Romano who asks Corday to attend: this surgery will be a test of their ability to work together. The surgery goes well. Afterwards, Benton discovers that he knows the boy's father, Isaac Price, who was in his class at high school. Corday is pleased - it will be easier to get blood samples for gene research - but Benton is not sure he wants Isaac to think they are just using Rodney as a test case. Benton relents and asks Isaac for blood samples from himself, his son and his ex-wife; Isaac agrees thinking it's in his son's best interest. Suddenly, Rodney's condition deteriorates: his blood does not clot and his lungs fill with blood. Despite Benton's valiant efforts, Rodney dies. Isaac, discovering that the tests were for research, refuses to allow an autopsy. Romano is furious and orders Benton to get consent but Peter refuses and tells Romano to get someone else to do it. Despite their run in, Benton later discovers from Corday that Romano has accepted him for his team.

4-9: "Obstruction of Justice"

Weaver believes Jeanie's accusation was no more than heat of the moment frustration. However, Jeanie is preparing her defence with some lawyers, friends of Maggie Doyle, and comes in to work refusing to accept her dismissal. She now believes Weaver was reacting to Jeanie's breach of her conditions of work in the ER a few weeks previously *[episode 4-4]*. Weaver informs Anspaugh and confides in West, who is setting up SPG in the ER, about her problems: he offers her the chance to give a paper at a SPG conference in the Caribbean the following week to get away from the pressures of the ER. Later, Jeanie and her lawyer confront Anspaugh and Weaver about Jeanie's dismissal: Anspaugh assures them that he will review the situation and, despite Kerry's objections, Jeanie is reinstated. Weaver confronts Jeanie about using her HIV status like this but Jeanie still thinks it had something to do with her dismissal. Jeanie returns

Weaver/
Jeanie

home to tell Al the good news but he has just been given a six month contract working on a construction site in Atlanta. That night, they part.

Corday/ Benton	A mother and daughter injured in a car accident are brought in to the ER. The mother is serious injured and Mark and Anna are unable to save her. Ellis West and Weaver manage to stabilize the daughter, Allison Beaumont, but fear she may need her leg amputating. Benton agrees but Corday and Romano insist there is a chance to save the leg by performing a fibula transplant. The surgery proceeds smoothly but in the final stages Allison crashes and Benton suddenly has to take over when Corday appears shocked at the consequences of her surgery. Allison is stabilized but in a coma and Corday is still shaken up by the experience. Did she decide to operate for the right reasons: saving the patient's leg or her lust for challenging surgery? Benton admits he has those same thoughts all the time.
Greene	Greene has agreed to let his solicitor, Herb Speevak, shadow him around the ER. Greene provides Herb with scrubs and insists that he can only follow him around but soon Herb is mistaken for a Synergix attending, and is handing out the advice he learned from an ER attending he hired for a few weeks to teach him the basics. Greene tries to keep Herb away from patients but is too late to intercept him using a defibrillator on a patient who had flatlined. The man is saved, much to Mark's surprise. Later, Herb tells Greene that the law suit against him has been dropped - Herb knows the Law family's lawyer - and thanks Mark for a thrilling day. He even gets to keep his scrubs.
Weaver/ Ross	A young man arrives in the ER insisting he requires Demerol. Carol is suspicious and Kerry insists on checking the man's clinic records before giving him any. The clinic has closed, which Weaver finds a convenient excuse, but leaves the case in Doug's hands. Later, she is angry to discover that Doug gave the man Demerol and discharged him.

Chase Carter, John's cousin, arrives in the ER with a swollen spider bite on his arm. As he is being treated, Chase explains to Carter that their grandfather is looking out for his successor and Carter is the hot favourite although he will have to give up medicine. Carter is not interested and returns to his other patients. A domestic violence case is brought in: the husband, a police officer, has been run over by his wife in their car. She has now taken a drugs overdose. Carter defends the wife's rights against another police officer, a friend of the husband, who is already helping to plot the legal case against the wife. He refuses to provide blood and stomach samples without the proper warrant and destroys the evidence. The police officer arrests Carter for obstruction of justice and takes him to the police station. Meanwhile, the couple are reunited and making out in a trauma room. "Carter went to jail for this?" asks Anna. Later, Anna bails Carter out and jokes that it's proving expensive having a rich guy as friend!

4-10: "Do You See What I See?"

It is Christmas Eve, 1997, and Herb Speevak is back in the ER with an actor and a photographer, recreating and recording his moment of glory for posterity. Mark has only to sign a few papers that afternoon and the Kenny Law suit will be over - he doesn't even have to give the apology demanded by the Law family. Meanwhile, Mark treats a woman who has the word 'whore' written in black marker on her stomach: she has been raped. Carol questions the woman while Greene performs an examination and treats her wounds. When she describes the violence of her attack, it reminds him too much of his own assault and he leaves. Later, he speaks to the woman again. She is angry at her attacker but realizes that hating him won't make the pain go away. The thought clearly plays on Greene's mind. That night he visits the Law family and apologizes. Chris says that he didn't assault Greene but was glad to hear that it had happened - but none of that will bring his brother back.

Carter

Weaver/   Weaver and Jeanie are still not on speaking terms. When
Jeanie   Weaver points out that by giving needles to a man with
          hepatitis she is breaking the law, Jeanie says the man
          won't report her but is not sure whether Weaver will.
          However, when Jeanie discovers she has forgotten her
          HIV medication, she has to turn to Weaver for emer-
          gency supplies. Weaver obliges without question and
          Jeanie thanks her. Meanwhile, Weaver has spent the
          night with Ellis West and agrees to accompany him to
          the Synergix conference in the Caribbean.

Carol   Carol prepares for a visit from Millicent Carter who is on
          her Christmas round of Carter-sponsored good causes.
          When she arrives, with Chase Carter dressed as Santa
          Claus, Carol is busy putting out the Christmas tree
          which has caught fire. After a hectic day, Millicent
          ominously says that she has seen all that she needed to
          see. Later, Carol receives a gift from the Carter Family
          Foundation: outside is beautiful Christmas tree, too tall
          for the ER. Carol is also handed a cheque for $150,000
          to continue the clinic.

Carter   George Henry insists that Carter let him perform an LP
          or intubation and then he can pass his ER rotation.
          Carter thinks that is a matter of opinion but is more than
          willing to get Henry off his hands. When a patient dies in
          trauma, Carter gets Henry to intubate the corpse - just as
          the man's brother arrives. Carter rushes the relative away
          while they pretend still to be operating. Later, Carter and
          Henry break the bad news to the relatives but to ease the
          wife's pain, Henry says the man's last thoughts were of
          Maria. Unfortunately the wife is called Angela! Mean-
          while, Carter speaks to Chase who has accompanied
          their grandmother to the hospital. In the back of the
          limousine, Carter finds Chase taking drugs.

Corday   Corday is preparing to fly back to England for Christmas
          when she suddenly hears that Romano wants to perform
          the second stage of Allison Beaumont's tib-fib surgery
          before the holiday. Corday is concerned: she feels guilty
          that the first stage put Allison in a coma [episode 4-9].

Nevertheless, surgery goes ahead. Just as Corday is about
to leave she hears that Allison has come out of her coma.
She tells her that her mother died in the ER. Corday
extubates Allison but finds that she has vocal chord
injuries from the accident. Corday calls for a head and
neck specialist. That evening she stays at Allison's
bedside instead of taking her flight home.

While treating Bart, a blind homeless man, Benton   Benton
touches the man's forehead and suddenly Bart is able to
see again. Anna can't find a logical explanation for the
effect of Benton's healing hands. Soon, Bart's friends
begin arriving in the ER asking for Benton to lay on
hands and cure their illnesses! Benton even appears to be
responsible for restoring a floor cleaner to working order
just by patting the janitor on the shoulder. Later,
however, Bart returns: he has lost his sight once more.
Benton discovers that Bart has a head tumour that, by
freak chance, allowed him to see one more time but is
terminal. Bart, however, seems content that he got to see
the park one last time.

Carol decides that her relationship with Doug should be   Carol/
made public but when she announces it to the staff they   Doug
merely start passing around their winnings. They knew
all along and had taken bets on when Carol and Doug
would come clean. With everyone present, Doug takes
the opportunity to propose. Everyone cheers as Carol
kisses him.

4-11: "Think Warm Thoughts"

Doug is keen to set a date for the marriage but Carol   Carol/
wants to take things slowly. She is unsurprisingly an-   Ross
noyed when her mother arrives demanding to know if   .
Doug's proposal of marriage is true: he asked for her
daughter's hand this morning. Carol has to explain that
she has been seeing Doug for the last eight months.
Doug comes in and hides from Carol, working in the free
clinic on his day off. By the end of the day, he is back in
her good books.

Weaver   Ellis informs Kerry that the figures for Synergix's first month in the ER are poor and he expects the second month's results to be worse. Weaver says that he can persuade Anspaugh to allow the SPG take-over; and if he can't, she can. (And then they exchange smutty phone calls: "Kerry Weaver, you are a bad, bad girl...") Anspaugh is resistant to their pressure and wants to hear the news from the trenches but by the end of the day it seems that SPG has won the contract. Weaver and West go back to his hotel to celebrate.

Jeanie   Anspaugh asks Greene to take charge of his son, Scott, who arrives complaining of abdominal pain. Scott was treated for cancer in the hospital ten months previously. Greene asks Jeanie to assist but Scott is short with them, and unhappy that a little stomach pain has to result in so much fuss. He refuses to let them take blood samples but Jeanie insists that she can take a sample without him feeling it. He challenges her and she disproves his doubts. Later, they talk about John Woo films as Scott gets x-rayed: he knows the drill and suspects that the tumour has returned. Sadly, Scott is proven right. Anspaugh, clearly impressed by Jeanie's efforts and friendship with his son, thanks her for all her help.

Corday   Corday tries to persuade Romano to let Allison have vocal chord surgery but Romano insists that Allison's insurance won't cover it. Corday visits Dr Kokowitz, a Chicago throat specialist, who she persuades to perform Allison's surgery for free. Romano is furious that she is questioning his commitment to Allison's best interests but later apologizes and schedules Allison's operation. Corday asks if she and Romano are still on good terms; he insists that they are "a match made in heaven."

Carter   Carter and Benton have been roped in to speak to second year medical students about their choice of rotation: Carter for the ER, Benton for surgery. One student, Laura Brown, has evidently taken interest in what both have to offer. After Carter's talk, Laura asks him to dinner but en route they find a man slumped in the snow. They rush him to the ER where Carter lets Laura watch him run some procedures only to discover that the man was drunk. Meanwhile, Laura becomes more interested in Benton's gory attempts to save another patient next door. Carter looks up to find his eager pupil has deserted to surgery.

Carol treats Mrs Riley, an elderly woman who is brought in by Susan, her meals-on-wheels lady. Mrs Riley is confused and dehydrated. As they put her into a gown, Carol sees the word 'whore' written in marker on her back - the rapist has struck again. The police are called once more. Greene says Mrs Riley's amnesia is probably a blessing but as the day draws on her memory slowly returns...

Carol

4-12: "Sharp Relief"

Carol arrives in the ER just as Doug is leaving. He asks that they meet later that day, after she has completed her paramedic ridealong: Doug has a surprise for her. In fact, the surprise is their wedding, which Doug has carefully organized in advance. He asks Mark to be his best man but to keep his plans secret: "Every other woman I went out with... I knew it was wrong. Now I want to spend the rest of my life with her."

Carol/
Ross

Romano and Benton operate on Scott Anspaugh to re-move an obstruction and discover that his cancer has returned. Jeanie tells Scott who reacts defiantly, insisting that he would rather die. Jeanie coaxes him round with two ring-side tickets to a hockey game. Anspaugh tells Jeanie that Scott needs more chemotherapy and asks her to be a part-time private duty care giver for his son. He tells her that Scott thinks highly of her, "as I do." Jeanie agrees. Jeanie tells Scott and sits by him in the ward while Donald Anspaugh looks on through the window.

Jeanie

Kerry is concerned to hear that the ER of another Chicago hospital has closed and emergency patients are being transferred to County and is prompted to investi-

Weaver

gate SPG's track record. In fact, 60% of SPG's trauma centres in the mid-west have been closed down. West gives her the party line and tells her not to worry, County ER won't close. "How could we?" she asks. "If everyone else closes, someone needs to handle the traumas." Weaver suggests that the hospital board delay their vote on the SPG take-over until she can do further work. Ellis asks to take her to dinner to talk over her concerns but Weaver insists that she wants to think alone, perhaps about both Synergix and her relationship with West.

Carter/ Anna

Chase arrives in the ER. He tells Carter that he stopped taking heroin two days ago and is clearly suffering the effects of withdrawal. John offers to help by putting Chase in a detox centre but won't prescribe compazine for him. They argue and Chase leaves. Anna tells Carter to let him go: she had a friend at med-school with a drug problem and knows what is happening. Carter is curt with her. Throughout the day, Carter gets telephone calls from Chase asking him for help and eventually John excuses himself from work on grounds of a family emergency. Chase is clearly near to breaking and has called his dealer who Carter tells to leave Chase alone. From the apartment, Carter nurses Chase and calls for some medication to help his cousin through the worst effects. Anna arrives with his prescription and helps. She explains to Carter that she wasn't entirely truthful earlier. It was her ex-boyfriend who had a drug problem: "I've done the detox dance more times than I can count." Carter thanks her for coming over. "What are friends for?"

Corday/ Benton

Corday excuses herself from the Anspaugh surgery to be present in the OR when Dr Kotlowitz reattaches Allison Beaumont's vocal chords. The Beaumont surgery is a terrific success and Allison should have her voice back in one or two weeks. To celebrate, Corday collars Benton and invites him for a drink. They end up at a British bar, playing darts, where Corday manages to convince Benton to drink Pimms after he loses a bet. The evening goes well: Benton is more than a little intoxicated and they are still dancing when the bar closes. Outside, there is an uncomfortable pause as they decide where to go next and end taking separate cabs home. Benton pauses to say that he really enjoyed the evening.

Carol's paramedic ridealong is with unit 57: paramedics Doris Pickman and Greg Powell. After spending some time in the station, they are finally called out on an emergency. An old woman, the latest victim of the serial rapist, is bleeding out and unresponsive. Powell's initial reaction is to shout that the woman is dead but Carol quickly takes over. The woman is brought to the ER where Greene takes over but is unable to save her. Meanwhile, Carol and Powell return to the woman's appartment. He explains that when he saw the old woman, it reminded him of finding his mother after she committed suicide. Carol tells him of her own suicide attempt. After they talk a little more, Greg leans over and kisses Carol. After work, Carol walks to reflect on her relationship with Doug. Back home, she finds Doug has been waiting, frantically calling around to find her. She explains that she has been thinking: she thinks that they are rushing into things and that she kissed Greg Powell. Doug storms out.

Carol/
Ross

4-13: "Carter's Choice"

It's six a.m. and there's a thick layer of snow on the ground, with the weather reports forecasting up to three feet later in the day. The ER is quiet, and Anna is sleeping in exam four: Carter looks at her for a moment before she wakes and he tells her Chase is still weak, but up and around - although he's evasive when Anna suggests the three of them should have dinner. Their breakfast plans are soon scotched by the arrival of a woman of seventy - the latest victim of the serial rapist who is still being pursued by the police - and a security guard who sustained multiple gun-shot wounds when he interrupted the crime. The woman's hips have been dislocated, but her vitals are normal and she will be all right. The security guard, however, dies despite Carter's

Carol/
Ross

attempts to save him. "No good deed goes unpunished," Greene remarks bitterly.

Greene   Cynthia's lease on her flat has expired, and her landlord is raising the rent: she suggests to Mark that she could move in with him, but he doesn't like the idea, and offers to help with her rent instead. Later, she asks an embarrassed Ross whether he thinks Mark doesn't think she's good enough, or is scared because he cares too much. Ross gives a non-committal reply, and tells Greene he needs to talk to her.

Benton/   Benton is nursing a hangover from his night out with
Corday   Corday, and is annoyed at Carla's decision to put baby Rees into day-care. Corday persuades him to have lunch with her, and frankly suggests that they should get together. Benton looks embarrassed and says he's not comfortable about the idea, but it is clear nevertheless that he's thinking about it. He agrees to go out to play darts - just darts - with her tonight...

Ross/   Ross notices Carol talking to Greg Powell in a corridor
Carol   *[see episode 4-12]* and quickly works out who he is. He demands that Carol shouldn't embarrass Ross in front of his friends, at which Carol laughs bitterly, reeling off a list of the times Doug did the same to her. But this isn't about getting even, she says, her voice breaking; it's about her needing some time. It's the one thing she's ever asked him for, she says. Later, he tells her he didn't mean to push her. "Take all the time you need," he says softly.

Weaver   Ellis West arrives in the ER having heard that Weaver is withdrawing her support for Synergix, despite the board's vote last night to begin negotiations. Weaver bitterly accuses him of using their relationship to get the contract and they part on bad terms, but later West tells her she was wrong, and he has withdrawn the contract: he only wanted it if it meant working closely with her.

Carter/   The police have caught the serial rapist at an abandoned
Anna   warehouse but he has a gun-shot wound to the chest, and

Malik, Conni and others react badly to the news that he will be brought to County for treatment. Carter and Anna treat him when he arrives, but because they only have four units of O negative left, he decides to 'auto-transfuse' - using the man's own blood to replace the blood he has lost. The man survives, but after work Anna confronts Carter and accuses him of withholding treatment. Carter denies it, but later turns up outside Anna's flat, and admits he wanted the rapist to die. "Was it wrong?" he pleads to Anna. "Are you sure?" No, Anna says, she's not sure, and takes his hand.

4-14: "Family Practice"

Mark returns to his parents' home in San Diego *[see episode 4-7]* after hearing that his mother Ruth has had a fall and broken her leg. David Greene meets him and Cynthia - who has accompanied Mark, to his obvious discomfort - at the airport and they go straight to the Naval Medical Centre, part of the retired navy community where the Greenes live. Mark is disturbed to find Ruth behaving in a deliriously uninhibited fashion, singing and making tactless remarks. The next day she undergoes a neuro exam, and is clearly distressed by her own mental state. The medical centre's Dr Sayers suspects her dementia has been caused by a series of small strokes, but Mark wants more tests, and demands a second opinion from a civilian.

Greene

As the tests continue, Mark seems increasingly agitated about Ruth's condition, David's ill health, their marriage, and his relationship with Cynthia. He learns that Ruth had been seeing a psychiatrist, and tells his father so when David confronts him about the fact that he's ordered Ruth to be tested for syphilis. The ensuing argument causes David to have an attack, and he too is taken to the medical centre.

Greene

With David recovering after his attack, Mark goes to see Dr Hemmings, the civilian specialist he has requested, who also happens to be a friend from med-school. She

Greene

agrees with Dr Sayers' diagnosis, although she knows it's not what Mark wanted to hear. Returning to the medical centre, Greene briefly helps with an incoming trauma case, the victim of a helicopter crash, while David looks on.

Greene   David, Mark and Cynthia bring Ruth home in a wheelchair, and the four of them talk for a while. Ruth is painfully frank in telling Mark and Cynthia they can't rely on sex to make their relationship work, and in a private conversation later, Cynthia tells Mark that although he's a "wonderful, beautiful person", he doesn't love her. Mark says he's sorry, that she means a lot to him and he didn't mean to lead her on, but the damage is done, and Cynthia wastes no time in leaving.

Greene   Later, Mark talks to his mother, who says she feels responsible for Mark and David's problems with each other. She blamed them both for the fact that she married before she was ready: they had only dated a couple of times when she became pregnant, and the relationship had already started to go wrong. She also tells Mark that his father passed up a promotion to admiral so he could return home to help Mark, who was being bullied at school. That night, she starts a small fire when she tries to make herself some broth, and David and Mark together put it out and help Ruth back to bed.

Greene   The following day, Mark goes to the docks with his father, as he did as a child. David reminisces about his work on a carrier ship, remembering the early morning feeling of the calm before the storm, knowing that in a moment the engines would start, and lives would be at stake. "Sound familiar?" he asks Mark, and he nods. David is proud of what Mark does, he tells him, and Mark thanks him for helping him get there. With David's hand on his son's shoulder, they head back home together.

'Family Practice' is the first time an episode of ER *features only one of the main characters, and it's a very different kind of episode: while there*

have been many storylines that have been emotionally affecting, none have touched quite such a raw nerve as this one. Ruth Greene's mental deterioration is so powerfully acted and scripted that it hurts to watch, particularly her scream of anguish during the neuro exam, and her innocent bemusement at being asked why people in glass houses shouldn't throw bricks. While the mutual pride and respect of father and son is a great cliché of American drama, that side of the story is also effective, and resolves Greene's emotional crisis much more satisfactorily than the brief conversation with Doug in 'Fathers and Sons'. And as for the inevitable break-up with Cynthia, no matter how impatient some of us may have been with her storyline by the end, you couldn't have helped feeling sorry for the poor girl as she finally realized she and Mark just weren't meant to be.]

4-15: "Exodus"

Corday's first day on a paramedic ridealong sees her attend to victims at a chemical plant explosion. Though warned not to get involved, just to observe and assist, she quickly finds herself involved in treating an elderly man, Leo Leipziger, trapped under a collapsed building. Corday gives Leo a morphine drip. Although his pulse is strong, his arm is pinned under concrete. Corday and the paramedic douse the man in motor oil for lubrication and raise the concrete by one inch. The attempt fails just as the building shakes once more: an explosion on the surface means that all paramedics are called out. Corday refuses to leave and orders more jacks to lift the concrete. Once in place, she rapidly pumps the jack, releasing the man but making the passage collapse around them. They escape just in time.

Corday

Carter is on an optics rotation although his heart is not in it and his skills are underdeveloped. His supervisor asks him to act as a consult on a glaucoma patient in the ER. Shortly after, a man is brought in from the trauma site covered in benzine. Weaver assists but soon collapses from exposure to the chemical. Randi also succumbs a few minutes later. Carter realises that the benzine, a highly toxic solvent has to be contained, and evacuates the ER - just as Corday rushes through the door with her

Carter

patient from the accident site with others. In the midst of the chaos, Carter takes control: all non-essential patients to be sent home, critical patients to the cafeteria, infected patients into the ambulance bay. While Anna and Carter evacuate patients, and Benton organises the cases in the cafeteria, Corday takes her patient to the OR. Carter moves an old woman who operates her own breathing bag. With Weaver incapacitated, Carter is made chief medical officer on duty.

Doug/   Ross sees a little girl, Sophie, who is suffering from
Carol   altered mental status, breathing problems and renal failure. Ross diagnoses an e-coli bacterial infection and insist upon dialysis. In the process of taking Sophie up to the OR, a fire alarm sounds and Doug and Carol find themselves and their patient trapped in the lift. Sophie only has twenty minutes of oxygen left. Doug tries to prise the door open just as the firemen find them but Sophie begins to crash as the oxygen runs out. They manage to force the door open and get a new oxygen tank just in time. Sophie recovers in paediatrics.

Corday   Romano and Corday scrub in to operate on Leo but their best shot is not enough: Leo's arm is amputated anyway.

Carter   Weaver finds herself in the makeshift ICU next to Mr Arteburn, one of her patients who has suffered a minor heart attack. Arteburn crashes. While Anna treats him, Carter rushes for ice-cold water. Plunging Mr Arteburn's face in the water initiates the diving reflex, slowing the heart rate and bringing him back. Working on the adrenaline, Carter shows his skills to the uppermost. Daniker, the fire captain, asks Carter to prepare disaster drills for his staff with the fire service - only to discover Carter is an intern. Daniker is suprised and congratulates Carter on his leadership during the crisis.

["Exodus" is one of those episodes that you wish would never stop. Right from the pre-credits, you are plunged into the feverish activity at the chemical plant explosion and Corday's furious attempts to save Leo. And when that is coming to a close, the evacuation of the ER under Carter's

command takes over. This is a superbly well-crafted episode, with both halves sharing a similar frantic pace and interlinked. Both Corday and Carter are shown to be immensely capable and dedicated: Carter in particular comes across as the real leader of the ER, as a talented physician who thrives on adrenalin. It's also one of the best directed episodes of the fourth series, with a lovely lingering high camera shot of the silent, empty ER eventually giving way to the flurry of activity which ensues as patients are moved back from the cafeteria, with Carter at its head. A brilliant, high-energy episode.]

4-16: "My Brother's Keeper"

Doug has stayed up all night preparing a presentation to the paediatrics department on his research. At the ER, Kerry tries to talk to him about her reservations about his study but he is called to look at a seizing five year old who has ingested a mystery chemical. The father, Keith Reynolds, explains that he has a lot of photography chemicals in the house. The boy comes round and says that his half-brother, Eric, gave him chemicals in a soda can. The father rushes off and starts shaking Eric but Doug intervenes: away from the father, Eric shows Doug cigarette burns on his arms from his dad. Eric gave his brother insecticide and developing fluid. Doug calls family services and tells the mother.

Ross/ Greene

Doug and Carol leave for the presentation. Doug comes under strong questioning from the floor, including Anspaugh and Kerry Weaver who arrives late. After, Doug accuses Kerry of ambushing him. Meanwhile, Doug hears that the wounds on Eric's arm may have been self-inflicted and that the boy has been trouble for some time. Despite his protests, it appears that Eric is to be committed.

Ross/ Weaver

Mark still has Cynthia's luggage and Ross suspects that Mark wants to see her again. But when Mark turns up at Cynthia's apartment, it's empty. Cynthia has not left a forwarding address and is ex-directory. Mark is having second thoughts about their breaking-up.

Greene

Romano tries to embarrass Corday by reading an article

Corday

on her in the newspaper about her fearless rescue of Leo Leipziper *[episode 4-15]*. Romano then hands her his six-month review of her efforts, and apologizes that it isn't as glowing as the newspaper article. Romano criticizes her focus: recently, she's been involved with vocal chords and paramedics, not trauma surgery. He invites her in on a new study.

Mark treats an elderly man who is suffering in the late stages of lung cancer as a result of smoking. As the man leaves, he sees Mark light up outside. Later, the man is brought back in arrest and Greene has to admit him. Some time later, Mark finds the man in arrest on the floor. Corday identifies an exit wound and they realise that the smoker shot himself. They call time of death. Mark destroys his pack of cigarettes.

Anna   Anna approves the transfer of a John Doe from a motor-cycle accident to the ER. When he arrives, she realizes that the other hospital has lied about his condition because the man has no insurance and they don't want to take care of him. Anna is shocked by the gross negligence, especially when it appears that the man will certainly die without surgery. Later, the man's son turns up and is told by Anna that his father has a slim chance from surgery but the chief of neurosurgery disagrees. Anna has to explain that she was overly optimistic but finds that the old man is being operated on - by the surgeon who transferred John Doe to her in the first place.

Mark   Mark obtains Cynthia's address and phone number from the telephone company. That evening, he arrives at Cynthia's new apartment and delivers her luggage. She has got her son back. Mark tries to explain that he made a big mistake breaking up with her but she simply responds, "You don't love me, Mark. I deserve better."

Corday   Corday tells Benton about her clash with Romano while they visit a natural history exhibition. They bump into Jackie, Peter's sister, which appears to make him embarrassed..

Jeanie supervises Scott Anspaugh's final dose of chemo-therapy. Scott asks to see her to go for a movie next week but she is back in the ER and doesn't know what her schedule is. Scott feels rejected and insists that he doesn't need her now and when she returns to his room she discovers that he left ten minutes ago. Jeanie goes to Scott's house and wins back his favour.

Jeanie

Six overdose cases are brought in, having taken a danger-ous new mix. Anna calls Carter over to her patient: it's Chase. He crashes and Carter takes over. He is in arrest for a long time and Carol fears brain damage but suddenly they capture a pulse. Chase is transferred to MICU where Anna comforts him. Carter's grandparents arrive and are horrified to discover that Carter knew of his cousin's drug use. He explains his attempts to detoxify Chase but Carter's grandfather is highly critical of John and calls his own doctor. Millicent doesn't blame Carter but insists that he blames them: "All your lives you have been indulged and considered it oppression." That evening, Carter stays at Chase's side.

Carter/
Anna

4-17: "A Bloody Mess"

As Benton snatches his scheduled fifteen minutes' quality time with baby Rees before he goes to daycare, Corday obtains Greene's permission to do a study of artificial blood (haemo-A) in the ER - without Romano's knowl-edge. Her first patient is an unnamed store-owner, with gunshot wounds to his chest. Meanwhile Morgenstern returns to the ER, telling his colleagues that his MI six months ago has given him a new perspective. But his performance in Corday's surgery is shaky, and the patient nearly dies. "Who the hell was that?" she asks Weaver afterwards, and is shocked to hear that he's the chief of emergency medicine.

Corday/
Benton

Making good on her promise to carry on being a friend even after the chemo has finished, Jeanie takes Scott

Jeanie/
Ross

rock-climbing - but his efforts to prove his strength backfire when he runs badly short of breath and has to be rushed to the ER. Ross runs some tests that reveal that his blood cell counts are very low. Suspecting that Scott's cancer may be back, he performs a bone marrow biopsy, despite Jeanie's objections. Weaver meanwhile presses Ross for his fellowship renewal papers, but instead he suggests himself for a new post of paediatric attending.

Benton/
Corday

Benton is called out of surgery with the news that Rees has a fever. Reluctantly he accepts Corday's offer of the use of her car to take him to Carla's restaurant, as long as he can drive. On the way, she suggests that he's uncomfortable about Carla seeing that he's dating a white woman. As he protests, he backs the car up too quickly and hits a middle-aged woman, who turns out to work for a law firm. Benton anxiously takes her - and Rees - to the ER, but is even more anxious when Carla arrives later and strikes up a casual conversation with Elizabeth. When Carla has gone, Peter irritably remarks that none of this would have happened if he'd taken the train, or a cab: "If I hadn't got involved," Corday sums up. "I didn't say that," Benton protests; "You didn't have to," Elizabeth replies.

Carter/
Anna

Anna treats a woman with a complicated pregnancy, whose husband accuses her of putting the child's life before his wife's because she is Catholic. Meanwhile, Carter is clearly exhausted, even falling asleep in the canteen. Anna asks him about Chase and he evades the question, saying it is still early in his recovery. Later, he goes to visit Chase, who it seems has suffered serious brain damage, and is unable to feed or dress himself.

Corday
Benton

Corday is angrily questioned about her use of 'fake blood' by the store-owner's son, who has been advised by the clearly bitter Romano. Later though, her patient is grateful and the son relents. Romano offers Corday a responsible position on his own haemo-A study but she declines, preferring to stay in the ER. At the end of the day she catches up an embarrassed Benton in the corridor, who makes a meal out of telling her he has to cancel their date. "I assumed that," she says breezily, holding out her hand. "I need my car keys."

Scott's biopsy has shown that his cancer is back: he needs a bone marrow transfusion, and more chemo. Carol has already opened up the clinic so that the staff can be tested as possible donors. Anspaugh is concerned that Ross is giving Scott PCA [patient controlled anaesthesia] and Greene tells Ross as much, asking to be kept informed in future: Ross merely replies that this is why they need a paeds attending. Later, Jeanie goes to see Scott with the news that eight possible marrow donors have been found. As Anspaugh has told her, he's in strong spirits: "My lucky number," he says, giving her a brave smile...

Jeanie/ Ross

4-18: "Gut Reaction"

It is the day of the ER's annual banquet and this year the organization has been left to Mark and Jerry. Inevitably, the result is absolute chaos: the flowers are not received at the venue, the band cancels and the food is eventually supplied by Jerry's mum. Nevertheless, the party goes ahead in full swing. Mark Greene explains why he threw the banquet. "Each day we work together as a family and because we're a family it's no secret that it's been a tough year for me... You stuck by me when I needed you... Thanks for being my family. I couldn't have made it without you."

Greene

Weaver has received a memo suggesting that a paediatrics attending may be appointed in the ER: Doug has spoken to the Dean. But Kerry is concerned that Ross has entirely the wrong attitude, as illustrated in his heavy-handed treatment of the mother of a young girl. In fact, Ross's persistence pays dividends as the child is revealed to have probable neurosepsis. Greene is further reassured of Doug's competence when he saves the life of a six year old girl by showing Mark how to intubate her using an innovative technique. Although Kerry is determined to

Ross/ Weaver/ Greene

315

fight the appointment of a paeds attending in the ER, Mark says that he is not so sure. Later he tells Doug that he should go for the job.

Carol/
Carter

Millicent Carter has sent Carol another cheque which has enabled her to buy more much-needed supplies for the clinic. However, later that day Carol hears that the cheque has been stopped and the medical supplies are being repossessed. Carter goes to his grandmother to defend the clinic. It becomes clear that Millicent is disenchanted with Carter and not Carol. She insists that Chase's situation shows that John cares nothing about the family, just their money. "Then keep your money," Carter tells her. Later, at the banquet, Carol kisses Carter. Whatever he said to his grandmother did the trick - the clinic's supplies have been paid for.

Benton/
Corday

Benton and Corday treat 71 year old Dr Lars Swanson, a retired physician, who is brought in by Allison Beaumont. Allison has become a trainee paramedic much to Corday's delight. Later, Benton replaces Corday on the Swanson laporoscopy, which is to be led by Morgenstern, a former student of Swanson's. The key-hole surgery is relayed to a TV screen where Benton sees Morgenstern probing the wrong area. Morgenstern becomes increasingly agitated by Benton's cross-examination and, despite Benton's warning, severs the gastric artery causing internal bleeding. Benton insists that they need to crack him and perform open surgery but Morgenstern is resistant. Corday arrives just in time to see Benton barge Morgenstern away from the operating table and crack Swanson's ribs. Despite his efforts, Dr Swanson dies. Later, Benton is asked by Anspaugh to prepare a report for a formal enquiry but on trying to recover the tape of the procedure Peter finds that there was none in the recorder. Morgenstern speaks to Benton afterwards and insists that Peter caused ruptured verises but Benton is persistent even though Morgenstern threatens to make the case a disciplinary matter for which Benton could be dismissed. Benton starts to entertain doubts about his own practice but

Corday reminds Benton that he was sure earlier. Whatever happens, it will be a case of Peter's word against Morgenstern's.

Carter insists that he and Anna are just friends but Carol says he's lame and tells him to ask Anna out! He does, and Anna agrees to go with him to the staff banquet. During the day, Anna asks Carter to take some bone marrow from her for a patient outside the hospital. He agrees - but seems more engrossed in her bottom as it appears from behind a sheet on the operating table! That evening, at the banquet, he broaches the subject of their going out but finds that she has just come out of a long term relationship and is not ready. They agree to be friends.

Carter/ Anna

Anspaugh tells his son Scott that the two possible bone marrow donors have failed to provide a match. Jeanie explains that there is a new chemotherapy-intensive treatment which could help Scott. Scott is unsure and asks Jeanie's opinion. When she says that it's a chance, he decides to go for the new therapy. Later Doug sees Scott and takes Jeanie aside. He explains that Scott may just have decided to take the chemotherapy, irrespective of the risks, because he has a crush on Jeanie and just wants to please her. Stage one of the therapy begins nevertheless and Scott crashes. Jeanie arrives just as the doctors manage to stabilize him. Later, she sits by Scott and tells him that he has to make his own decisions and that she will love and respect him whatever decision he makes. Scott bursts into tears: he doesn't want any more chemotherapy. Jeanie accepts his decision and kisses him lightly.

Jeanie

4-19: "Shades of Gray"

It is the day of Scott Anspaugh's funeral. Jeanie practises a hymn she plans to sing at the service in the shower. She visits Donald Anspaugh before the funeral. Scott left her a box he wanted her to have containing soap opera digest - suddenly Jeanie realizes where he got all those future plots! At the funeral, Jeanie changes her mind and sings 'Time of your Life', one of Scott's favourites, instead of her hymn.

Benton   Before a review committee on Dr Swanson's death, Benton admits that he pushed Morgenstern aside to crack the patient's chest, believing that Morgenstern was in the wrong. The two begin to argue once more but Kayson intercedes. The committee is set up and suspends Benton despite Morgenstern's objections: Peter is taken off surgical rotation until a formal inquiry is held on Dr Anspaugh's return. However, when he is about to leave, Greene asks Benton to assist on an emergency case: Greene hasn't suspended him from the ER. They rush the patient up to the OR where Benton begins the clamp and run procedure before he is dismissed by Morgenstern, who arrives a little later. After the surgery, Morgenstern finds Benton. He watched the laporoscopy tape, which had been in his possession all the time, and found Benton was right. He apologizes: he had let the situation get out of hand. His two final acts as Chief of ER are to reinstate Benton and to resign.

Anna/   A pregnant woman is brought to the ER with serious
Weaver   injuries. Anna discovers that the woman was in the middle of an abortion when an explosion at the clinic caused a wall to fall on her. The woman begins to haemorrhage and Weaver orders that they finish the abortion in the ER. Anna refuses and leaves. Later, Weaver tells Anna that she had a duty to her patient but failed her because of a moral objection to abortion which Anna denies. Later, a peaceful protestor tries to convert Anna to her cause but Anna accuses her of exciting the extremists by her propaganda. Meanwhile, Weaver speaks to the woman who is preparing to leave: this is not her first abortion. Weaver suggests that she use contraception but the young woman is abusive and leaves. Weaver explains to Anna that the patient's wishes come first but Anna says that if the same situation arose again she can't be sure that she wouldn't do the same thing.

Doug treats Zoe, a young girl who was present at the **Ross** clinic for a pre-natal check up. Her boyfriend, Donny, had accompanied her and came with her to the ER. Although the baby is fine, the girl has a pulmonary embolism and has to be stabilized and intubated. However, Zoe's brain is starved of oxygen and she has to be kept alive on a ventilator for the sake of the unborn child. Zoe's parents arrive and are hostile to Donny. Unfortunately, because he and Zoe are underage, Zoe's parents are left to make the decision to keep Zoe alive until the baby is born or perform an emergency c-section. After some time, they decide to let the baby run closer to full term but Donny is to be excluded from its life.

Mr Newton brings in his elderly father who has been **Carter** lying in his own filth in bed for several days. Carter is horrified to discover bedsores, a further sign of neglect, and calls social services who agree to put the old man in an extended care facility. Mr Newton is horrified at Carter's actions and leaves to get his lawyer. However, when old Mr Newton becomes more coherent he explains to Carter that he wants to die in his own bed. Carter tries to revoke the social worker's decision but it is too late. He apologizes as the old man is taken away.

Corday is called to treat one of the paramedics injured at **Corday/** the clinic explosion only to discover that it is Allison **Benton** Beaumont. Allison asks Corday to perform the procedures but again surgery is difficult and Allison is close to death. Romano tells Corday it is hopeless but she is abusive and continues to work to save Allison. Her surgery is successful but Corday is frustrated. She tells Benton, "You can put them back together, but you can't keep them that way." Later that night, after Benton is reinstated, he visits Corday at her apartment. "I lost my mentor today," he tells her, "and the hospital - they lost a great surgeon." As he explains how he should have told Morgenstern how much he appreciated him, he and Corday kiss.

4-20: "Of Past Regret And Future Fear"

Benton/
Corday

After spending the night together, Benton leaves to attend his son's baptism while Corday heads to County. At the church, Benton feels excluded: his niece is contemptuous of his choice of new girlfriend while he has to share parental duties with Carla's new boyfriend. Then at the hospital, he finds that Romano has invited Corday to lunch to discuss her work. In Doc Magoo's, Corday tells Romano that she has thought about staying in the autumn but it is clear that he doesn't really want to talk about that. Eventually, he asks her out on a date. She apologetically rejects his offer and lets him guess that she has a policy of not fraternizing with work-mates. Romano seems relieved - "For a while there I thought I was competing with Peter Benton." But he also seems a little bitter about being rejected and on seeing Benton in on his day off, performing surgery with Corday, says he's glad to see he's not the only surgeon without a life!

Carol
Ross

Carol has severe misgivings about inviting her mother around for brunch although Doug is persistent. Mrs Hathaway does not arrive alone: she brings a gentleman friend, Haviere, who she has been seeing for some time. Doug finds the whole situation funny but Carol is fretful. At work, Carol takes care of Paul Kinturner, a 31 year old security guard who has suffered severe chemical burns from hydrofluoric acid. As the acid will draw calcium from the man's cells, Greene tries to counter the effects with calcium intravenously but is told by a toxicologist that such extensive exposure is always fatal. Carol volunteers to sit by the man's bedside after Greene breaks the news. She discovers Paul has a six and a half year old daughter, Molly, whom he hasn't seen since she was six months old. Kinturner asks Carol to arrange for his savings to be given to Molly but is adamant that his daughter shouldn't think that he is buying her forgiveness. Carol finds the mother and tries to convince her to let Molly see her father: Carol didn't get the chance to say goodbye to her father. Nevertheless, the mother refuses to let Molly go through this experience.

Kinturner is upset at his ex-wife's decision but is persuaded by Carol to write a final note to his daughter, which he dictates to her. As she reads it back to him, Mr Kinturner dies. Later, Carol tells Doug that she had never thought about whether her father was asking for her. After her father's death, her mum always complained about relying on men. Now her mum is happy and she's the one holding back. "Truth is, I'm scared to death of losing you, Doug."

Carter arrives at the Kenner Institute and meets his grandmother. Chase is deteriorating: he's losing more activity down his left side. Carter is determined not to accept the truth but seeing Chase seems to confirm the analysis. Later that day, Millicent talks to Carter about his future. She appreciates the freedom that comes with financial independence but wants him around. His grandfather is too proud to come to Carter, but would like Carter to go to him. They ask him to finish his residency then practise part-time - they need him to run the business. However, Carter is adamant: he wants to be a doctor, there's nothing else for him.

Carter

Kerry treats Mrs Wynbock, an elderly woman who is having trouble shaking off the flu. At first, Weaver diagnoses atypical pneumonia contracted from birds but a mix up at the labs reveals that she has HIV. Kerry explains that there was a mix-up and that they have tested for HIV but Wynbock's fiancée takes Kerry aside and confesses that he has the infection and asks her not to tell his partner. Kerry insists that the couple have to talk.

Weaver

Doug treats a baby, Josh McNeil, who was born addicted to heroin. The mother, however, is taking her son's prescription of methadone for herself, leaving the baby in withdrawal. The baby is admitted. Later, Doug is angered when he discovers that the mother has abandoned Josh in the hospital.

Ross

Carter and Anna are chatting outside when a taxi pulls

Carter/ Anna

up. Anna recognizes the man who steps out and heads over: Dr Max Rocher, the boyfriend with whom she is still involved. They briefly kiss, though Anna then looks over to Carter somewhat apologetically.

4-21: "Suffer The Little Children"

Jeanie   Jeanie wakes with a cough and a temperature. At County she gets a chest film which she asks Weaver to look at. Weaver says that it's too early to tell anything and that another chest film is needed. She tells Jeanie to put the patient's name on the next one. When Jeanie brings the next film, she tells Weaver that it is hers. Weaver promises that there will always be a job in the ER for Jeanie, whatever her viral count, and they decide to draw some blood. Thankfully, the results are positive. Jeanie is a little run-down while the rough time she has had with Al and Scotty has made her forgetful, which has affected her treatment. Kerry offers to listen to Jeanie if she wants to talk about it. Jeanie decides to take her up on her offer.

Ross/   Josh McNeil *[episode 4-20]* is ready to begin a process of
Carol   long-term withdrawal with an ex-nurse who will act as a foster mother. However, Doug later hears that Josh is being returned to the mother who has since moved in with her aunt who will take care of the baby if the mother can't. Doug persuades the social worker to return Josh to the ER so that he can fill in some forms and send the baby home with all his medication. It is a stalling tactic and once inside the ER Doug says Josh has pneumonia and will need to be on an IV overnight. Instead, he begins a 12-18 hours rapid detoxification of the child under deep sedation, a new procedure still being pioneered. Carol is concerned by Doug's decision but insists on helping him. Soon their shifts are over and Carol has to avoid Weaver. Meanwhile, Ross lies to Greene about the medication he needs for a patient.

Corday/   Corday pesters Benton to take her to a jazz club on the
Benton   south side. Benton says that it isn't a good idea. At work, they meet in a locker room and kiss. Romano enters but

they are not sure if he saw them together. Later, Romano hints to Corday that she may not have a future in County, leading her to suspect that he saw her and Benton earlier and is preparing to withdraw her scholarship. Benton confronts Romano and insists that punishing Corday for her relationship with him is unfair but Romano claims he didn't see them. Nevertheless, he congratulates Benton on his 'excellent choice.' That evening, Benton agrees to take Corday to the jazz club on the south side. He says that all his feelings about her skin colour won't change overnight. "I'm trying to work through this, you've got to trust me, okay?"

Anna showed Max the sights last night. He is in Chicago to conduct a feasibility study for a proposed paediatrics unit in the ER and is coping well with his addiction. Anna is concerned that Carter will judge Max on the negative things she has told him and insists that he is a good guy. Carter is concerned that she and Max are back together again but she says that she is not sure. Throughout the day, he is curt to Max, who is nevertheless impressed by Carter's diagnostic capabilities, especially with one 11 year old, Sam Adams, who is brought in suffering mysterious breathing problems. Meanwhile, Anna plays supporting cast to a hammy tele-evangelist who is given permission to broadcast her 'death-bed' appeal from the hospital. Later that day, Carter tells Anna that he thinks Max is trouble. He hopes that he is wrong, but that is what he thinks.

Anna/ Carter

Weaver is annoyed that Dr Max Rocher's study has been sprung on them and suspects that Doug Ross has initiated it to show up how the ER handles paediatrics cases: Doug is angling for a paediatrics attending position in the ER. Kerry tries to bog Max down in charts but Greene insists that Max should be given free rein to see the ER in operation. Kerry is angry that Mark appears to be giving Max support to help Doug get an attending's position but he insists that's not true: he thinks that a paediatrics unit or an attending is un-necessary. Meanwhile, Josh McNeil suffers a setback and

Weaver/ Ross/ Carol/ Greene

crashes. Greene hears the flatline and rushes into the room to find Doug performing the rapid detoxification without consent. Doug tries to explain but Mark refuses to hear him out. Weaver is furious and rushes the baby to intensive care, demanding that Ross explain himself to hospital administration. Greene is angrier: "You lied to me, Doug. You looked me right in the face and lied to me."

4-22: "A Hole In The Heart"

Ross/   Weaver and Ross arrive in PICU with Josh McNeil. The
Weaver   attending physician argues that the rapid detoxification
            should be continued for the baby's benefit though
            Weaver is more concerned with hospital policy. Ross is
            defiant: "I just want to make sure that this boy gets a
            decent shot at a normal life. I don't care about your rules
            or regulations." Weaver hopes he doesn't care about
            being an ER paediatrics attending either because he's just
            lost all chance at that.

Greene/   Greene asks for an appointment to see Anspaugh as soon
Carol   as possible. In the meantime he speaks to Carol and
            encourages her to say that she was doing her duty as a
            nurse in assisting Doug but she maintains that what she
            and Doug did was in the child's best interests. Mark and
            Kerry agree to attend the Ross enquiry together but soon
            discover that Ross has already seen Anspaugh, Kayson
            and Max Rocher about the case without them. He has
            admitted to overstepping the line but the senior staff
            members have supported his actions.

Ross   Once the detoxification is complete, Ross extubates Josh
            although it is too early to say if the baby will be okay.
            Later, Vicky McNeil, Josh's mother, arrives and asks to
            see her son. When she hears of the treatment, she asks
            Doug if he can do the same for her. Although he gives
            her the names of some physicians who could perform the
            procedure on adults, he fears that it won't take away the
            psychological addiction.

Meanwhile, Weaver arranges an Executive Committee Review of the case. Ross hands his incident report to Greene and Weaver but Mark is unwilling to let Doug get away with lying to him. Doug insists that Josh was more important than rules but Greene is annoyed that he wasn't able to intervene. Doug insists that this situation is not about the baby but Mark's inability to treat Doug as an equal. Their argument is cut short as Carol calls them over to an urgent case...

Ross/ Greene

With her authority already challenged by Ross's misdemeanour, Kerry is frustrated to discover that she will not be automatically promoted to ER Chief now that Morgenstern has resigned. Anspaugh tells her that a nation-wide search will be made for the best candidate but he is pleased to hear that she will apply. Throughout the day, she is engaged in disputes, firstly with Greene whom she accuses of letting Doug Ross get away with frequent abuses and with an insurance company which refuses to pay a $500 bill for one of her patients. Under the constant pressure, she resigns as acting head of the ER and storms out as Greene tries to calm her down. However, when Randi asks who will now look at the budget forms, Kerry takes them.

Weaver

Corday receives notification from Romano that he is discontinuing her sponsorship but when she tries to find him she discovers that he has left for a conference in Costa Rica. Benton is unaware of Corday's situation until she asks Anspaugh in the middle of surgery if she can apply for a position in County. Anspaugh says that she has missed the deadline but Corday is persistent: she wants to stay in the US. After surgery, Benton tells Corday that he thinks her desperate attempts to stay on are not helpful but she is more concerned that he does not appear passionate about her desire to stay.

Benton/ Corday

Lydia asks Carter if he has seen any percoset, a strong painkiller that she left lying around but which has suddenly gone missing. Carter is immediately suspicious of Max who was once addicted to painkillers. Carter tells

Carter/ Anna

Anna but she accuses him of being low - Max has told her that he's clean. Carter says that is what Chase told him. Later, Max tells Anna that he is about to recommend a paediatrics unit in the ER and may consider running it, if they offer, but it depends on where he stands with Anna. Eventually, the subject comes round to the missing percoset. Although he didn't take it, he says she'd be crazy not to suspect him.

Carol   Carol treats Mr Nabel who tried to commit suicide during an argument with his wife. Although he insists that it was a moment of insanity, the psych consult is called. Carol later discovers that the man has been in three times, a sure sign of a cry for help. Later he returns again, covered in blood and apologizing. As Carol checks him out, he hands her a gun and says that there weren't enough bullets. Carol runs outside to Nabel's car and calls Doug and Mark over. Nabel has shot his wife, son and daughter. Quickly, all three are brought into the ER. The daughter is stabilized but the mother has spinal injuries. The son is bleeding out, a hole in his right ventricle, and is rushed straight to surgery...

SECTION FOUR

Prognosis
[Series Five]

The emergency room of County General, like any highly pressurised working environment, is heavily dependent on team dynamics. The members of staff on which we have focused in compiling the files in this dossier work together exceptionally well, and recent events have stressed the importance of ensuring that they continue to do so, to maintain the ER's high standards of performance.

Mark Greene continues to be the lynchpin of the ER, and his new found interest in the paramedic services should provide him with extra interest until such time as he can be offered tenure. The board is particularly pleased to retain John Carter as second year resident, now that the issue of his salary is resolved, and hopes that he will prove himself as a teacher as well as a physician. Meanwhile, Elizabeth Corday has taken the unusual choice of starting her training anew as an intern in order to stay at County General, which will benefit the hospital greatly - though is to be hoped that her decision is based on professional rather than personal interests.

The departure of Dr Morgenstern as chief of emergency medicine has left a significant gap at the head of the ER team. Although Kerry Weaver has performed well as acting chief, she would not be the board's first choice as a permanent replacement, and she has therefore been re-designated 'interim chief' while a new candidate is sought. At the other end of the management scale, the free clinic operated by Nurse Hathaway continues to be an unqualified success, assisted by the appointment of Lynette Evans as the clinic's nurse practitioner.

The most significant development in the team dynamic of the ER recently has been the recent reorganisation of paediatric care. The departure of Dr Del Amico in summer 1998, in part due to the lack of a paediatric ER department, therefore represents unfortunate timing as well as being a significant loss to the team. With one third of emergent cases falling into the paediatric category, the ER will benefit greatly from the new specialist department and the new post of paediatric attending, now held by Doug Ross.

Certain members of the board, however, remain sceptical about the wisdom of putting Dr Ross in such a responsible position. The rapid detoxification of Josh McNeil, although successful, was a serious breach of the rules for which Dr Ross has recently completed a thirty-day period of probation, but it is far from clear that he has learned the lessons of the incident. It is the board's earnest hope that the paediatric attending position will provide him with a greater insight into the importance of procedure and protocol, and that there will be no further incidents. In the final analysis, the proper functioning of the ER team within our established procedures must take precedence over any one individual, however skilled. No one is indispensable.

[Despite its seemingly unassailable position as America's top drama show, consolidated by the record-breaking sum paid by NBC to commission the fifth series, ER has something to prove in 1999. With Carter's student days and two internships now complete, it seems the writers are seizing the opportunity to make changes to the show, to keep its story lines fresh and interesting. Kellie Martin has brought a breath of fresh air to the show as med-student Lucy Knight, introduced in the first episode of series five. The opportunity to meet our favourite characters anew through her eyes showed just how much some of them have changed, particularly Benton (seen briefly in a clinch with Corday) and a particularly ill-tempered Carter.

Of course, the big question for this year is whether the show can survive without George Clooney as Dr Ross. His decision to leave has been zealously publicised for the last year and a half, creating an expectation in some quarters that he would leave during series four - with many journalists circulating rumours about his grisly death at gunpoint. In fact George's contract was always going to take him into the fifth series, and at time of writing it seems the way will be left open for guest appearances. Surprisingly though, the show's producers have apparently taken the decision to write out Dr Ross mid-way through the series rather than at the end, leaving half a dozen or so episodes for the show to establish that it can go on without him. Consequently, by the time you read this George's last episode should already have been broadcast in the US.

So, will this be a disaster for ER? *Admittedly, there will be a substantial contingent of George's fans who, having watched the show only to see their hero, will stop watching once he has gone. In story terms too, the character of Ross is important because of the conflict that arises between him and others, notably Weaver and Greene, and because of the romantic saga with Carol. (One question that hasn't been answered yet is where Ross's departure leaves that relationship: hopefully the writers realise how badly many of us would react to a break-up.) But in a show with the kind of writers and actors* ER *has, to talk of any one character being vital to its success is actually nonsense. The fourth series actually had something of a surfeit of characters, and Ross actually had very little to do for much of it. Provided the writers continue to come up with good story lines for the characters they have,* ER *can ride out and even flourish the departure of any individual, even George Clooney. Which is not to say, of course, that we won't miss him...]*

Appendices

Appendix One
The Actors

Appendix Two
Episode List

Anthony Edwards was best known, before *ER*, for his role as Tom Cruiseís best friend in the blockbuster film *Top Gun*, and a recurring role in the TV series *Northern Exposure*. His other credits include feature films *The Client, Pet Sematary II, Revenge of the Nerds* and *Revenge of the Nerds II: Nerds in Paradise*, and TV movies from *Hometown Boy Makes Good* in 1974 to *In Cold Blood* in 1996, in which he was cast against type as Dick Hickock. In 1998 he starred alongside Sean Connery and Gillian Anderson in *If They Only Knew*, otherwise known as Dancing *About Architecture*.

George Clooney was a familiar face from a large number of television roles before landing his role as Doug Ross, featuring in series such as *Sisters* and *Roseanne*, and coincidentally a situation comedy called *ER* in the mid-eighties. He failed to secure the role taken by Brad Pitt in the feature film *Thelma and Louise*, but has since found fame in Hollywood with starring roles in *Batman and Robin, One Fine Day* and the acclaimed *Out of Sight*. Born in Lexington, he is the son of broadcaster Nick Clooney and the nephew of singer Rosemary Clooney (who played Mary Kavanagh in two episodes of *ER*).

Sherry Stringfield worked solidly since leaving university in New York, at first on stage then in television including a regular role in the daytime drama *Guiding Light*. She left her role as one of the regular characters on *NYPD Blue* to star as Dr Susan Lewis in *ER*. Her decision to leave the show in 1996 was reportedly driven by a desire to lead a ënormal lifeí with her boyfriend in New York away from the gruelling schedule and fame of a top-rated drama series.

Noah Wyle was raised in Los Angeles and attended an exclusive boarding school in Ojai, California for four years. He has appeared in feature films such as *A Few Good Men, Swing Kids, There Goes My Baby* and *Crooked Hearts*, and co-starred in the TV mini-series *Blind Faith* and the TV movie *Guinevere of Camelot*. With George Clooney, he also guest-starred as a doctor in an episode of *Friends*, and has featured in several films over the last couple of years, including *The Myth of Fingerprints*.

Julianna Margulies was born in New York, and graduated from high school in New Hampshire with a Bachelor of Arts degree. Her first professional acting role was in Steven Segalís action movie *Out for Justice* in 1991, which was followed by a recurring role in *Homicide: Life on the Street* and guest roles in *Law and Order* and *Murder, She Wrote*. She recently starred in the 1996 feature film *Traveller*. In 1995 she won the Emmy award for Best Supporting Actress in a Drama Series for her role as Carol Hathaway.

Gloria Reuben was born in Toronto, Canada, and has starred in feature films including *Nick of Time, Timecop and Wild Orchid 2*, and TV movies including *Confessions: Two Faces of Evil, Dead Air, Percy and Thunder* and *Shadowhunter*. Before moving to Los Angeles to begin her acting career, Gloria was a professional model.

Laura Innes became one of the regular *ER* cast in series three after playing Kerry Weaver as a recurring character for the second series, for which she was nominated for an award by the US organisation Viewers for Quality Television. Her other acting credits include the TV series *Louie* and *Wings*, the 1978 feature film *The Fury* and a number of TV movies, including *See Jane Run, And the Band Played On*, and *Judith Krantzis ëTorch Song'*.

Mario Bello starred with Scott Bakula in the US drama *Mr and Mrs Smith* before joining *ER* at the end of the third series as Anna Del Amico. She also had guest roles on various shows including *Nowhere Man* and *Due South*, and extensive credits in New York theatre including the world premiere of *The Killer Inside Me*. She left *ER* in 1998, between the fourth and fifth series, to pursue her film career.

Kellie Martin joins *ER* for the fifth series and will bring a legion of adoring fans to the show, judging by the number of Internet sites devoted to her. With a string of credits from movies *Jumpin' Jack Flash* and *Matinee* to providing voices for cartoon series such as *Taz-Mania* and *A Pup Named Scooby Doo*, she drew attention to herself in 1996 with a role in the critically disastrous *Crisis Center*, conceived as a sci-fi version of *ER*...

Alex Kingston enjoyed a successful acting in career in Britain before being snapped up for ER, starting as a 15-year-old bully in *Grange Hill* and working her way up to the lead role in *Moll Flanders*. As a member of the Royal Shakespeare Company she appeared in productions of *Much Ado About Nothing*, *King Lear* and *Love's Labours Lost*.

Eriq La Salle worked extensively in television and films before taking the role of Dr Benton in *ER*. His film credits include *Color of Night*, *Drop Squad*, *Jacobis Ladder* and *Coming to America*. Television credits include *Under Suspicion* and a series regular role in *The Human Factor*, as well as a number of TV movies including *Empty Cradle*, *Circumstantial Evidence*, *What Price Victory*, *Leg Work*, and *War Stories*.

Appendix Two
Episode List

No.	Episode Title	Writer	Director	Remarks
1-00	Pilot (aka 24 Hours)	Michael Crichton	Rod Holcomb	Feature length pilot episode. Called *ER: The Movie* for video release. Carol's suicide attempt

Series One

No.	Episode Title	Writer	Director	Remarks
1-1	"Day One"	John Wells	Mimi Leder	First appearance of Taglieri and Cvetic.
1-2	"Going Home"	Lydia Woodward	Mark Tinker	First appearance of Kayson and Mary Kavanagh (Rosemary Clooney, aunt of George).
1-3	"Hit and Run"	Paul Manning	Mimi Leder	First appearance of Langworthy and Walt.
1-4	"Into That Good Night"	Robert Nathan	Charles Haid	
1-5	"Chicago Heat"	John Wells★	Elodie Keene	★Teleplay by John Wells, from a story by Neal Baer. First appearance of Chloe Lewis and Linda Farrell.
1-6	"Another Perfect Day"	Lydia Woodward★	Vern Gillum	★Teleplay by Lydia Woodward, from a story by Lance A Gentile. First appearance of Patrick.
1-7	"9½ Hours"	Robert Nathan	James Hayman	First appearance of Benton's mother and Bob.
1-8	"ER Confidential"	Paul Manning	Daniel Sackheim	Last appearance of Cvetic.
1-9	"Blizzard"	Lance A Gentile★	Mimi Leder	★Teleplay by Lance A Gentile, from a story by Neal Baer and Paul Manning. First appearance of Hicks.
1-10	"The Gift"	Neal Baer	Felix Enriquez Alacalá	Mary Kavanagh returns.
1-11	"Happy New Year"	Lydia Woodward	Charles Haid	First appearance of Jackie.
1-12	"Luck Of The Draw"	Paul Manning	Rod Holcomb	First appearance of Deb Chen.
1-13	"Long Day's Journey"	Robert Nathan	Anita W Addison	First appearance of Jeanie Boulet and

			Diane Leeds.	
1-14	"Feb 5, '95"	John Wells	James Hayman	
1-15	"Make of Two Hearts"	Lydia Woodward	Mimi Leder	
1-16	"The Birthday Party"	John Wells	Elodie Keene	
1-17	"Sleepless In Chicago"	Paul Manning	Christopher Chulack	
1-18	"Love's Labor Lost"	Lance A Gentile	Mimi Leder	Jodi O'Brien case.
1-19	"Full Moon, Saturday Night"	Neal Baer	Donna Deitch	First appearance of 'Wild Willie' Swift and Al Boulet.
1-20	"House of Cards"	Tracey Stern	Fred Gerber	Last appearance of Deb Chen.
1-21	"Men Plan, God Laughs"	Robert Nathan	Christopher Chulack	
1-22	"Love Among The Ruins"	Paul Manning	Fred Gerber	
1-23	"Motherhood"	Lydia Woodward	Quentin Tarantino	Death of Benton's mother. Birth of Suzie Lewis.
1-24	"Everything Old Is New Again"	John Wells	Mimi Leder	Carol's 'wedding'. Last appearance of Taglieri and Diane Leeds.

Series Two

2-1	"Welcome Back Carter!"	John Wells	Mimi Leder	First appearance of Weaver, Harper Tracy, Shep, Raul, Loretta, Holda.
2-2	"Summer Run"	Lydia Woodward	Eric Laneville	
2-3	"Do One, Teach One, Kill One"	Paul Manning	Felix Enriquez Alacalá	First appearance of Randi and Chia-Chia. Chloe abandons Suzie.
2-4	"What Life?"	Carol Flint	Dean Parisot	
2-5	"And Baby Makes Two"	Anne Kenney	Lesli Linka Glatter	Last appearance of Chia-Chia.
2-6	"Days Like This"	Lydia Woodward	Mimi Leder	First appearance of Vucelich.
2-7	"Hell and High Water"	Neal Baer	Christopher Chulack	Ross rescues Ben Larkin from storm drain.
2-8	"The Secret Sharer"	Paul Manning	Thomas Schlamme	
2-9	"Home"	Tracey Stern	Donna Deitch	
2-10	"A Miracle Happens Here"	Carol Flint	Mimi Leder	First appearance of Mr and Mrs Rubadoux.

2-11	"Dead of Winter"	John Wells	Whitney Ransick	
2-12	"True Lies"	Lance A Gentile	Lesli Linka Glatter	
2-13	"It's Not Easy Being Greene"	Paul Manning	Christopher Chulack	
2-14	"The Right Thing"	Lydia Woodward	Richard Thorpe	Last appearance of Mr Rubadoux. First appearance of Ray Ross.
2-15	"Baby Shower"	Carol Flint★	Barnet Kellmann	★Teleplay by Carol Flint, from a story by Belinda Casas-Wells and Carol Flint.
2-16	"The Healers"	John Wells	Mimi Leder	Death of Raul. Chloe Lewis returns.
2-17	"The Match Game"	Neal Baer	Thomas Schlamme	
2-18	"A Shift In The Night"	Joe Sachs	Lance A Gentile	ER stretched to limits.
2-19	"Fire In The Belly"	Paul Manning	Felix Enriquez Alacalá	First appearance of Dale Edson.
2-20	"Fevers of Unknown Origin"	Carol Flint	Richard Thorpe	Last appearance of Harper Tracy.
2-21	"Take These Broken Wings"	Lydia Woodward	Anthony Edwards	Al Boulet tests positive for HIV.
2-22	"John Carter, M.D."	John Wells	Christopher Chulack	Jeanie tests positive for HIV. Carter graduates but misses ceremony.

Series Three

3-1	"Dr. Carter, I Presume"	John Wells	Christopher Chulack	Last appearance of Shep. First appearance of Gant and Carla Rees.
3-2	"Let The Games Begin"	Lydia Woodward	Tom Moore	First appearance of Anspaugh.
3-3	"Don't Ask, Don't Tell"	Jason Cahill★	Perry Lang	★Teleplay by Jason Cahill, from a story by Paul Manning and Jason Cahill. First appearance of Maggie Doyle and Abby Keaton.
3-4	"Last Call"	Samantha Howard Corbin★	Rod Holcomb	★Teleplay by Samantha Howard Corbin from a story by Samantha Howard Corbin and Carol Flint.
3-5	"Ghosts"	Neal Baer	Richard Thorpe	First appearance of Charlie (Kirsten Dunst).

336

3-6	"Fear Of Flying"	Lance A Gentile	Christopher Chulack	
3-7	"No Brain, No Gain"	Paul Manning	David Nutter	
3-8	"Union Station"	Carol Flint	Tom Moore	Last appearance of Susan Lewis. Lydia and Al Grabarsky marry.
3-9	"Ask Me No Questions, I'll Tell You No Lies"	Barbara Hall★	Paris Barclay	★Teleplay by Barbara Hall, from a story by Neal Baer and Lydia Woodward.
3-10	"Homeless for the Holidays"	Samantha Howard Corbin	David Guggenheim	
3-11	"Night Shift"	Paul Manning	Jonathan Kaplan	Death of Gant. Last appearance of Abby Keaton.
3-12	"Post Mortem"	Carol Flint	Jacque Toberen	First appearance of Greg Fischer and Nina Pomerantz.
3-13	"Fortune's Fools"	Jason Cahill	Michael Katleman	Hathaway suspended.
3-14	"Whose Appy Now?"	Neal Baer	Felix Enriquez Alacalá	
3-15	"The Long Way Around"	Lydia Woodward	Christopher Chulack	Carol involved in armed robbery. (Guest star: Ewan McGregor.)
3-16	"Faith"	John Wells	Jonathan Kaplan	Hathaway re-instated.
3-17	"Tribes"	Lance A Gentile	Richard Thorpe	
3-18	"You Bet Your Life"	Paul Manning	Christopher Chulack	
3-19	"Calling Dr. Hathaway"	Jason Cahill and Samantha Howard Corbin★	Paris Barclay	★Teleplay by Jason Cahill and Samantha Howard Corbin, from a story by Neal Baer.
3-20	"Random Acts"	Carol Flint	Jonathan Kaplan	Greene assaulted. Last appearance of Greg Fischer. First appearance of Anna Del Amico.
3-21	"Make A Wish"	Lydia Woodward★	Richard Thorpe	★Teleplay by Lydia Woodward, from a story by Joe Sachs. Benton and Carla's baby born two months premature.
3-22	"One More For The Road"	John Wells	Christopher Chulack	Carter asks to leave surgical program.

THE ER FILES

<table>
<tr><td colspan="5" align="center">**Series Four**</td></tr>
<tr><td>4-1</td><td>"Ambush"</td><td>Carol Flint</td><td>Thomas Schlamme</td><td>'Live' episode, two versions recorded. First appearance of Corday. Morgenstern suffers MI.</td></tr>
<tr><td>4-2</td><td>"Something New"</td><td>Lydia Woodward</td><td>Christopher Chulack</td><td>First appearances of Cynthia and George Henry.</td></tr>
<tr><td>4-3</td><td>"Friendly Fire"</td><td>Walon Green</td><td>Felix Enriquez Alcalá</td><td></td></tr>
<tr><td>4-4</td><td>"When the Bough Breaks"</td><td>Jack Orman</td><td>Richard Thorpe</td><td></td></tr>
<tr><td>4-5</td><td>"Good Touch, Bad Touch"</td><td>David Mills</td><td>Jonathan Kaplan</td><td>First appearance of Romano.</td></tr>
<tr><td>4-6</td><td>"Ground Zero"</td><td>Samantha Howard Corbin</td><td>Darnell Martin</td><td>First appearance of Ellis West.</td></tr>
<tr><td>4-7</td><td>"Fathers and Sons"</td><td>John Wells</td><td>Christopher Chulack</td><td>Doug, Mark and Carol only.</td></tr>
<tr><td>4-8</td><td>"Freak Show"</td><td>Neal Baer</td><td>Darnell Martin</td><td></td></tr>
<tr><td>4-9</td><td>"Obstruction of Justice"</td><td>Lance Gentile</td><td>Richard Thorpe</td><td>First appearances of Allison Beaumont, Chase Carter. Last appearance of Al Boulet.</td></tr>
<tr><td>4-10</td><td>"Do You See What I See?"</td><td>Jack Orman</td><td>Sarah Pia Anderson</td><td>*Teleplay by Jack Orman from a story by Linda Gase.</td></tr>
<tr><td>4-11</td><td>"Think Warm Thoughts"</td><td>David Mills</td><td>Charles Haid</td><td>First appearance of Scott Anspaugh. Swift appears.</td></tr>
<tr><td>4-12</td><td>"Sharp Relief"</td><td>Samantha Howard Corbin</td><td>Christopher Chulack</td><td></td></tr>
<tr><td>4-13</td><td>"Carter's Choice"</td><td>John Wells</td><td>John Wells</td><td>Last appearance of Ellis West.</td></tr>
<tr><td>4-14</td><td>"Family Practice"</td><td>Carol Flint</td><td>Charles Haid</td><td>Greene, Cynthia at Greenes' home, San Diego.</td></tr>
<tr><td>4-15</td><td>"Exodus"</td><td>Walon Green & Joe Sachs</td><td>Christopher Chulack</td><td>ER evacuated.</td></tr>
<tr><td>4-16</td><td>"My Brother's Keeper"</td><td>Jack Orman</td><td>Jacque Toberen</td><td>Last appearance of Cynthia.</td></tr>
<tr><td>4-17</td><td>"A Bloody Mess"</td><td>Linda Gase</td><td>Richard Thorpe</td><td>Morgenstern returns.</td></tr>
<tr><td>4-18</td><td>"Gut Reaction"</td><td>Neal Baer</td><td>T R Babu Subramaniam</td><td>Last appearance of Scott Anspaugh.</td></tr>
<tr><td>4-19</td><td>"Shades of Gray"</td><td>Samantha Howard Corbin</td><td>Lance Gentile</td><td>Morgenstern resigns.</td></tr>
<tr><td>4-20</td><td>"Of Past Regret And Future Fear"</td><td>Jack Orman</td><td>Anthony Edwards</td><td>First appearances of Josh McNeil, Max Rocher.</td></tr>
<tr><td>4-21</td><td>"Suffer The Little Children"</td><td>Walon Green</td><td>Christopher Misiano</td><td></td></tr>
<tr><td>4-22</td><td>"A Hole In The Heart"</td><td>Lydia Woodward</td><td>Lesli Linka Glatter</td><td></td></tr>
</table>